Communications
in Computer and Information Science 1014

Commenced Publication in 2007
Founding and Former Series Editors:
Phoebe Chen, Alfredo Cuzzocrea, Xiaoyong Du, Orhun Kara, Ting Liu,
Krishna M. Sivalingam, Dominik Ślęzak, Takashi Washio, and Xiaokang Yang

More information about this series at http://www.springer.com/series/7899

Silvester Draaijer · Desirée Joosten-ten Brinke ·
Eric Ras (Eds.)

Technology Enhanced Assessment

21st International Conference, TEA 2018
Amsterdam, The Netherlands, December 10–11, 2018
Revised Selected Papers

 Springer

Editors
Silvester Draaijer ⓘ
Faculty of Behavioural
and Movement Sciences
Vrije Universiteit Amsterdam
Amsterdam, The Netherlands

Desirée Joosten-ten Brinke
Welten Instituut
Open University of the Netherlands
Heerlen, The Netherlands

Eric Ras
Luxembourg Institute of Science
and Technology
Esch-sur-Alzette, Luxembourg

ISSN 1865-0929   ISSN 1865-0937 (electronic)
Communications in Computer and Information Science
ISBN 978-3-030-25263-2   ISBN 978-3-030-25264-9 (eBook)
https://doi.org/10.1007/978-3-030-25264-9

This Springer imprint is published by the registered company Springer Nature Switzerland AG
The registered company address is: Gewerbestrasse 11, 6330 Cham, Switzerland

Preface

The objective of the International Technology-Enhanced Assessment Conference (TEA) is to connect researchers, policy-makers, and practitioners with innovative ideas and research to address current challenges and advances in the field of e-Assessment. The aim is to advance the understanding and application of information technology to the assessment process (e-assessment) through peer-reviewed contributions from the research, policy, and practice sector. This volume of conference proceedings provides an opportunity for readers to engage with refereed research and a few practice papers that were presented during the 21st edition of this conference, which took place in Amsterdam, The Netherlands, at the Vrije Universiteit Amsterdam, during December 10–11 2019. Each paper was reviewed by at least three experts and the authors revised their papers based on these comments, discussions during the conference, and comments by the editors. In total, 14 submissions from 34 authors were selected to be published in this volume. These publications present a wide variety of studies in technology-enhanced assessment and research. The publications show that technology is still gaining more and more momentum in all phases of assessment as well as in the many difference assessment domains (i.e., school education, higher education, and performance measurement at the workplace). We see a progression in research and technologies that further automate phases in assessment.

Several contributions focus on generating and designing test items, automatic generation, and effects of providing rich feedback, but there are also contributions relating to assessment and privacy, MOOCs, collaborative problem solving and fraud. The papers will be of interest for educational scientists, policy-makers, and practitioners who want to be informed about recent innovations and obtain insights into technology-enhanced assessment. We thank all reviewers, contributing authors, the keynote speaker, sponsors, and the hosting institutions for their support.

May 2019

Silvester Draaijer
Desirée Joosten-ten Brinke
Eric Ras

Organization

General Chairs

Silvester Draaijer	Vrije Universiteit Amsterdam, The Netherlands
Desirée Joosten-ten Brinke	Open University of The Netherlands and Fontys, University of Applied Sciences, The Netherlands

Program Committee Chairs

Silvester Draaijer	Vrije Universiteit Amsterdam, The Netherlands
Desirée Joosten-ten Brinke	Open University of The Netherlands and Fontys, University of Applied Sciences, The Netherlands
Eric Ras	Luxembourg Institute of Science and Technology, Luxembourg

Program Committee

Koen Aesaert	Ghent University, Belgium
Dietrich Albert	University of Graz, Austria
Ilja Cornelisz	Vrije Universiteit Amsterdam, The Netherlands
Geoffrey Crisp	University of New South Wales, UK
Mary Dankbaar	Erasmus University Medical Center, The Netherlands
Sven De Maeyer	University of Antwerp, Belgium
Jeroen Donkers	Maastricht University, The Netherlands
Silvester Draaijer	Vrije Universiteit Amsterdam, The Netherlands
Mariana Durcheva	TU-Sofia, Bulgaria
Chris Edwards	The Open University, UK
Theo Eggen	Cito/University of Twente, The Netherlands
Maka Eradze	Tallinn University, Estonia
Inger Erikson	BI Norwegian Business School, Norway
Giuseppe Fiorentino	Accademia Navale di Livorno, Italy
Lot Fonteyne	Ghent University, Belgium
Gabriele Frankl	Alpen-Adria Universität Klagenfurt, Austria
Lester Gilbert	University of Southampton, UK
Michael Goedicke	University of Duisburg-Essen, Germany
Dai Griffiths	University of Bolton, UK
Anna Guerrero	Universitat Oberta de Catalunya, Spain
José Janssen	Open University, The Netherlands
Rianne Janssen	Katholieke Universiteit Leuven, Belgium
Amanda Jefferies	University of Hertfordshire, UK
Martin Johnson	Cambridge Assessment, UK
Desirée Joosten-ten Brinke	Open University, The Netherlands

Sally Jordan	Open University, UK
José Paulo Leal	University of Porto, Portugal
Christine Lippens	Universiteit Antwerpen, Belgium
Nabin Maharjan	The University of Memphis, USA
Ivana Marenzi	L3S Research Center, Germany
Hélène Mayer	Luxembourg Institute of Science and Technology, Luxembourg
Kelly Meusen	HZ University of applied Sciences, The Netherlands
Rob Nadolski	Open University, The Netherlands
Kate Outhwaite	Anglia Ruskin University, UK
Margus Pedaste	University of Tartu, Estonia
Hans Põldoja	Tallinn University, Estonia
Eric Ras	Luxembourg Institute of Science and Technology, Luxembourg
M. Elena Rodriguez	Universitat Oberta de Catalunya, Spain
Ellen Rusman	Open University, The Netherlands
Venkat Sastry	Cranfield University, UK
Christian Saul	Fraunhofer, Germany
Cor Sluijter	Cito, The Netherlands
Michael Striewe	University of Duisburg-Essen, Germany
Esther Tan	Open University, The Netherlands
Dirk Tempelaar	Maastricht University, The Netherlands
Nathan Thompson	ASC, USA
Alison Twiner	The Open University, UK
Thomas Daniel Ullmann	The Open University, UK
Marieke Van der Schaaf	Utrecht University, The Netherlands
Bernard Veldkamp	University of Twente, The Netherlands
Peter Vlerick	Ghent University, Belgium
David Walker	University of Sussex, UK
Denise Whitelock	The Open University, UK
Karsten D. Wolf	Universität Bremen, Germany
Li Zhang	George Mason University, USA

Sponsors

DigitalEd (www.digitaled.com)
Grasple (www.grasple.com)
WiseFlow (www.uniwise.dk)
Xebic (www.xebic.com)
Questionmark (www.questionmark.com)
Teelen (www.teelen.nl)
Aurora Network (https://aurora-network.global/)

Contents

Dynamic Generation of Assessment Items Using Wikidata

Michael Striewe[(⊠)]

University of Duisburg-Essen, Gerlingstraße 16, 45127 Essen, Germany
michael.striewe@paluno.uni-due.de

Abstract. Automated generation of assessment items can provide large item pools for formative assessments with little effort. However, if the generation process produces self-contained items, these need to be updated or re-generated each time the data source used for generation changes. This paper describes and discusses an alternative approach that dynamically retrieves item content from Wikidata using SPARQL queries. The paper compares four different examples and discusses both benefits and limitations of this approach. Results show that the approach is usable for a broad range of different items for formative assessment scenarios and that limitations are manageable with acceptable effort.

Keywords: Assessment item generation · Wikidata · SPARQL

1 Introduction

Before an assessment can be conducted, an appropriate set of assessment items needs to be prepared. There are several ways of how to do this, including manual creation of individual items, automated generation of items, and import of existing items from a repository. Depending on the assessment scenario, there may also be a difference in the effort needed: A formal summative assessment may require a small set of well-calibrated and well-tested items, resulting in a high effort per single item. An informal formative assessment may require a much larger set of similar but not equal items, resulting in a high effort to construct a large item pool.

If we consider a very simple item for geography training as an example, we can create roughly 200 single items to ask for the capital of one of the countries in the world. It is surely a tedious task to create all these items manually. Automated generation of assessment items can help in this case [1]. If the assessment is conducted in a traditional way (such as a paper-based written exam), the generation needs to be done "offline" during the assessment preparation. If the assessment is performed as an e-assessment, the item generation can also happen "online" dynamically while the assessment is conducted. In either case, some data source is needed that contains some pieces of data that make up the actual content of the generated assessment items. In the case of "offline" generation, the data source is only needed once during the generation process, as the result of that process is a set of static self-contained exercises that can be used independent of the original data source. Notably, this implies the need to update or re-generate the assessment items once the contents of the original data source changes.

© Springer Nature Switzerland AG 2019
S. Draaijer et al. (Eds.): TEA 2018, CCIS 1014, pp. 1–15, 2019.
https://doi.org/10.1007/978-3-030-25264-9_1

In the case of our geography training items, this is indeed likely to happen, as sometimes countries change their name, the name of their capital, or split into two or more new countries.

Dynamic "online" generation can also use self-contained items by encoding the full data set from the data source within the item. In this case, the e-assessment system will make a random selection of one of several possible values for specific parts of the item content. This technique is usually based on item templates and is well supported by standardized item formats [2]. However, this also implies the need to update the item once the original data source changes. Moreover, the data set used to generate item content may be too large to be encoded locally within the item, or single pieces of data used within an item are too large or too complex to be encoded locally within the item. Considering the geography item again, it may be feasible to encode a list of 200 countries and their capitals within an assessment item. Nevertheless one can consider other items in which it might be necessary to encode 200 maps of these countries within the item as well, which might be a much more complex endeavor.

An alternative is dynamic item generation relying on external data sources. In this case, the item does not contain actual data but just technical information on where to find appropriate data. This paper describes and discusses a template-based approach for generating assessment items dynamically within an e-assessment system. The approach makes use of an external data source by connecting to Wikidata via SPARQL queries. The paper compares four different cases to describe the application of the approach and to explore its benefits and limitations. The goal is to answer the question in which contexts dynamic item generation is possible and whether the challenges and limitations that might occur can be handled with acceptable effort.

The paper is organized as follows: Sect. 2 reports on related work in the field of assessment item generation. Section 3 discusses the technical background of the proposed approach. Section 4 compares four different examples of exercises using the proposed approach and discusses individual benefits and limitations for each of them. Section 5 closes the paper with conclusions and future work.

2   Related Work

The idea of assessment item generation is not new, but has been discussed already some years ago. However, many approaches solely generate answer options for single-choice or multiple-choice items [3–8] or focus on items that ask *what?*, *how?* or *why?*-questions [9]. While both are useful applications, they do explore neither the possible range of item types nor the possible range of competency levels. This paper discusses a larger range of possible applications, as it also includes a sample for a cloze text item as well as a sample for an item testing application and analysis competencies.

Foulonneau and Ras [10] report several different processes for item generation with different starting points such as learning resources or domain models. The same paper also mentions important research questions such as item quality (which is also discussed in e.g. [6]), inclusion of complex item elements such as multimedia resources and the use of the semantic web as a potential data source. Some of these questions are not yet answered and do appear also at various places in the comparison presented in this paper. However, this paper solely uses a generation process starting with structured data and does not explore different processes with other starting points.

Foulonneau also analyzed an approach using SPARQL and DBpedia to generate assessment items automatically [11]. Different to the approach in this paper, the generation process produced self-contained items using the QTI format. It does thus not solve the problem of updating items when the underlying data source changes. Nevertheless, some of the technical details from that approach are similar to the ones from the approach in this paper.

Closely related to automated item generation is automated question generation [12], which is also used in the context of education, but does not necessarily produce questions that can be used as assessment items in an automated assessment system. Instead, it can also be used in tutorial systems [13] or argumentation support systems [14].

3 Technical Background

The approach presented in this paper is based on the e-assessment system JACK [15]. Among its item types, this system offers item types for single/multiple-choice-items as well as cloze texts and drop-down-menus. The system also employs a template-based approach for these kinds of items, in which variables can be used as placeholders for item content. The item definition may contain expressions for each variable that are evaluated dynamically right before the item is delivered to a user [16]. In the same way, expressions can be used when evaluating user input for cloze texts. The expression language used within JACK is able to perform many operations on strings, numbers, and lists and can redirect calls to external systems such as computer algebra systems [17]. The general definition of items in JACK happens by creating XML documents. In a simple exercise, one document describes the item template including placeholders and another document lists the operations to be performed to fill these placeholders. No specific tool support for writing these documents is available at the moment. Nevertheless, university teachers are usually able to define exercises on their own with only minimal technical support after they have received a half-day training.

For using external data source, the expression language and the expression evaluator have been extended in such a way that it allows evaluating SPARQL queries. SPARQL is a structured query language for data stored in Resource Description Framework (RDF) format [18]. This format allows describing virtually any kind of data in a "subject-predicate-object" style, where both subject and object are so-called entities. If we consider the author of this paper to be an entity with ID e123 and this paper to be an entity with ID e456, we can use a predicate with ID p789 and the meaning "has authored" the express the authorship of this paper via the tuple (e123, p789, e456). A SPARQL query like "e123 p789?papers" would return a list of all entities authored by author e123.

A large database project using this format is the Wikidata project [19], in which for example Amsterdam is represented as an entity with ID Q727[1]. The Wikidata project

---

[1] https://www.wikidata.org/wiki/Q727.

also offers a SPARQL endpoint that allows accessing the database content by posing SPARQL queries. Thus, the approach for using dynamic item generation with Wikidata and SPARQL in JACK results in the following workflow:

1. An item author defines an item template including one or more variables.
2. The item author defines an expression containing a SPARQL query for each of the variables.
3. Optionally, the item author also defines an expression containing another SPARQL query and a reference to the user input as a rule for determining the item result.
4. Each time the item is delivered to a user JACK retrieves a value for each variable by posing the SPARQL query to Wikidata. JACK then inserts the results in the item template and displays the item.
5. If defined in step 3, JACK also poses a SPARQL query to Wikidata after a user has submitted an answer to determine the item result.

The SPARQL endpoint of Wikidata is usually able to answer each query within less than 500 ms, which causes no relevant delay in delivering items.

4   Comparison of Four Sample Cases

In this section, we present and discuss four examples of assessment items using dynamic item generation. For each example, a motivation is given on why to realize this item via dynamic item generation. Afterwards the actual realization of the item is explained alongside a sample instance of that item. All examples are shown in their original phrasing in German with translations of key element provided in the figure caption. Each example is concluded by a discussion of individual benefits and limitations.

4.1   Case 1: Archaeological Sites

Figure 1 shows a sample instance of an item for the first case[2]. The idea for the item origins from a brainstorming session with archaeologists on the use of e-assessment in their domain. One part of the basic studies in archaeology is historical geography in which students acquire basic knowledge about ancient cities, archaeological sites and their geographical location. It is important to know geographical locations to be able to take part in scientific discussions in that domain. Consequently, training sessions in that domain include assessment items asking for geographical locations of ancient cities or archaeological sites.

Prerequisites. The technical design of an appropriate item definition seems to be possible, as the necessary data is available on Wikidata. In particular, Wikidata offers entities representing the concepts of cities (Q515[3]), archaeological sites (Q839954[4])

---

[2] Item live-demo: https://jack-demo.s3.uni-due.de/jack2/demo?id=63144.

[3] https://www.wikidata.org/wiki/Q515.

[4] https://www.wikidata.org/wiki/Q839954.

Aufgabe "Römische Städte und archäologische Stätten"

Frage 1

Welche der folgenden Städte oder archäologischen Stätten liegt in der römischen Provinz Germania inferior?

Antworten:

- ☐ Augusta Treverorum
- ☐ Durnomagus
- ☐ Icorigium
- ☐ Marcomagus

Fig. 1. Screenshot for a sample exercise instance for case 1. The English translation of the question is "Which of the following cities or archaeological sites is located in the Roman province Germania inferior?".

and ancient Roman provinces (Q182547[5]), as well as properties describing the geographical location (P131[6]).

Realization. As shown in Fig. 1, the item contains a short question naming the Roman province and offers four answer options, from which at least one is correct. The technical realization is straightforward: A SPARQL query asks for all available ancient cities and archaeological sites that are located within an ancient Roman province and retrieves a list of tuples containing the city or site name and province name. From this list, the e-assessment system randomly draws four elements. The province named in the first element is used in the question and the city or site names of the four elements form the answer options. This way it is assured that at least one answer option is correct. Answer options are shuffled into random order, so that users cannot know which one was the first.

Benefits. The main benefits is the expected one of reduced need for data encoding and updating. The list of possible answer options is quite large, as there exist hundreds of relevant places all over the Roman Empire. Thus, it would be inefficient to have this encoded directly in the item definition. Moreover, additional places may join this list when new findings are made, which would require updating all items using such a list.

As an additional benefit, it is also possible to make the SPARQL query more specific to include only e.g. places from a specific period or places of a certain size (if appropriate data is available). This can be used to customize training sessions more specifically to the current contents of a lecture or to gain more precise control over the selection of distractors.

Limitations. The main limitation in this case is the high dependency on data completeness and quality in the underlying data source. At the time of writing this paper,

---

[5] https://www.wikidata.org/wiki/Q182547.

[6] https://www.wikidata.org/wiki/Property:P131.

the data quality for ancient cities and archaeological places in Wikidata is quite poor. Despite the fact that there are hundreds of relevant places and almost every ancient Roman province recorded in Wikidata, the query used in the item definition returns only 54 places. From these, 36 are located within the ancient Roman province "Germania Inferior". There are two reasons for that: First, for many places property P131 is not set for the respective ancient Roman province, so that the query cannot detect this connection. Second, results must be filtered to match the language of the item template (in order to avoid e.g. using an English name in an assessment item phrased in German), but not all places might have names recorded in the requested language. This is a problem somewhat similar to the naming problem reported in [11], where the same person was known by different names. In the particular case of historic places, a place might by commonly known by its Latin name in one language, but by a different name in another language. This limitation can be avoided by using the approach only with data from data sources that have a sufficient quality or by contributing to the Wikidata project to help to improve data quality directly. The latter is possible with minimal training, as Wikidata offers a web-based interface for browsing and editing its contents.

4.2   Case 2: Chemical Compounds

Figure 2 shows a sample instance of an item for the second case[7], which looks somewhat similar to the one in the previous case. The idea for this item was born after a brainstorming session with the chemistry department of the author's university. Basic competencies in chemistry include the ability to identify chemical compounds by looking at a graphical representation of their molecule structure. Training sessions thus include items showing molecule structures and asking for the name of the chemical compound.

Prerequisites. Although the item looks very similar to the on in the previous case, the technical design is a bit more complex: Wikidata offers entities representing the concepts of chemical compounds (Q11173[8]), as well as properties describing the chemical structure (P117[9]). However, the graphical representation of the chemical structure is not provided directly by Wikidata, but as a link to an image resource hosted in the Wikimedia Commons project [20].

Realization. As shown in Fig. 2, the item contains a short question including the graphical representation and offers four answer options, from which one is correct. To achieve that, a SPARQL query asks for all available chemical compounds and retrieves a list of tuples containing the name and chemical structure. Drawing randomly directly from this list may result in four compounds with very different structures that are too easy to distinguish. Hence, the query retrieves an additional representation of each chemical structure in the canonical SMILES notation [21], which is available via

---

[7] Item live-demo: https://jack-demo.s3.uni-due.de/jack2/demo?id=63140.

[8] https://www.wikidata.org/wiki/Q11173.

[9] https://www.wikidata.org/wiki/Property:P117.

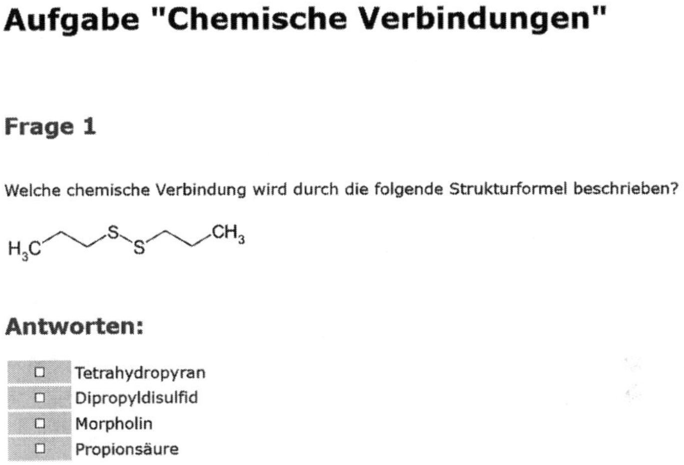

Aufgabe "Chemische Verbindungen"

Frage 1

Welche chemische Verbindung wird durch die folgende Strukturformel beschrieben?

Antworten:

- ☐ Tetrahydropyran
- ☐ Dipropyldisulfid
- ☐ Morpholin
- ☐ Propionsäure

Fig. 2. Screenshot for a sample exercise instance for case 2. The English translation of the question is "Which chemical compound does the following molecule structure describe?".

property P233[10]. Results are then filtered to only include elements with the same size of the SMILES representation with a predefined length in the range of 6 to 12. This simple heuristic limits the list of query results to ones that are more similar to each other. From this filtered list, the e-assessment system finally randomly draws four elements and uses the first as the correct answer as in case 1.

Benefits. Similar to case 1, the list of possible answer options is quite large, as there exist hundreds of chemical compounds. Even with filtering for a specific length of the SMILES representation, each filtered list has 89 to 151 entries. Moreover, a graphical representation is needed for each of them. Thus, it would be both inefficient and complex to have this encoded directly in a self-contained item definition. Hence, the expected main benefit of reduced need for data encoding applies here again.

As an additional benefit, it is also possible to make the SPARQL query more specific to include only specific chemical compounds.

Limitations. Loading graphical representations from the Wikimedia Commons project (or any other source) includes an additional external data source in the process. This may introduce additional errors, as e.g. Wikidata may point to the wrong image within Wikimedia or the image may contain the wrong data. This limitation can be avoided by carefully checking data quality before using several sources or by using the approach with own data sources with known quality.

The heuristic described above may also be insufficient to create items of the desired didactical quality in terms of selecting good distractors. For example, the heuristic does not look for molecules including a least some similar atoms. This limitation can be avoided by including more sophisticated filter functions in the item definition to get

---

[10] https://www.wikidata.org/wiki/Property:P233.

more fine-grained control of the selected data. This may require to extend the capabilities of JACK or to write sophisticated SPARQL queries.

4.3   Case 3: Geography Data

Figure 3 shows a sample instance of an item for the third case[11]. The idea for this item comes from plans for a curriculum on data literacy that is organized around different competencies for data collection, data handling and data analysis. Central competencies in this context are abilities to read, understand and compare data. Training sessions can thus include item in which a (small) dataset is provided and some statements are given that must be identified as true or false with respect to the given data. Different to the cases discussed above, the resulting items thus do not tackle the competency level of knowledge, but application and analysis competencies. Nevertheless, multiple-choice items are usable for that purpose.

The sample item shown in Fig. 3 uses some data about countries in the European Union to generate statements about size, population and related topics. However, the general idea of this item is not specific to geography data, but also applicable to other data sets.

Prerequisites. The particular item from Fig. 3 makes use of the fact that the European Union is represented in Wikidata by entity Q458[12] and properties exist for area (P2046[13]), population (P1082[14]), memberships (P463[15]) and capitals (P36[16]). Notably, Wikidata also offers options to express area information in different (metric and non-metric) units.

Realization. As in the previous cases, the realization starts by retrieving tuples of data using a specific SPARQL query. In this case, a data tuple is retrieved for each country being a member of the European Union. Each tuple contains name, area and population of the country as well as name, area and population of its capital. To make data comparable, area sizes are normalized to be returned in square kilometers. Two random tuples from the result list are chosen to be included in the item.

Four statements are generated from the chosen data where each generated statement may be true or false. Whether a true or false statement is generated is decided randomly for each statement. The first statement is always concerned with areas and is true or false with respect to the factor of area size between the two countries or one country and the capital of the other country. As a simple heuristic for producing false statements, the generator always computes the right factor but swaps country or city names for the wrong statement. This reflects the fact the students sometimes do the right calculations but make mistakes in the interpretation of results. Similarly, the second

---

[11] Item live-demo: https://jack-demo.s3.uni-due.de/jack2/demo?id=63131

[12] https://www.wikidata.org/wiki/Q458.

[13] https://www.wikidata.org/wiki/Property:P2046.

[14] https://www.wikidata.org/wiki/Property:P1082.

[15] https://www.wikidata.org/wiki/Property:P463.

[16] https://www.wikidata.org/wiki/Property:P36.

Aufgabe "Daten verstehen und vergleichen"

Frage 1

Betrachten Sie zunächst die folgenden Daten zu zwei europäischen Staaten.

Land	Österreich	Kroatien
Fläche des Landes in km²	83879	56594
Einwohnerzahl des Landes	8572895	4284889
Hauptstadt	Wien	Zagreb
Fläche der Hauptstadt in km²	414.87	641
Einwohnerzahl der Hauptstadt	1840573	790017

Welche der folgenden Aussagen sind korrekt?

Antworten:

☐ Das Land Kroatien ist flächenmäßig etwa 1.5-mal größer als das Land Österreich.
☐ Das Land Österreich hat etwa 10.9-mal mehr Einwohner als die Stadt Zagreb.
☐ Das Land Kroatien hat eine geringere Bevölkerungsdichte als die Stadt Zagreb.
☐ Etwa 2% der Einwohner von Kroatien leben in der Hauptstadt Zagreb.
☐ Keine der Aussagen ist richtig.

Fig. 3. Screenshot for a sample exercise instance for case 3. The question asks to look at the data for two European countries and to judge whether the following statements are correct. The answer options provide four different statements about area size, population, population density and the share of people living in a capital or the share of area the capital has with respect to the whole country. The fifth option should be ticked if all four statements are wrong.

statement is about population size and works with a factor and potentially swapped names as well. The third statement is about population density and may compare countries or cities among each other as well as countries with cities. False statements are generated in this case by miscalculations by factor 10. The fourth statement is about the share of people living in a capital or the share of area the capital has with respect to the whole country. Again, miscalculations by factor 10 are used here to generate false statements. The fifth statement is generic and only true if all generated statements are false.

Notably, after computing factors, density and shares some additional decisions and calculations are necessary to make sure that all factors and shares a rounded to a sensible number of decimal places.

Benefits. Different to the first two cases, neither the size of the data set nor its complexity is a real issue in this case. In fact, it is not even necessary to show real data in this item, as it would also work with completely random numbers and generic names like "Country A" or "City X". However, one of the goals of a data literacy curriculum is to enable students to understand and evaluate data they encounter in everyday life, such as in the news or in scientific publications. Thus, it is at least helpful to include up-to-data real data also in training sessions to allow students to check the plausibility of results by comparing calculation results to common knowledge.

This can also be used to make exercises more appealing, for example by first asking students about their favorite sports team and then using data for that team in the exercises.

Limitations. No serious limitations have been encountered during the design of this item. Improvements to the existing item are possible by a more sophisticated text generation for false statements that might explicitly consider additional typical calculation or interpretation mistakes. As an alternative, the item format can be changed so that statements need to be completed as cloze-texts. Then it is no longer necessary to generate false statements based on assumptions about typical mistakes. Instead, user input needs to be evaluated by comparison with the correct solution.

4.4   Case 4: German Governors

Figure 4 shows a sample instance of an item for the fourth case[17]. Different to the previous cases, this is not a multiple- or single-choice-item, but an item with input text fields and a drop-down menu. The item is not motivated by a specific didactical purpose or context. Instead, it is included in this comparison to demonstrate additional options for using SPARQL queries. The general idea of the item is to allow students a free input with only very few limitations and then use Wikidata as a data source to verify the correctness of the answer. Therefore, the sample item in Fig. 4 provides a drop-down-list of German states and allows students to select freely one of them for which they also have to name the incumbent governor. As in case 3, the general idea of the item is not limited to that particular domain, but applicable in other domains.

Prerequisites. Different to the cases discussed so far, the use of Wikidata as a data source happens in two steps in this case. The first step is to generate contents for the drop-down menu included in the item. This is possible for the sample item, as entities representing German states can be identified by a "is a"-property (P31[18]) pointing towards entity Q1221156[19], which represents German states.

The second step is to check whether the input in the text fields is equivalent to the name of the governor of the selected state or of a German state at all. This is also possible, because property P6[20] returns an entity representing the current head of government.

Realization. Similar to the two different ways of using the data source, the realization is also split into two parts. The first part is a simple query asking for German states. An additional check for the absence of property P576[21] (which denotes the date or point in

---

[17] Item live-demo: https://jack-demo.s3.uni-due.de/jack2/demo?id=62162.

[18] https://www.wikidata.org/wiki/Property:P31.

[19] https://www.wikidata.org/wiki/Q1221156.

[20] https://www.wikidata.org/wiki/Property:P6.

[21] https://www.wikidata.org/wiki/Property:P576.

Aufgabe "MinisterpräsidentInnen deutscher Bundesländer"

Frage 1

Geben Sie den Namen eines amtierenden Ministerpräsidenten oder einer amtierenden Ministerpräsidentin eines deutschen Bundeslandes an.

| | | amtiert in | | |
| Vorname | Nachname | | Bundesland | |

Fig. 4. Screenshot for a sample exercise instance for case 4. The question asks to provide the name of an incumbent German governor and the state he or she is head of. The states are provided as a drop-down list.

time on which an organization was dissolved) has to be included to make sure that the result excludes abandoned historic states.

The second part consists of two different SPARQL queries. The first query retrieves the head of government for the state selected by the student. The result of the query is compared to the text input to find out whether it is equivalent or at least the last name is correct. This allows giving partial credit in cases of a mistake in the first name. The second query asks for German states in which a person with the name entered by the student is head of government. This allows giving partial credit in cases in which the named person is indeed a governor, but not in the selected state.

Benefits. As in cases 1 and 2 above, the main benefit is the reduced need for updates to the item. Due to elections that take place in a regular frequency but not at the same time for all states, an item like this will never use the same data for a long time. Checking items like this after every election is a tedious task that can easily be avoided by using Wikidata as demonstrated here.

As a secondary benefit, it is also possible to include some more queries in the evaluation process so that for example partial credit is also possible if a student enters a former governor instead of the current one.

Admittedly, it seems to be quite unlikely that the amount or naming of German states will change in the future. Thus loading the contents for the drop-down-list from an external data source may actually be not necessary for the sample item. However, in other domains appropriate contents for a drop-down-list may be more likely to change, so that the general benefit is still valid.

Limitations. Different to the other three cases, this one includes several SPARQL queries where some of them also include student input. This may result in two problems: First, issuing several queries may slow down the performance of the assessment system, even if each single query does not consume much time. That problem is hard to avoid, as that alternative is to retrieve larger data sets with less queries and perform additional queries just locally in the assessment system within these data sets. This may reduce the time needed to query an external system, but adds time for data processing. Another strategy to avoid this limitation is the possibility to cache data returned by the SPARQL query. This can increase performance at least in cases when a large number of students uses the same items within a short period. However, caching data for a longer time contradicts the concept of dynamic "online" generation of item content and will thus reduce its benefits. For the sample item, it should nevertheless be possible to cache data for some hours or even days for the governor names and even for much longer periods for the state names. As caching is a general system feature, the limitation requires development effort to JACK. Teacher cannot solved it individually in the item design.

Second, students may try to compromise the system by entering malicious input if they know that their input becomes part of a query. That problem must be tackled by introducing some extra checks to sanitize or reject malicious input. However, this is possible for future JACK development and does not induce other limitations.

4.5 Summary

A short summary of the conceptual and technical features of the four cases discussed above is provided in Table 1. Each case has some individual features that makes it unique in comparison to the other cases. This demonstrates that the general approach of using SPARQL queries for dynamic item generation and using Wikidata as a data source is usable in a brought range of different domains and scenarios. The benefits in all cases included less data encoding in the item definition or more up-to-date data within the item. This is exactly what was expected from the approach. The limitations included a wider range of individual issues, where most of them can be avoided with little extra effort. Possible additional actions that may be needed include the use of sophisticated filter or checking functions and careful management of data sources or data quality. Both actions are anyway known from the work necessary to produce high quality assessment items, so that these extra actions indeed do not induce a high additional effort.

Table 1. Summary of the conceptual and technical features of the four cases.

	Case 1 (Archaeological sites)	Case 2 (Chemical compounds)	Case 3 (Geography data)	Case 4 (German governors)
Item type	Multiple-choice	Single-choice	Multiple-choice	Cloze text and drop-down menu
Competency level	Knowledge	Knowledge	Application and analysis	Knowledge
Content of (initial) data set	Names of 54 sites and their roman province	Names and image-URLs of 89 to 151 chemical compounds	Data sets for 27 European countries	Names of 16 German states

(*continued*)

Table 1. (*continued*)

	Case 1 (Archaeological sites)	Case 2 (Chemical compounds)	Case 3 (Geography data)	Case 4 (German governors)
Additional processing of data for item generation	no	no	yes	no
Additional external resources included in item	no	yes	no	no
Additional SPARQL queries for answer evaluation	no	no	no	yes

5 Conclusions and Future Work

This paper presented an approach on how to use SPARQL queries and Wikidata to generate assessment items dynamically within an automated assessment system. The comparison of four cases demonstrated that the approach is usable in a brought range of different domains and scenarios. Some limitations might occur during the design of assessment items. It is possible to avoid these limitations with little effort in most cases. Some limitations require teachers to be careful in selecting their data sources, while other limitations can be solved with a one-time development effort in JACK.

In turn, a large bank of items can be created that update automatically as the underlying data sources is updated. Data quality and appropriate mechanisms to select good distractors automatically for single-choice and multiple-choice questions have been identified as the main challenges that need future research and development.

Besides that, future work includes to explore two directions in more detail: First, text generation (as shown in case 3) seems to be an interesting technique to generate more sophisticated items based on the plain data retrieved from Wikidata or any other source. The technique is not limited to generating answer options, but can also be used to generate questions or corrective feedback. Second, checking answers against external data sources (as shown in case 4) can also be extended for granting partial credit or generating automated corrective feedback.

Acknowledgements. The author would like to thank Gerwin Rajkowski for his work on implementing a first prototype for SPARQL query integration within JACK as part of his bachelor's thesis. The German Federal Ministry of Education and Research founded parts of the research for this paper with grant number 01PL16075.

References

1. Gierl, M., Lai, H., Zhang, X.: Automatic item generation. In: Mehdi Khosrow-Pour, D.B.A. (Ed.) Encyclopedia of Information Science and Technology, 4th edn., pp. 2369–2379. IGI Global, Hershey (2018)
2. IMS Global Learning Consortium: IMS Question & Test Interoperability Specification. http://www.imsglobal.org/question/. Accessed 19 Oct 2018
3. Mostow, J., Jang, H.: Generating diagnostic multiple choice comprehension cloze questions. In: Proceedings Workshop on Innovative Use of NLP for Building Educational Applications, 136–146 (2012)
4. Al-Yahya, M.: OntoQue: a question generation engine for educational assesment based on domain ontologies. In: 11th IEEE International Conference on Advanced Learning Technologies, 393–395 (2011)
5. Gierl, M.J., Lai, H., Turner, S.R.: Using automatic item generation to create multiple-choice test items. Med. Educ. **46**, 757–765 (2012)
6. Lai, H., Gierl, M.J., Touchie, C., Pugh, D., Boulais, A.-P., Champlain, A.D.: Using automatic item generation to improve the quality of MCQ distractors. Teach. Learn. Med. **28**, 166–173 (2016). Routledge
7. Afzal, N., Mitkov, R.: Automatic generation of multiple choice questions using dependency-based semantic relations. Soft. Comput. **18**, 1269–1281 (2014)
8. Susanti, Y., Iida, R., Tokunaga, T.: Automatic generation of english vocabulary tests. In: 7th International Conference on Computer Supported Education (CSEDU), 77–87 (2015)
9. Iwane, N., Gao, C., Yoshida, M.: Question generation for learner centered learning. In: 13th IEEE International Conference on Advanced Learning Technologies, 330–332 (2013)
10. Foulonneau, M., Ras, E.: Assessment item generation, the way forward. In: CAA 2013 International Conference (2013)
11. Foulonneau, M.: Generating educational assessment items from linked open data: the case of DBpedia. In: García-Castro, R., Fensel, D., Antoniou, G. (eds.) ESWC 2011. LNCS, vol. 7117, pp. 16–27. Springer, Heidelberg (2012). https://doi.org/10.1007/978-3-642-25953-1_2
12. Le, N.-T., Kojiri, T., Pinkwart, N.: Automatic question generation for educational applications – the state of art. In: van Do, T., Thi, H.A.L., Nguyen, N.T. (eds.) Advanced computational methods for knowledge engineering. AISC, vol. 282, pp. 325–338. Springer, Cham (2014). https://doi.org/10.1007/978-3-319-06569-4_24
13. Olney, A.M., Graesser, A.C., Person, N.K.: Question generation from concept maps. Dialogue and Discourse **3**(2), 75–99 (2012)
14. Le, N.-T., Nguyen, N.-P., Seta, K., Pinkwart, N.: Automatic question generation for supporting argumentation. Vietnam J Comput. Sci. **1**, 117–127 (2014). https://doi.org/10.1007/s40595-014-0014-9. Springer-Verlag New York, Inc.
15. JACK website. http://www.s3.uni-duisburg-essen.de/en/jack/. Accessed 19 Oct 2018
16. Schwinning, N., Striewe, M., Savija, M., Goedicke, M.: On flexible multiple choice questions with parameters. In: Proceedings of the 14th European Conference on e-Learning (ECEL) (2015)
17. Schwinning, N., Kurt-Karaoglu, F., Striewe, M., Zurmaar, B., Goedicke, M.: A framework for generic exercises with mathematical content. In: Proceedings of the International Conference on Learning and Teaching in Computing and Engineering (LaTiCE), 70–75 (2015)
18. RDF website. https://www.w3.org/RDF/. Accessed 19 Oct 2018

19. Wikidata project. https://www.wikidata.org/wiki/Wikidata:Main_Page. Accessed 19 Oct 2018
20. Wikimedia Commons project. https://commons.wikimedia.org/wiki/Main_Page. Accessed 19 Oct 2018
21. SMILES website. http://daylight.com/smiles/. Accessed 19 Oct 2018

Students' Attitudes Towards Personal Data Sharing in the Context of e-Assessment: Informed Consent or Privacy Paradox?

Ekaterina Muravyeva$^{(\boxtimes)}$ (iD), José Janssen, Kim Dirkx,
and Marcus Specht

Open University, Welten Institute,
Valkenburgerweg 177, Heerlen, The Netherlands
{kmu,jja,kdi,msp}@ou.nl

Abstract. Modern technologies increasingly make use of personal data to provide better services. Technologies using biometric data for identity and authorship verification in the context of e-assessment are a case in point. Previous studies in e-health described a privacy paradox in relation to consent to personal data use: even when people consider protection of their personal data important, they consent fairly readily to personal data use. However, the new European Data Protection Regulation (GDPR) assumes that people give free and informed consent. In the context of e-assessment, this study investigates students' attitudes towards personal data sharing for identity and authorship verification purposes with the aim of optimising informed consent practice. Students with special educational needs or disabilities (SEND) were included as a specific target group because they may feel more dependent on e-assessment. The findings suggest that a privacy paradox exists in the context of e-assessment as well. Furthermore, the results indicate that students are more reluctant to share video recordings of their face than other personal data. Finally, our results confirm the effect found in previous studies on e-health: those feeling a stronger need for technologies, in this case SEND students, are more inclined to consent to personal data use. Implications for informed consent practice are discussed.

Keywords: Informed consent · Personal data · Sensitive data · e-Assessment · Decision-making · Privacy paradox

1 Introduction

1.1 General Problem

Personal data are defined by Art. 4 of the new European Data Protection Regulation (GDPR) [27] as "any information relating to an identified or identifiable natural person ("data subject")". The data subject's consent constitutes the legal ground for personal data use. Consent is "any freely given, specific, informed and unambiguous indication of the data subject's wishes by which he or she [...] signifies agreement to the processing of personal data relating to him or her" [27]. This definition of consent makes clear that consent should be informed. Nevertheless, a growing number of studies show that even when people consider protection of their personal data very important, they demonstrate little interest in reading information on personal data use [1, 10, 12, 15, 30]. Only 20% of internet users pay attention to the details of requests for personal data use before giving consent [12]. This contradiction between attitudes towards protection of personal data and actual behaviour is referred to as the *"privacy paradox"* [23]. Various reasons have been suggested to explain this paradox: lack of awareness, lack of perceived choice, or inhabitation (as people are overloaded with requests for personal data use, they develop a habit of simply consenting without being informed) [4, 14]. A study by Wilkowska, and Ziefle [33] investigating the acceptance of e-health technology revealed that less healthy people appear less concerned about the secure storage of their personal data. In this respect, Burgess [6] speaks of a possible trade-off between the benefits and risks involved: despite *awareness of the risks*, people may feel tempted or more or less forced to consent.

Even those who *read* the information provided, do not always feel confident that they *understand* the information. In the context of medical research the proportion of people who understand different elements of the information varies from 52% to 76% [31]. Among internet users, only 21% are confident that they completely understand the information [8, 9]. The same study showed that internet users do not want to spend more than 5 min reading the information. In this respect, Hallinan, Forrest, Uhlenbrauck, Young, and McKinney [16] identified the following barriers to comprehension: poor presentation, challenging legal language, and a disconnect between what is expected and what is actually explained. Although this study was carried out in the context of medical research, which may have affected the expectations in specific ways, the same barriers could still be a threat in other domains.

Whether the decision to consent is *a freely made decision* is also difficult to determine. In a study conducted by Custers, Van der Hof, and Schermer [9], participants reported experiencing peer pressure or dependency on a website that required personal data. They also felt rushed or having limited time to make a decision. The way in which consent is obtained (digital, paper, verbal) may also influence a decision-making process [5, 26, 34]. A digital consent form provides many different opportunities, such as using hyperlinks in the text for additional information, photo and video materials for visualisation, and navigation through the text [19, 32]. However, too many details can create stress and concern [29, 31], and reading from the screen can create fatigue and make understanding and remembering difficult [20, 28]. This appears to be the case especially when feedback on progress is poor so that it is not immediately clear how much text still has to be read [1, 21]. A successful informed consent procedure often involves more than one communication model, for instance, written and verbal, including a face-to-face interaction with a knowledgeable person [7, 18].

Additionally, in the case of *identity and authorship verification technologies for e-assessment* [22, 24], it is not easy to explain exactly how personal data are used. A variety of instruments can be used to verify students' identity: face recognition, voice recognition, analysis of keystroke dynamics and forensic (writing style) analysis. For authorship verification, forensic analysis and plagiarism detection software can be applied. It is a challenge to ensure that students read the information and indeed understand how these instruments function, to enable an informed decision. Considering the issues identified in previous studies with respect to awareness, information uptake and comprehension, the current study investigates whether the same issues apply in the context of e-assessment.

1.2   Research Questions

Is there a privacy paradox in regard to students' attitudes and behaviour towards personal data sharing in the context of e-assessment? To investigate this general issue, the current study addresses the following questions:

Q1: How do students feel in general about sharing personal data?
Q2: How do students behave in regard to sharing personal data: do they read the information provided, and if so, how much time do they spend reading it?
Q3: To what extent do students understand the information provided?
Q4: Do students who appear concerned about sharing personal data spend more time reading the information?
Q5: Is there a relation between time spent reading and information comprehension?
Q6: Do the results for the above questions differ significantly for students with special educational needs or disabilities (SEND)?
Q7: Do the results for the above questions differ significantly depending on students' demographic characteristics (sex, age and level of education)?

The answers to these questions will be discussed in terms of their implications for improving the informed consent procedure.

Figure 1 provides a mapping of the research questions on the concepts introduced in the General Problem description.

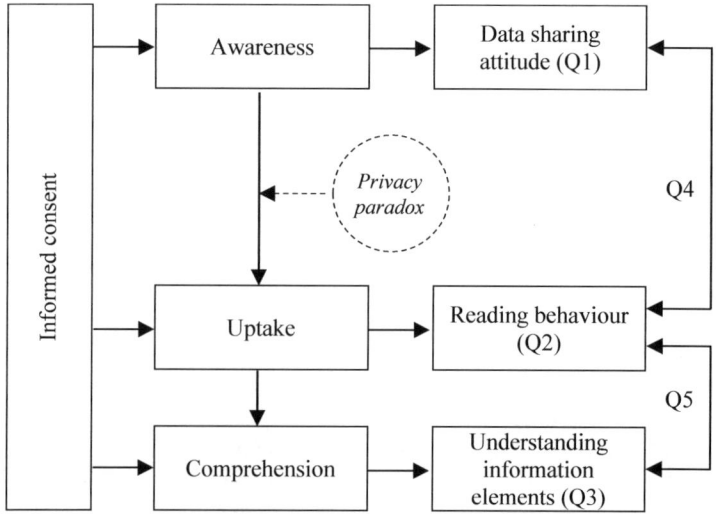

Fig. 1. A mapping of the research questions on the theoretical concepts.

Students' awareness will be assessed by examining their attitude towards personal data sharing: their perceptions of the risks and dangers involved in sharing personal data in general and sensitive personal data in particular. Information uptake is investigated by means of self-reported reading behaviour. The privacy paradox actually indicates a tension between these concepts of awareness and uptake: concerns over personal data sharing are not reflected in uptake behaviour. Therefore, we will analyse the relation between attitudes and actual behaviour. Finally, comprehension will be investigated through self-reported levels of understanding of various information elements, and we will explore the relation between understanding and reading behaviour.

2 Method

2.1 Design

For this study, a mixed-methods explanatory design was adopted [17]. Following an online survey investigating attitudes towards personal data sharing in the context of e-assessment as well as the clarity of the information provided, the findings were discussed in greater depth through a focus group interview. The questions regarding personal data sharing and informed consent were included in a larger questionnaire that was designed in the context of the TeSLA project pilot (https://tesla-project.eu/), which aimed to test and evaluate the TeSLA technology for identity and authorship verification for e-assessment. The results reported here pertain to students of the Open University of the Netherlands.

2.2 Participants

The online survey was completed by 228 students from various faculties of the Open University of the Netherlands. As a special target group, 35% of the participants were SEND students. Of the participants, 71% were female, and more than half were over the age of 40. These figures reflect the overrepresentation of female and older students in the Open University student population as a whole. A focus group interview was conducted with four students, including three SEND students.

2.3 Material

Informed Consent. The informed consent procedure was conducted in Dutch and included an information letter and a consent statement. The information letter contained 996 words. The text was split into small paragraphs, each with a separate title, addressing the purpose of data collection, collection and processing details, and contact information. Data subject rights such as the right to withdraw consent and to access, change and delete the collected data were presented in two separate paragraphs, together with instructions on how to exercise these rights. The consent statement contained 303 words and was presented at the end of the information letter.

Online Questionnaire. Data were collected using the Bristol Online Survey (BOS) tool (https://www.onlinesurveys.ac.uk/) and included background information (sex, age, level of education, SEND) as well as questions related to reading the information (yes/no), time spent reading (in minutes), level of understanding of various information elements (scale of 1 to 5, where 1 is completely unclear and 5 is completely clear), and willingness to share various types of personal data (yes/no).

Focus Group Interview Questions. During the focus group interview, students were prompted to elaborate on their experiences with personal data sharing, informed consent procedures and decision-making with respect to the pilot. As SEND students were overrepresented, considerable attention was paid to align the TeSLA technology with their needs and disabilities.

2.4   Procedure

Two sampling procedures were used, depending on the specific target group. SEND students were invited to take part in the study via e-mail by the Open University advisor for SEND students. Other students were invited following a two-stage sampling procedure. In the first stage, teachers of relevant courses were invited to participate in the pilot. These teachers were then asked to invite students enrolled in the courses to participate in the pilot. They were invited through an announcement and were subsequently presented with informed consent through which they could either accept or decline personal data use. For SEND students, a dedicated course environment was created to realise an experience with informed consent as well as with the TeSLA technology similar to that of the students enrolled in regular courses. Students who gave consent were asked to complete the online questionnaire and whether they would be willing to participate in a follow-up focus group interview. These students were later invited by e-mail for an interview.

2.5   Data Analysis

The quantitative data were analysed using the IBM Statistical Package for the Social Sciences Version 24 [13]. Analyses included chi-square and t-tests to determine group differences. Kendall's tau-b was used to determine relations: first, between time spent reading and understanding various information elements and second, between demographic characteristics (sex, age, and educational level) and students' behaviour through the informed consent procedure. For the focus group, a written report was produced.

3   Results

Q1: How do students feel about sharing personal data?

45% of the participants see the need to share personal data as a main disadvantage of identity and authorship verification technology. When asked more specifically whether they are prepared to share particular types of personal data, 9% appear unprepared to share any data. Others are willing to share, but their willingness depends heavily on the type of data. Table 1 lists different types of personal data distinguished in the questionnaire and willingness to share. Of those who are prepared to share personal data, only approximately one in two participants is prepared to share video recordings of their face, whereas still images of their face appear much less sensitive.

Table 1. Willingness to share personal data.

	% students willing to share
Image of face	70.6
Recording of voice	62.3
Keyboard dynamics	61.8
Video recording of face	47.8
	$n = 204$

Students participating in the focus group interview had no concerns and felt comfortable sharing different types of personal data. They explained that they were aware that if any concerns arose later, they could still withdraw their consent and ask that the collected data be deleted. One of them commented about not seeing much difference between sharing personal data in the context of e-assessment and being monitored by a supervisor during regular examinations in a study centre.

Q2: How do students behave in regard to sharing personal data: do they read the information provided, and if so, how much time do they spend reading it?

We asked the participants whether they had read the information provided prior to giving their consent: 84% of them said they had done so. When asked about the time spent reading the information, the answers of those who had read the information ranged from 0 to 30 min ($M = 5.36$, $SD = 4.059$). We recorded these answers in three categories according to our estimation of what was a reasonable (expected) time to take up the information provided: 0–3 min (less than expected), 4–8 min (expected), over 8 min (more than expected). Table 2 shows the answers for those participants who indicated that they had read the information. 37% spent less time reading the information than we expected. Considering the 5 min reading limit suggested by the study of Custers, Van der Hof, and Schermer [9], we found that 78% of participants in this study spent 5 min or less reading.

Table 2. Time spent reading the information.

	% students
0 to 3 min	36.9
4 to 8 min	43.1
Over 8 min	20.0
	$n = 190$

During the focus group interview, one participant said that he read the information superficially without paying special attention to the details. He explained that he feels overloaded with requests for personal data use on the internet, and that he often provides his consent without reading the information. The other participants said that they read the information carefully, but they did not have any concerns about providing their personal data because they trust their educational institution.

Q3: To what extent do students understand the information provided?

Comprehension of the information provided was measured by asking the participants to indicate to what extent specific information elements were clear to them. Ideally, all information should be completely clear to all participants. Table 3 shows that, depending on the specific information element, one in ten to one in four participants did not find the information clear enough. The information provided on the type of data was least clear. However, when asked about questions they possibly had, only 11 students said they had questions. Their questions confirmed that they were not sure how the data would be used (for instance, "Which assignments will be used, exactly?" or "What personal data will be collected from me?").

Table 3. Clarity of different information elements.

	% clear/completely clear
Purpose of data collection	88.4
Data subject rights	82.7
Collection and processing details	81.7
Contact information	81.4
Types of personal data	76.5
	n = 225

Students participating in the focus group interview initially indicated that the information was clear except one who considered the information insufficient. However, during the discussion, several questions arose. They wanted to know when and how they could withdraw their consent, whether they needed to give a reason for withdrawing, and how the educational institution could guarantee that the collected data would be deleted. Answers to the first two questions were provided in the information letter, but apparently, this information had not been taken up. In addition, students noted that even after being informed, there is little choice for those students who have no opportunity to go to a study centre for final examinations.

Q4: Do students who appear concerned about sharing personal data spend more time reading the information?

Those who see personal data use as a main disadvantage and/or are unwilling to share video recordings of their face do not appear to spend more time reading the information.

Q5: Is there a relation between time spent reading and information comprehension?

No relation was found between self-reported time spent reading and understanding of the various information elements. However, understanding of the various information elements appears strongly correlated: when the participants indicated that they understood one element, they were likely to understand other elements as well.

Q6: Do the results for the above questions differ significantly for SEND students?

It is noteworthy that at a general level, the survey results indicated that SEND students are more likely to consider that the TeSLA technology for identity and authorship verification meet their needs ($\chi2 = 14.364$, $df = 1$, $p < .001$). These findings, are confirmed by SEND students commenting, for example, that e-assessment "is a convenient additional option that makes it unnecessary to travel to a study centre". Even when they do not feel a direct personal need: "Despite my disability, I am able to come to a study centre to take an exam. But I think it is a very good initiative that is worth investigating". However, it is important to note that some SEND students actually prefer taking examinations at a study centre: "I personally prefer to take exams at the Open University. But I understand why you do this research. A lot of students will benefit from it". Another SEND student indicated that she would regret losing face-to-face examinations as an opportunity to meet other students.

Despite a different general perception of this technology with respect to compliance with SEND, the responses of SEND and non-SEND students are the same in regard to the assessment of the potential disadvantages of this technology: they equally perceive the need to share their personal data as a main disadvantage. Moreover, the results for SEND students do not differ significantly in terms of overall willingness to share personal data. However, when we examine willingness to share particular types of data, there is one exception, which involves precisely the most sensitive type of data in the context of e-assessment, namely, video recordings. Of the SEND students participating in the survey, 60% are willing to share video recordings of their face compared to 42% of non-SEND students ($\chi2 = 6.637$, $df = 1$, $p < .05$).

Q7: Do the results for the above questions differ significantly depending on students' demographic characteristics (sex, age, and educational level)?

No relation was found between sex, age and the questions above. However, there appears to be a small but significant correlation with educational level: those with a higher education degree feel more concerned about sharing video recordings of their face ($r_\tau = .147$, $p < .05$).

4   Conclusions and Discussion

Personal data use is considered a main disadvantage of technology for identity and authorship verification by almost half of the students who participated in this study. Approximately one in ten students reported that they are unwilling to share any personal data at all. The majority are willing to share their personal data, although it depends on the type of data and, to some extent, student characteristics. Overall, students are least willing to share video recordings of their face, especially students with a higher education degree. Interestingly, SEND students are more willing to share this most sensitive type of data. This difference is possibly related to the fact that they are more dependent on these technologies, and they indicated that the TeSLA technology meets their needs. This finding is in line with the study of Wilkowska, and Zielfe [33] describing a relation between a sense of dependency and concern about secure storage.

Approximately 20% of participants did not find the information provided clear. This percentage does not appear satisfactory, although we are not aware of any benchmark, and 100% clarity is probably difficult to achieve. Compared to the figure of 76% at best in the medical domain, 80% of students taking part in this study indicated that the information was clear, which might be an optimal percentage. The information provided on the type of data was least clear. This may be because this information was not under a separate header and, as a result, did not attract the proper attention.

Regarding our research question on whether a privacy paradox appears to exist in the context of e-assessment, we made the following observations. A substantial number of participants (37%) spent 3 min or less reading the information, whereas we expected people to require at least 4 min to get a proper understanding. Furthermore, we cannot say that those who expressed a concern about sharing personal data were likely to spend more time reading the information provided. Finally, the participants who said they had questions regarding the information did not tend to pose those questions. These findings indicate that a privacy paradox exists in the context of e-assessment.

A possible explanation suggested in the focus group interview is that the decision to consent is based not on the information provided but rather on a sense of confidence and trust in the institution requesting personal data. When a request for personal data comes from a well-known and trusted institution, the decision can be more easily made, and the data subject does not feel a need to be fully informed. Despite the fact that not everything was clear, students still decided to participate in the study and share their personal data. This again points to a privacy paradox. Additionally, the effect of habitation described by Böhme, and Köpsell [4] appeared to be an explanation during the focus group interview, where participants commented that information uptake was not feasible considering the vast number of requests for personal data use on the internet. These and other effects merit further investigation, although our primary focus is on developing an informed consent procedure that enhances informed decision-making.

5   Limitations and Future Work

The digital consent form used in this study was designed in the context of the TeSLA project. Following a design-based research approach [11, 24], the findings of the current study will inform a re-design of this initial version of the consent form. For instance, the information on types of data will be described in a separate paragraph, under a separate header, to attract proper attention. Additionally, we will investigate ways to facilitate the data subjects in asking questions.

While the current study was based on self-reported data, a follow-up study should provide us with more objective measurements. To this end, we are planning a study in which students' reading behaviour will be closely timed and monitored using an eye tracker device, and information uptake and comprehension will be assessed through a short knowledge test. A particular challenge for this follow-up study will be to mimic a real-life scenario, encouraging students to behave as they would if presented with informed consent while studying in their home environment.

Acknowledgement. This project has been co-funded by the HORIZON 2020 Programme of the European Union. Project number: 688520 – TeSLA – H2020 – ICT – 2015/H2015 – ICT – 2015. This publication reflects the views of the authors only, and the European Commission cannot be held responsible for any use, which may be made of the information contained therein.

References

1. Ackerman, R., Lauterman, T.: Taking reading comprehension exams on screen or on paper? A metacognitive analysis of learning texts under time pressure. Comput. Hum. Behav. **28**(5), 1816–1828 (2012)
2. Awad, N., Krishnan, M.: The personalization privacy paradox: an empirical evaluation of information transparency and the willingness to be profiled online for personalization. MIS Q. **30**(1), 13–28 (2016)
3. Bansal, G., Zahedi, F.M., Gefen, D.: Do context and personality matter? Trust and privacy concerns in disclosing private information online. Inf. Manag. **53**(1), 1–21 (2016)
4. Bohme, R., Kopsell, S.: Trained to accept? A field experiment on consent dialogs. In Proceedings of the 28th International Conference on Human Factors in Computing Systems, pp. 2403–2406 (2010)
5. Bossert, S., Strech, D.: An integrated conceptual framework for evaluating and improving "understanding" in informed consent. Trials **18**(1), 1–8 (2017)
6. Burgess, M.: Proposing modesty for informed consent. Soc. Sci. Med. **65**, 2284–2295 (2007)
7. Cohn, E., Larson, E.: Health policy and systems consent process. J. Nurs. Sch. **39**(3), 273–280 (2007)
8. Custers, B.: Click here to consent forever: expiry dates for informed consent. Big Data Soc. **3**(1), 1–6 (2016)
9. Custers, B., Van der Hof, S., Schermer, B.: Privacy expectations of social media users: the role of informed consent in privacy policies. Policy and Internet **6**(3), 268–295 (2014)
10. Dienlin, T., Trepte, S.: Is the privacy paradox a relic of the past? An in-depth analysis of privacy attitudes and privacy behaviours. Eur. J. Soc. Psychol. **45**(3), 285–297 (2015)
11. Edelson, D.C.: Design research: what we learn when we engage in design. J. Learn. Sci. **11**(1), 105–121 (2009)
12. Elsen, M., Elshout, S., Kieruj, N., Benning, T.: Onderzoek naar privacyafwegingen. https://www.centerdata.nl/. Accessed 21 Mar 2019
13. Field, A.: Discovering Statistics Using IBM SPSS Statistics, 5th edn. Sage Publications Ltd, Thousand Oaks (2017)
14. Greener, S.: Unlearning with technology. Interact. Learn. Environ. **24**(6), 1027–1029 (2016)
15. Hallam, C., Zanella, G.: Online self-disclosure: The privacy paradox explained as a temporally discounted balance between concerns and rewards. Comput. Hum. Behav. **68**, 217–227 (2017)

16. Hallinan, Z., Forrest, A., Uhlenbrauck, G., Young, S., McKinney, R.: Barriers to change in the informed consent process: a systematic literature review. Ethics Hum. Res. **38**(3), 1–10 (2016)
17. Ivankova, N.V., Creswell, J.W., Stick, S.L.: Using mixed-methods sequential explanatory design: from theory to practice. Field Methods **18**(1), 3–20 (2006)
18. Kadam, R.: Informed consent process: a step further towards making it meaningful! Perspect. Clin. Res. **8**, 107–112 (2017)
19. Kretzschmar, F., Pleimling, D., Hosemann, J., Füssel, S., Bornkessel-Schlesewsky, I., Schlesewsky, M.: Subjective impressions do not mirror online reading effort: concurrent EEG-eyetracking evidence from the reading of books and digital media. PLoS One **8**(2), 1–11 (2013)
20. Mangen, A., Walgermo, B.R., Brønnick, K.: Reading linear texts on paper versus computer screen: effects on reading comprehension. Int. J. Educ. Res. **58**, 61–68 (2013)
21. Myrberg, C., Wiberg, N.: Screen vs paper: what is the difference for reading and learning? Insights **28**(2), 49–54 (2015)
22. Noguera, I., Guerrero-Roldan, A.E., Rodríguez, M.E.: Assuring authorship and authentication across the e-Assessment process. In: Proceedings of the 19th International Technology Enhanced Assessment Conference, TEA2016, pp. 86–92 (2017)
23. Norberg, P.A., Horne, D.R., Horne, D.A.: The privacy paradox: personal information disclosure intentions versus behaviours. J. Consum. Aff. **41**(1), 100–126 (2007)
24. Okada, A., Whitelock, D., Holmes, W., Edwards, C.: e-Authentication for online assessment: a mixed-method study. Br. J. Educ. Technol. **50**(2), 861–875 (2019)
25. Plomp, T.: Educational Design Research: An Introduction. In: Plomp, T., Nieveen, N. (Eds.), Educational Design Research, pp. 10–51. Enschede: Netherlands institute for curriculum development (2013)
26. Pollach, I.: A typology of communicative strategies in online privacy policies: ethics, power and informed consent. J. Bus. Ethics **62**(3), 221–235 (2005)
27. Regulation (EU) 2016/679 of the European Parliament and of the Council of 27 April 2016 on the protection of natural persons with regard to the processing of personal data and on the free movement of such data, and repealing Directive 95/46/EC. http://eur-lex.europa.eu/legal-content/EN/TXT/PDF/?uri=CELEX:32016R0679&from=EN. Accessed 21 Mar 2019
28. Sidi, Y., Ophir, Y., Ackerman, R.: Generalizing screen inferiority - does the medium, screen versus paper, affect performance even with brief tasks? Metacognition Learn. **11**(1), 15–33 (2016)
29. Steinfeld, N.: I agree to the terms and conditions: (How) do users read privacy policies online? An eye-tracking experiment. Comput. Hum. Behav. **55**, 992–1000 (2016)
30. Taddicken, M.: The "Privacy Paradox" in the social web: the impact of privacy concerns, individual characteristics, and the perceived social relevance on different forms of self-disclosure. J. Comput.-Mediated Commun. **19**(2), 248–273 (2014)
31. Tam, N.T., Huy, N.T., Thoa, L.T.B., Long, N.P., Trang, N.T.H., Hirayama, K., Karbwang, J.: Participants' understanding of informed consent in clinical trials over three decades: systematic review and meta-analysis. Bull. World Health Organ. **93**(3), 186–198 (2015)
32. Tamariz, L., Palacio, A., Robert, M., Marcus, E.N.: Improving the informed consent process for research subjects with low literacy: a systematic review. J. General Internal Med. **28**(1), 121–126 (2012)
33. Wilkowska, W., Ziefle, M.: Perception of privacy and security for acceptance of e-Health technologies. In: Proceedings of the 5th International Conference on Pervasive Computing Technologies for Healthcare, Pervasive Health 2011, pp. 593–600 (2011)
34. Yoshida, A., Dowa, Y., Murakami, H., Kosugi, S.: Obtaining subjects' consent to publish identifying personal information: current practices and identifying potential issues. BMC Medical Ethics **14**(1), 1–9 (2013)

Students' and Teachers' Perceptions of the Usability and Usefulness of the First Viewbrics-Prototype: A Methodology and Online Tool to Formatively Assess Complex Generic Skills with Video-Enhanced Rubrics (VER) in Dutch Secondary Education

Ellen Rusman[(⊠)], Rob Nadolski, and Kevin Ackermans

Welten Institute, Open University of the Netherlands, Valkenburgerweg 167,
Heerlen, The Netherlands
{Ellen.Rusman,Rob.Nadolski,Kevin.Ackermans}@ou.nl

Abstract. Rubrics support students in learning complex generic (21st century) skills, as they provide textual descriptions of skills' mastery levels with performance indicators for all constituent subskills. If students know their current and strived-for mastery level, they can better determine subsequent learning activities towards skills mastery. However, text-based rubrics have a limited capacity to support the formation of mental models of a complex skill. Video-enhanced rubrics (VER) with video modeling examples have the potential to improve and enrich mental model formation, feedback quality, and thus improve students' performance.

In the Viewbrics-project we therefore developed, through design-based research, a methodology for the formative assessment of complex skills with Video-Enhanced Rubrics (VER), precipitated in an online tool. This paper describes the features of the first prototype of this online tool and the results of a stakeholder evaluation of its perceived usefulness and usability, by means of a questionnaire and card-sorting exercise, with 7 teachers and 21 students of two secondary schools.

The evaluation of this first prototype showed that both teachers and students evaluated the online tool and formative assessment methodology as handy, usable, helpful and feasible for learning complex skills, although some recommendations were made to further improve the design of the tool.

Keywords: Video · Rubrics · (Formative) assessment · Complex skills · Feedback · Mental model · Technology-enhanced assessment · 21st century skills

1 Introduction

Complex generic skills (also called '21st century skills') are internationally seen as increasingly important for society and education [1]. However feasible teaching and assessment methodologies to support their practice are still lacking. Complex skills

© Springer Nature Switzerland AG 2019
S. Draaijer et al. (Eds.): TEA 2018, CCIS 1014, pp. 27–41, 2019.
https://doi.org/10.1007/978-3-030-25264-9_3

consist of constituent subskills which orchestration require high cognitive effort and concentration [2, 3], and repetitive practice over a longer time in order to master them. Complex generic skills are important for all kinds of work, education and life in general, but are not specific for a domain, occupation or task. Complex skills can be applied to a broad range of situations and subject domains [4]. Many schools are struggling with the integration of complex skills in their curriculum [5]. Dutch teachers explicitly indicated that, although they are aware of the importance of practicing skills and do try to pay attention to them in their lessons, it is often not done very explicitly, structure and regularly [6].

The Viewbrics-methodology and online tool are designed to provide both teachers and pupils with structured support to formatively assess and provide high quality feedback while practicing skills in first two classes in secondary schools on the athenaeum/gymnasium level. It also adds Video-enhanced Rubrics (VER) to the current educational practice: an integrated feedback and reflection format of textual rubrics and video modeling examples.

The targeted mastery level of a skill is often expressed by means of a text-based (analytic) rubric. Rubrics are often-used instruments to (formatively) assess complex generic skills and to support students. They provide descriptions of skills' mastery levels with performance indicators for all constituent sub-skills, thus making expectations explicit [7]. When students acquire insight in their performance compared to the targeted mastery level of a complex skill, they can better monitor their learning activities and communicate with teachers [8, 9].

However, many aspects of the strived-for behavior in complex skills refer to motoric activities, time-consecutive operations and processes that are hardly captured in text (e.g. body posture or use of voice during a presentation). Text-based rubrics have a limited capacity to convey contextualized and 'tacit' observable behavioral aspects of a complex skill [10, 11]. Tacit knowledge or 'knowing how' is interwoven with practical activities, operations and behavior in the physical world [11].

However, we expect that these restrictions can be overcome with video-enhanced rubrics (VER), which are developed through a design research approach [17] in close collaboration with teachers and students and subsequently studied in a comparative experimental study on their potential effects within the Viewbrics-project (www.viewbrics.nl). A video-enhanced rubric (VER) is the synthesis of video modeling examples and a text-based analytic rubric. The VER is presented to the learner in a digital formative assessment format and methodology. We expect video-enhanced rubrics to foster learning from the observation of video modeling examples [12–14], thus supporting mental model formation, when combined with textual performance indicators.

For example, Van Gog et al. found an increased performance of task execution when a video-modeling example of an expert was shown [12, 15] and De Grez et al. found comparable results while learning presentation skills [13]. Furthermore, text supposedly leaves more room for personal interpretation of the performance indicators of a complex skill than video. More room for interpretation may negatively influence the mental model formation of a skill and has an adverse effect on feedback consistency of assessors. When teacher trainees compare their own performance with video-modeling examples they tend to 'overrate' their own performance less during self-reflection than without these examples. Teacher trainees also improved insight into their performance compared to the targeted mastery level of a complex skill [16].

Overarching research on mastering complex skills [2] indicates that the learning process and skills' acquisition are positively influenced by modeling examples, variety of application context as well as frequent feedback. Finally, video modeling examples also capture 'know-how' (procedural) knowledge and may also include 'know-why' (strategic/decisive) knowledge. Know-why knowledge can be used during practicing a skill as well as while providing feedback.

Concluding, based on theory, we expect that the use of video modeling examples (illustrating behavior associated with skills mastery levels in context) with information in different modalities (moving images, sound), combined with text-based rubrics, will foster a more concrete and consistent mental model of a complex skill amongst students and teachers than solely using text-based rubrics. We expect a more concrete and consistent mental model of a complex skill to improve quality of feedback given by teachers or peers during skills training, and subsequently result in more effective or efficient skill mastery. This study reports on the design of a first prototype of the overall formative assessment methodology, the accompanying online tool and on perceptions of students and teachers on both usefulness and usability of (parts of) the tool.

2 The 'Viewbrics' Project

The Viewbrics project is a three year research and development project structured in two major phases. In the first major phase of the project we develop and study, by means of design research, a methodology for the formative assessment of complex skills with Video-Enhanced Rubrics (VER), precipitated in an online tool. In this phase, a design research approach is chosen [17], in which teachers (from different disciplines), students and researchers collaborate in a core team and evaluate the methodology and online tool in cycles. The team is supplemented with additional design expertise, like e.g. script-writing, multimedia, programming and interface experts, when needed. For the validation of the three rubrics and the video-modeling examples a broader group of teachers and students were involved (e.g. by means of a MOOC on formative assessment). The second major phase of the project is dedicated to an empirical study in which the formative assessment methodology and online tooling is implemented and studied in two secondary schools on its effects on mental model development as well as on the mastery of complex skills of students. This paper reports on one of the steps taken within the design research phase of the Viewbrics-project, during which the formative assessment methodology with VER's and associated online tooling was developed.

The design research process is structured in three steps dedicated to developing and testing various versions of the video-enhanced rubrics and the digital 360 degree feedback instrument with different (groups of) stakeholders (researchers, teachers, students).

In this paper we report on the results of a stakeholder evaluation with students and teachers of two lower secondary education classes (athenaeum/gymnasium). This pilot aimed to answer and collect feedback on three questions, namely:

1. To what extent is the overall Viewbrics methodology and foreseen design and functionality of the complete online tool perceived as useful by both teachers and students?
2. To what extent is the first working prototype, containing parts of the foreseen functionality of the complete online tool, perceived as usable by both teachers and student?
3. What feedback do teachers and students have to improve the online tool both on perceived usability as well as usefulness?

However, before we do, we first describe the features of this prototype portrayed in relation to the Viewbrics-methodology and foreseen functionality of the complete online tool.

3 The Design and Functionality of the First Prototype of the Viewbrics-Online Tool

Depending on the role (student-learner, student-peer assessor, teacher, administrator) the complete Viewbrics online tool will support different types of working processes. In this paper we describe the formative assessment methodology, associated processes and interfaces from the **student-learner perspective** to provide an impression of the complete foreseen design of the online tool. The first working prototype of the Viewbrics-online tool contains a sub-set of this foreseen functionality, namely the (self- and peer) assessment functionality. Stakeholders were informed through a presentation and mock-ups about all steps of the complete formative assessment methodology and foreseen design of the online tool. The overall formative assessment process supported by the Viewbrics methodology is visualized in Fig. 1 and consists of five main steps.

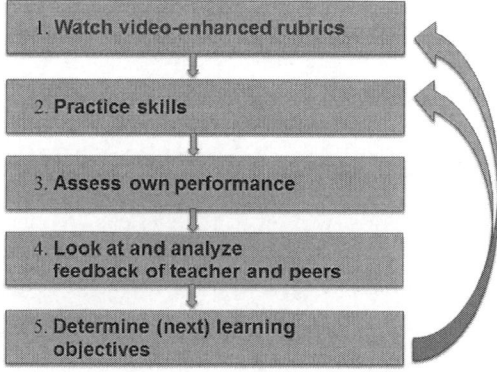

Fig. 1. Formative assessment process in Viewbrics from the student's perspective

Below we describe these five steps and present the major interfaces associated with this formative assessment process:

Step 1 - 'VER watching': Students watch video-enhanced rubrics (VER) with video-modeling examples and information processing support (by means of a questioning mechanism [18]) in the online tool, in order to form a mental model of a complex generic skill and an impression of the expected mastery level. They first watch the complete video, then they process the video modeling examples by means of questions linking the video to the rubrics and then they proceed to the page where they can watch the video modeling examples in fragments associated with a subskill (Fig. 2) and review the complete video. This step was not yet available in the online tool during the evaluation of the first prototype, however we include it in the paper, as it illustrates and provides insight in the complete Viewbrics-formative assessment methodology.

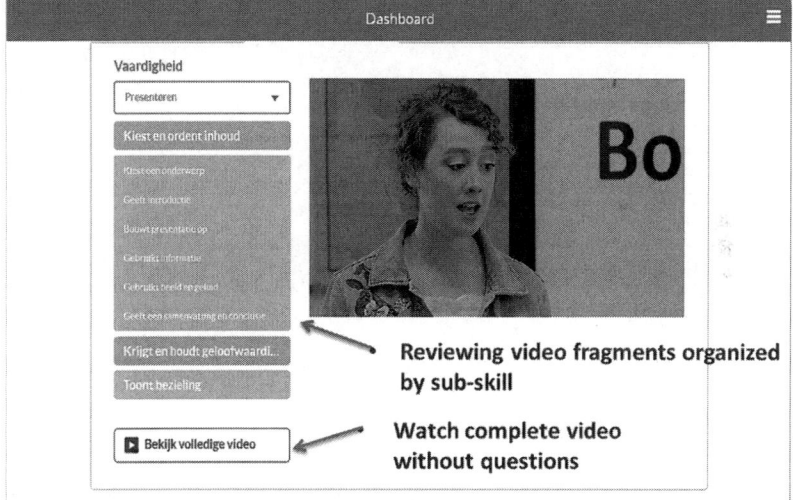

Fig. 2. Reviewing video fragments of modeling examples by sub-skill in rubric

Step 2 - 'Practicing a skill': Students go 'into the real world' in order to practice a skill in the context a teacher provided them with and with the impression of skilled behaviour they formed by looking at the VER.

Step 3 - 'Self-assessment': Based on their own experience with practicing their skill, students self-assess their performance by means of the rubrics in the online tool. Rubrics are organized in skills clusters and sub-skills (Fig. 3). Each sub-skill is described in a rubric with four performance level descriptors (Fig. 4). Only after completing the self-assessment, students can look at the 360-degree feedback of peers and the teacher (who assess a students' performance while practicing by scoring the rubrics and providing additional tips and tops per skills' cluster).

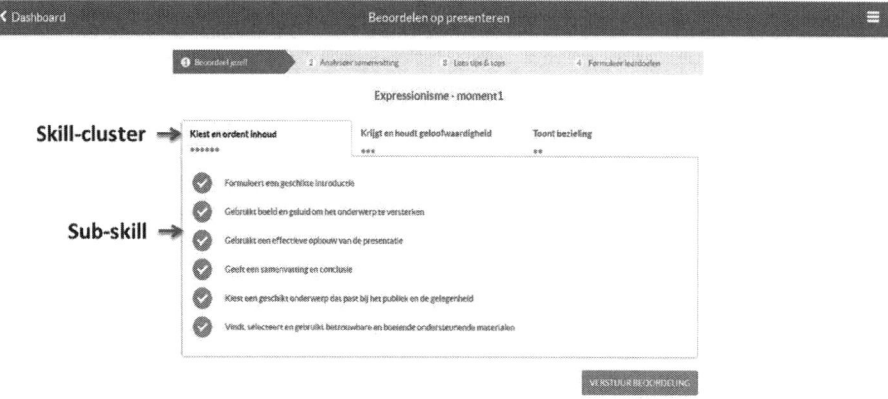

Fig. 3. Self-assessment by means of reflection on subskills within a skill-cluster

Fig. 4. Scoring a rubric with four mastery level descriptions per sub-skill

Step 4 - 'Analysis of feedback': The feedback provided by peers and teacher is visualized in a 'skill performance feedback wheel' representing students' performance score on the subskills of a complex skill in blue (Fig. 5). This visualization allows students to see at a glance, on what skills they may still improve and what skills they performed well on. Performance growth or decline between assessment moments are visualized in performance level highlights (red for shrinkage, green for growth) (Fig. 6) and the top 3 skills that went either well or less well are presented below the wheel. All provided tips and tops are summarized in a feedback report. Students analyze this information and determine what went well and what subskills may still need improvement.

Step 5 - 'Determine (next) learning objectives': Students describe their learning objectives in the online tool based on their analysis, to determine where to focus on during their next practicing session (Fig. 7). This information becomes part of their formative assessment report of one specific assessment moment (M1) in time, to be used and referred to for future practice.

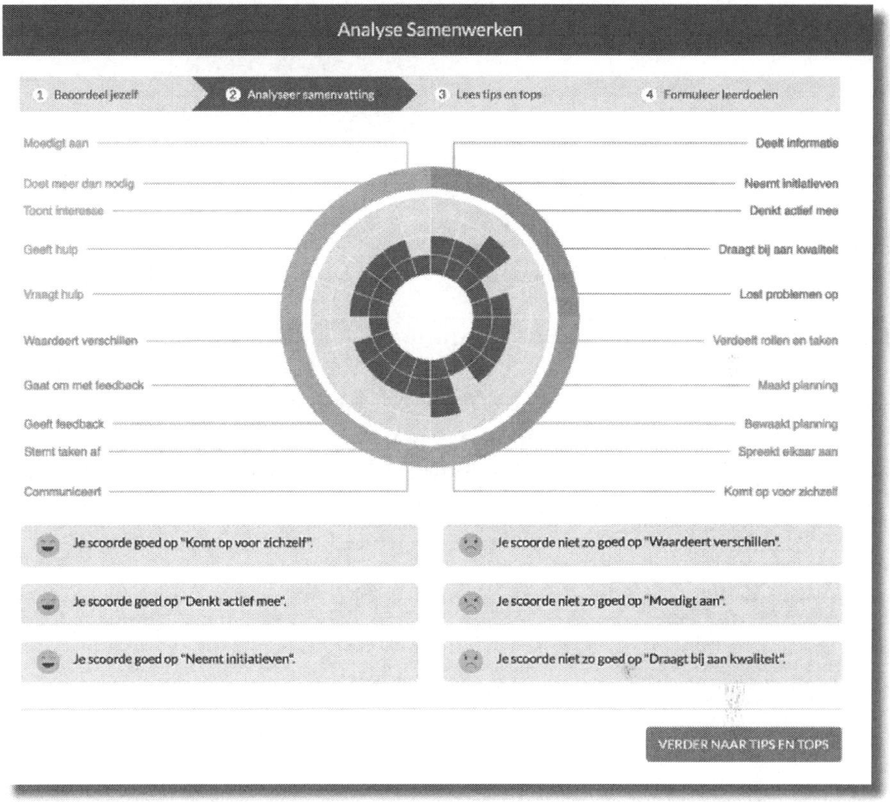

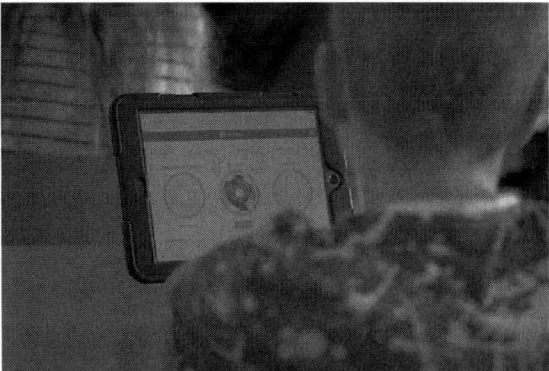

Fig. 5. 'Skill performance feedback wheel' representing students' performance scores

Fig. 6. Complex skill growth visualization on dashboard

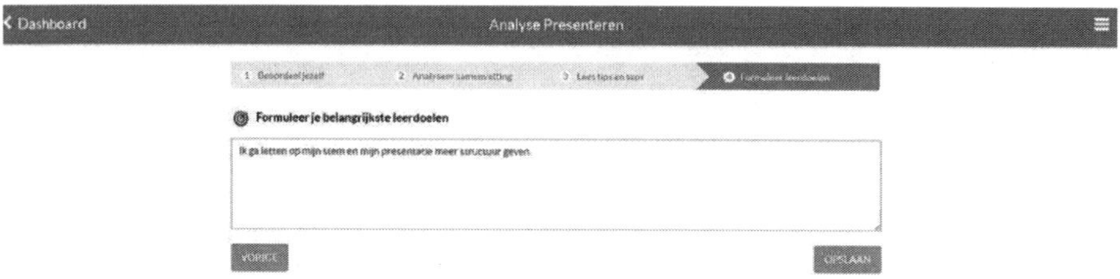

Fig. 7. Description of skills' learning objectives for next practicing sessions

4 Stakeholder Evaluation Method

During this stakeholder evaluation the overall interface design, the flow of the methodology and perceived usability and usefulness of the formative assessment methodology and online tool were evaluated by student and teachers. Not all steps could be evaluated in the working prototype, mainly due to developmental and practical reasons, however the overall foreseen design of the tool was presented by means of mock-up screens.

The video-enhanced rubrics with video-modeling examples (step 1) were not yet implemented in this version of the system, as the video-modeling examples were at that time still in production. Additionally, we could not let all students practice all skills for themselves (step 2), as that would take too much time. Therefore we asked them to recall a setting in which they had previously practiced a complex skill. Additionally, we asked them to peer-assess a 'dummy student', which performance was recorded and displayed to both teachers and students. The working prototype contained formative assessment functionality with text-based rubrics and we could therefore simulate an assessment setting and process including step 3 till 5 for one skill, namely "presenting" which is how we approached this stakeholder evaluation.

4.1 Participants

21 students and 7 teachers of two secondary school classes in their first school year, from two different schools, participated in this evaluation study. 13 students were from school number 1, 8 students from school number 2. Students were between 12 to 14 years old. 1 teachers was from school number 1, 6 from school number 2.

4.2 Materials

This evaluation study is part of a broader research project, for which parents of students were informed by means of a letter and signed an informed consent form, allowing their children to participate in research activities. To conduct the evaluation, students and teachers received a short presentation with some background on the project, a written instruction with the various steps they needed to follow during the evaluation and two (self-and peer) assessment tasks, an account on the Viewbrics online tool, a video with a 'dummy' student's presentation that they needed to assess, two questionnaires (1 for each evaluation round) repeating three open questions and an online card sorting exercise [19]. Card sorting is a participatory, user-centered usability technique used to gain a deep understanding of participant's mental models and insight in how they make sense of the domain or subject under consideration.

The three open questions in the questionnaire addressed the users perceptions with regard to the overall usability and usefulness of the system:

- What did you think worked well? (name the specific parts of the system and describe what you liked best)
- What did you think worked less well? (name the specific parts of the system and describe what you liked less)
- Do you have a tip or idea to improve the part of the system that you liked less?

The online card sorting exercise contained an instruction and 48 adjectives, evenly balanced between positive and negative designations. Examples are 'attractive', 'distracting', 'annoying', 'practical' etc. Furthermore, it contained 6 open fields, with space for additional explanations.

4.3   Design and Procedure

Both students and teachers were introduced to the online tool through a presentation, outlining the background of the project, the purpose of the evaluation and a short overview of the functionality of the tool. During this presentation they were also asked to provide any 'negative' feedback on the online tool when feasible and applicable, as this would allow us to further improve it. Then students and teachers performed the stakeholder evaluation of the online tool in three main steps, which deviated partly depending on their role (Table 1).

In the written introduction of the online card sorting task we once again asked participants to also provide 'negative' feedback when applicable, as this would allow us to further improve the tool. Unfortunately, not all students and teachers could join the complete session, therefore some respondents are lacking in the card sorting task. 2 teachers and 20 students could complete the whole card sorting task.

Table 1. Evaluation procedure from students' and teachers' perspective.

Student procedure	Teacher procedure
1. Assess a peer's performance:	1. Assess a student's performance:
• Watch the video with the presentation performance of a 'dummy' student	• Watch the video with the presentation performance of a 'dummy' student
• Assess this student with the help of the online tool, using the rubrics and 'tips and tops' functionality	• Assess this student with the help of the online tool, using the rubrics and 'tips and tops' functionality
• Answer the questionnaire with 3 open questions on this part of the system	• Start the 'self-assessment' activity of the assessed student
	• Answer the questionnaire with 3 open questions on this part of the system

(continued)

Table 1. (*continued*)

Student procedure	Teacher procedure
2. Assess your own performance: • Assess your own presentation performance of a presentation you did in the past • Analyze the information in the 'skill performance feedback wheel' and the tips and tops (some 'dummy' tips and tops were provided in the tool) • Formulate your subsequent learning objectives and share them with your teacher • Answer the questionnaire with 3 open questions on this part of the system	2. Formulate key feedback tip to improve student's performance: • Look at and analyze the most recent feedback scores of the 'dummy' student • Formulate a key feedback tip • Answer the questionnaire with 3 open questions on this part of the system
3. Describe your experience: • Choose six cards with adjectives, describing your experience with the online tool best • Explain in a few sentences why a specific word describes your experience	3. Describe your experience: • Choose six cards with adjectives, describing your experience with the online tool best • Explain in a few sentences why a specific word describes your experience

5   Results

5.1   Questionnaires

Looking at the results of the questionnaires, as well as the card sorting exercise, it appeared that the information acquired through the card sorting task was more detailed and precise then the information provided in the questionnaires. Therefore, we here only report the information from the questionnaires that was complementary to the information acquired through the card sorting task in Table 2.

5.2   Card Sorting Exercise

2 teachers and 20 students participated in the card sorting exercise (as some had to leave due to other duties). A total of 36 different words were used by both teachers and students to describe their experience with the system. 22 of the selected words were positive 'adjectives', 12 negative and 2 neutral (ordinary, technical).

As a threshold for further reporting of student results we used a criterion of $\geq 25\%$: a word had to be selected independently by a minimum number of students in order to be reported in Table 3. 9 words thus remained. In the explanations, students had the tendency to describe the same adjective in different words, but in many cases didn't provide additional information. Therefore, we only included explanations in the table that provided additional information. If explanations were similar, we choose the most informative 'key' explanation in the table and included the number of similar explanations between brackets. The words of teachers were considered separately (Table 4).

Table 2. Information acquired through student's & teacher's questionnaires

	Students	Teachers
Worked well	- clarity of the assessments - through smileys you could easily see how good or bad a performance was/helped to provide a quicker assessment - students can simply assess someone else, without the person knowing who assessed their performance - you could easily discover how it worked, for example: how to score the rubrics and the tips and tops. - good that you could also assess yourself - circle in which you saw what went well/less well and the associated summary	- highlights in the text were useful as it is quite a lot of text - there are choices to make when teachers assess students. To obtain an overall picture and assess their performance this can work quickly and well - rubrics are clear, quite extensive, good that tips/tops are available - students can formulate a learning objective for the next time and a teacher can monitor this - students have an overview of the elements of a presentation that go well and that do not (yet) go well - the wheel provides a quick overview and it is good that students can compare their performance
Worked less well	- sometimes you wanted to assess in between, but that was not possible, then it was just too good or just too bad - I think you should remove the 'no tips/tops' button, so that you have to provide arguments - it sometimes took a while to load a page - you can kind of cheat and assess yourself better	- subjects/headers at the top of a rubric was not indicated clearly. Add extra highlights - after clicking 'no tips/tops' for the 2nd sub-skill, this was automatically indicated for the 3rd sub-skill - sometimes there are other reasons for an assessment score then indicated in the rubric. Thus, the rubric score and tips/tops can be contradictory - color use is unclear => use of 2 'flat' colors in text - no explanation of the colored diagram provided. I do not understand the sequence of learning objectives and the core tip of the teacher
Suggestions	- play videos automatically before you can complete the rubric - put tips and tops in a square, so that the assessed person will see that at a glance - no self-assessment	- add: a color legend? 2 brighter colors? explanation to the diagram? - Provide a concise summary of data, this is clearer for the teacher, but mainly also for students - Refine cubes [in the wheel] and add further explanations

Table 3. Overview of selected words by students (selected by $\geq 25\%$).

Word	Frequency	Percentage	'Key' explanations
Handy	12	60%	More handy then just writing/you don't have to write (3); The program is well-thought through; Time-saving and safe; You can quickly fill in your opinion and it is very clear; It helps to receive good quality feedback; Handy that students can also provide feedback; You can see clearly on what you still have to work on and where not; It can make an assessment of a presentation more easy for teachers
Clear	10	50%	It is well-organized and intuitive (2); You see clearly where you have to go to complete a task (2); comprehensible (2); Information is clear, clustered and well-written (2); You see very well what you can still improve, and what you are already good at; Easy to use
Usable	8	40%	Very well usable (5); It is fine/easy to use; It is very useful to see if you did your presentation well. Also, for the teacher; You can quickly fill in what you think and it is very clear
Fun	8	40%	It was fun and interesting (4); It's nice that you know what you did well; It is fun to work with because you can also give your own opinion; Its nice while it keeps up with the time; It looks nice
Helpful	6	30%	It makes sure you are consistent, hopefully; Through this you have no paperwork; It is very helpful because you can see what you should do better next time; People can fill in their real opinion; It went much easier through those texts under the smileys
Easy	6	30%	You can quickly fill in what you think and it is very clear; Easy to learn; It is easy once you've found where to go; You can do this quickly and easily
Ordinary	5	25%	It was simply a good site; It looks a bit boring; It is not really original
Logical	5	25%	It is quite logical how it works (2); The information was logical (2)

Table 4. Overview of selected words by teachers

Word	'Key' explanations
Usable (2):	1. If the school system is ready for this, it can be useful to measure and keep track of progress. 2. Through a reasonably easy click pattern you can assess students well, both by peers and the teacher
Understandable:	After a short instruction it is easy to use. Explanations for teachers are clear
Accessible:	With a few exceptions, I think everyone could easily work in this way
Original:	Until now I have only worked with paper and this does not result in individual reactions. Here students have to provide their own opinion and that seems more pleasant to me
Unhandy:	For the time being not useful yet, because experience shows that certainly not all teachers can handle digital systems with this type of assessments, also because they have to use it during a presentation. I assessed the performance afterwards and got the impression that I should have done this during the presentation. It therefore requires certain (still to be developed) skills of the teacher
Practical:	Students receive their assessment fast and can quickly read and process their feedback themselves. It is always digitally available and can be used to discuss progress
Time-consuming:	It will take a long time for all teachers to perceive this as a useful tool and so it will be time consuming in the beginning. A lot of information available and choices to be made in the beginning

6   Conclusions and Discussion

With regard to usefulness (research question 1) and usability (research question 2) of the overall Viewbrics methodology, student and teachers participating in this stakeholder evaluation study evaluated the usability of the Viewbrics formative assessment methodology and online tool overall overwhelmingly positive, although depending on their perspective (student/teacher) stressed different aspects of and perceptions on its usefulness. Both groups evaluated the Viewbrics online tool as handy, usable and helpful. Additionally, students perceived it as clear, fun, easy, ordinary and logical and teachers as innovative, understandable, accessible, original and practical.

With regard to feedback for improving the first prototype's usability as well as usefulness (research question 3), some teachers mentioned that they perceived Viewbrics as 'unhandy' and 'time-consuming'. However, their explanations revealed that this was mainly caused by teachers' digital and media skills, not by inherent characteristics of the Viewbrics methodology and online tool. Interestingly and contradictory, students found the system clear, easy, logical and fun, whereas teachers expressed their concern whether Viewbrics might be too complicated and sometimes unclear for students.

Students' perception of the 'self-assessment' phase in the methodology also appeared to be contradictory: some students indicated it as very useful to reflect on their own performance, however some of them indicated it as a risk to commit 'fraud'.

We interpreted this latter remark as something stemming from a more 'summative assessment' perspective, where this information would be also used to give them a final assessment and a grade. As this methodology is designed and developed to provide formative feedback and reflection assistance for the mastery of complex skills, to foster student's growth, this perspective is in principle not applicable. However, this illustrates the way some students (as well as teachers) are still thinking about assessment in general. Both students and teachers provided concrete suggestions, e.g. regarding the explanation and visualization of the 'wheel', in order to further improve the online tool. These suggestions will be evaluated and considered for implementation in the tool.

We here proposed and (partly) evaluated an innovative and integrated way to foster the accomplishment of (generic) complex skills, by combining a formative assessment methodology with video-enhanced rubrics (VERs) and an online feedback tool, called 'Viewbrics' (www.viewbrics.nl). This pilot study and the foreseen follow-up quasi-experimental study of the Viewbrics methodology and (the design of the) associated online tool may contribute both to our knowledge on how to support the acquisition of (generic) complex skills as well as concrete ways to do so in educational practice within secondary schools.

This evaluation of a prototype is part of the first major phase of the Viewbrics-project, in which a design research approach is adopted in order to, together with teachers, students, researchers and other relevant stakeholders and professionals (e.g. multimedia, human-computer interaction), co-design and create a usable and useful formative assessment methodology and online tool with video-enhanced rubrics (VERs).

In the second major phase of the project, effects of implementing this formative assessment methodology and online tool on the formation of 'rich' mental models of a complex (generic) skills as well as on the acquired mastery level of a skill and perceived feedback quality (more consistent and concrete) amongst students and teachers in secondary education will be studied. In this second phase, the Viewbrics methodology is implemented and effects are studied in two schools, by using a quasi-experimental design comparing three groups, namely a (1) control-, (2) Viewbrics methodology and online tool with text-based rubrics-, (3) Viewbrics methodology and online tool with video-enhanced rubrics-group within each school. Results will be reported as part of future research efforts.

Acknowledgement. We would like to gratefully acknowledge the contribution of the Viewbrics-project, officially called 'Formative assessment of complex skills with video-enhanced rubrics in secondary education', a three-year research and development project funded by the Netherlands Initiative for Education Research (NRO), project number 405-15-550.

References

1. Voogt, J., Roblin, N.P.: A comparative analysis of international frameworks for 21st century competences: implications for national curriculum policies. J. Curric. Stud. **44**, 299–321 (2012)

2. Kirschner, P., Van Merriënboer, J.: Ten steps to complex learning a new approach to instruction and instructional design. In: Good, T.L. (ed.) 21st Century Education: A Reference Handbook, pp. 244–253. Sage, Thousand Oaks (2008)

3. Galligan, F., et al.: Advanced PE for Edexcel. Heinemann Educational Publishers, Oxford (2000)

4. Bowman, K.: Background paper for the AQF Council on generic skills, Canberra (2010)

5. Rusman, E., Martínez-Monés, A., Boon, J., Rodríguez-Triana, M.J., Villagrá-Sobrino, S.: Gauging teachers' needs with regard to technology-enhanced formative assessment (TEFA) of 21st century skills in the classroom. In: Kalz, M., Ras, E. (eds.) CAA 2014. CCIS, vol. 439, pp. 1–14. Springer, Cham (2014). https://doi.org/10.1007/978-3-319-08657-6_1

6. Thijs, A., Fisser, P., van der Hoeven, M.: 21E Eeuwse Vaardigheden in Het Curriculum Van Het Funderend Onderwijs. Slo, p. 128 (2014)

7. Andrade, H., Du, Y.: Student perspectives on rubric-referenced assessment. Pract. Assess. Res. Eval. **10**, 1–11 (2005)

8. Panadero, E., Jonsson, A.: The use of scoring rubrics for formative assessment purposes revisited: a review. Educ. Res. Rev. **9**, 129–144 (2013)

9. Schildkamp, K., Heitink, M., Van Der Kleij, F., Hoogland, I., Dijkstra, A., Kippers, W.: Voorwaarden voor effectieve formatieve toetsing - een praktische review, Enschede (2014)

10. Berry, O., Price, M., Rust, C., Donovan, B.O., Price, M., Rust, C.: Teaching in higher education know what i mean? Enhancing student understanding of assessment standards and criteria. Teach. High. Educ. 37–41 (2007)

11. Westera, W.: On the changing nature of learning context: anticipating the virtual extensions of the world. Educ. Technol. Soc. **14**, 201–212 (2011)

12. van Gog, T., Verveer, I., Verveer, L.: Learning from video modeling examples: Effects of seeing the human model's face. Comput. Educ. **72**, 323–327 (2014)

13. De Grez, L., Valcke, M., Roozen, I.: The differential impact of observational learning and practice- based learning on the development of oral presentation skills in higher education. High. Educ. Res. Dev. **33**, 256–271 (2013)

14. Rohbanfard, H., Proteau, L.: Live vs video presentation techniques in the observational learning of motor skills. Trends Neurosci. Educ. **2**, 27–32 (2013)

15. van Gog, T., Rummel, N.: Example-based learning: integrating cognitive and social-cognitive research perspectives. Educ. Psychol. Rev. **22**, 155–174 (2010)

16. Baecher, L., Kung, S.C., Jewkes, A.M., Rosalia, C.: The role of video for self-evaluation in early field experiences. Teach. Teach. Educ. **36**, 189–197 (2013)

17. Plomp, T., Nieveen, N.: Educational design research: an introduction. In: Plomp, T., Nieveen, N. (eds.) Educational Design Research, pp. 10–51. Netherlands Institute for Curriculum Development, Enschede (2013)

18. Ackermans, K., Rusman, E., Brand-Gruwel, S., Specht, M.: The dilemmas of formulating theory-informed design guidelines for a video enhanced rubric. In: Ras, E., Guerrero Roldán, A.E. (eds.) TEA 2017. CCIS, vol. 829, pp. 123–136. Springer, Cham (2018). https://doi.org/10.1007/978-3-319-97807-9_10

19. Last, J., Simmons, S., Keene, C.: Card sorting-design research techniques

Assessing Learning in MOOCs Through Interactions Between Learners

Francis Brouns$^{(\boxtimes)}$ (iD) and Olga Firssova (iD)

Welten Institute, Open University of the Netherlands,
P.O. Box 2960, 6401 DL Heerlen, The Netherlands
{francis.brouns, olga.firssova}@ou.nl

Abstract. This paper presents a retrospective analysis of learning in a MOOC as reconstructed from the conversations that learners conducted in MOOC group forums while performing the course tasks. A mixed method approach was applied to analyze the quantity and the quality of these conversations. Two activity patterns were distinguished – in groups with higher activity levels, there were more individual contributions (posts) on more course themes and these contributions were broader spread throughout the course. In high activity groups there was also more interaction between participants, i.e., more questions, answers, explanations and elaborations. The presented study demonstrates how modeling interactions in group forums helps to elicit individual and emerging group knowledge construction and thus supports defining MOOC learning, informs MOOC design and provides insights on how assessing MOOC learning can be automated.

Keywords: Assessing learning · Learner interactions · Knowledge building · Text analysis · MOOC learning · Mixed methods

1 Theoretical Framework

After a decade of growth, Massive Open Online Courses (MOOCs) may still be seen as a trend that develops next to the mainstream of the 21st century education. The growth is, however, spectacular. Major institutions in Higher Education including world top universities have already developed and offered open learning for altogether millions of learners all over the world. The body of knowledge on MOOCs, MOOC learners, MOOC design and MOOC technologies grows exponentially and the width of topics MOOC researchers are getting a better grip on is diverse.

The theoretical underpinnings of learning in massive online open education are, however, still under construction. MOOCs can be conceptualized, set up and run by their providers in a multitude of ways. MOOC participants enrolling in MOOCs pursue diverse goals, among which course completion is not necessarily one they pursue [1]. Individual learners' goals are known to vary and to be susceptible to change depending on their concrete (first) experiences and/or on other factors that may shape, hinder or re-shape the learning process [2].

The open access, "free" character and the absence of boundaries at curriculum level make learning in a MOOC and possible outcomes of this learning fuzzy, little

© Springer Nature Switzerland AG 2019
S. Draaijer et al. (Eds.): TEA 2018, CCIS 1014, pp. 42–54, 2019.
https://doi.org/10.1007/978-3-030-25264-9_4

predictable and thus little congruent with the mainstream curriculum-based learning. The question arises how using other mechanisms than compliance with pre-defined learning objectives or course completion can be used to define MOOC learning. This study addresses this question. Such a mechanism does not, however, need to be a separate effortful activity. An adjacent question is how (and to what extent) assessing MOOC learning can be automated.

Individual learning is an internal process. Construction of knowledge, though, involves verbal interaction with others when learning goals or outcomes are made explicit and communicated in some form, when there is collaborative effort involved [3–5] or when the interaction is a by-product of individual learning activity, such as, for example, student seatwork [6]. Interactions that take place in online learning environments and are made "visible" with the help of technologies help to understand both what is learned and how it is done at both individual and group level [7]. The literature on technology enhanced learning in general and more specifically on computer mediated communication (CMC) and computer supported collaborative learning (CSCL) accumulated in the past decades of active use of computers for learning and teaching provides theoretical frames for understanding how exchanges in online learning environments contribute to learning and joint knowledge construction. This literature contains instrumentation for its analysis in the form of content coding schemes that are geared towards a particular instructional context or learning design [8–12].

The CSCL literature legacy can be used in the conceptualization, analysis and assessment of MOOC learning when learners' active contributions to MOOCs in the form of posts, conversations and sharing experiences, ideas and artefacts are taken into account. While the first open online courses that followed the principles of learning in networks, the so called cMOOCs, and the first massive knowledge consumption courses, the xMOOCs, represented two distinct strands in open education movement, recent generations of MOOCs build upon the legacy of both strands combining in different constellations (elements of) "production and consumption" of knowledge with active and social learning elements [13–16].

This paper will zoom into learners' interactions in a MOOC environment as a way to establish the boundaries of and lay the ground for operationalizing MOOC learning. The main aim of the study was to explore methodologies to capture indicators of learning from learners' contributions in search for semi-automated assessment of evidence of learning or knowledge construction. The next section first describes a framework for knowledge construction in online learning that combines aspects of individual learning with social learning and creation of (cultural) artefacts [5, 17].

1.1 Knowledge Building in Online Learning Environments

Various researchers have developed theories and models to explain how learners learn or how learning in communities might be facilitated. Models and frameworks like the Knowledge Building model by Scardamalia and Bereiter [18–20] or the often used Interaction Analysis model by Gunawardena, Lowe, and Anderson [21] model contributions of individual learners to shared knowledge construction. These models and frameworks are often based on underlying assumptions the researchers have on how learning occurs and therefore are specific and fine-grained. Such granularity limits applicability, in particular when effortful and time consuming detailed analysis of content or discourse is not feasible. As one of the aims of the current study was to look for a technology-based solution and analysis methods that potentially can be automated, an approach based on general principles of learning through interaction was taken as point of departure.

1.2   Learning Attribution in Online Learning Environments

Paavola and Hakkarainen [17] combine three metaphors of learning in order to develop an emergent approach to understanding learning against the current societal trends and challenges: the acquisition metaphor (a monologue), the participation metaphor (a dialogue) and the knowledge-creation metaphor which sees learning as a trialogue, with interaction between learners through (cultural) artefacts they develop together.

In a way, Stahl [4, 5] connects these metaphors by conceptualizing the individual knowledge construction as a process embedded in a shared learning experience - as continuous interaction between personal and social learning. Individual knowledge is, in this view, externalized through public utterances and is constructed through discourse and interaction with others based on the exchange of utterances, clarifications, building on each other's input, resolving controversies and negotiating meanings.

Externalizations take on various forms, such as teacher or learner monologue of dialogue between both, conversations between groups of learners, exchanges that involve few or many participants, remain superfluous or go deep, are anchored in sharing documents and artefacts or not.

Artefacts that are created and shared with others make it possible for all to engage in interaction and discourse around these artefacts, elaborate and build on the existing knowledge in order to construct new knowledge on both the individual and group level [17]. Analysis of utterances of individual learners and exchanges between learners together with analysis of artefacts can shed light on what is learned and the quality of this learning. At the same time such analysis can help to evaluate the richness of the environment in which individual and group conversations and learning through conversations occur [7, 22].

In an electronic learning environment learning becomes visible to others through exchanges between learners who can respond to each other in real time (i.e., through chat) and asynchronously (i.e., through discussion boards or social media). Learning is thus also visible for those who are not directly involved in conversations but might benefit from reading available exchanges and reflecting on them at a later moment. "Invisible" learning of these silent learners might in its turn become visible if they eventually join an on-going conversation or start a new one and thus contribute to exchanges that act as instantiations and at the same time as both sources and triggers of individual and collaborative knowing [5]. Thus, individual learning as an internal monologue and social interaction as a dialogue transform into collaborative learning and knowledge creation [17].

1.3 Modelling Personal and Shared Knowledge Construction Through Discourse in a Shared Online Learning Environment

In his model Stahl demonstrates the interdependence of individual and collaborative knowledge building without further specifying kinds of knowledge and actors involved. Garrison, Anderson and Archer [23] provide such a specification defining cognitive, social and teaching presence as essential elements or constituent parts of the learning process in an online environment. According to Garrison et al. [23], cognitive presence manifests itself in articulations of event triggers, exploration of ideas through sustained information exchange and formulating new ideas. Social presence refers to learners presenting themselves and communicating with others in order to connect, initiate and maintain interaction, and/or build up a relationship, increase or maintain trust. Social presence allows participants in an online exchange to develop a sense of belonging in a community and establish or strengthen a personal identity. The sense of belonging is in its turn reported to be positively associated with motivation, satisfaction, performance and the degree of perceived learning. The third element, teaching presence is related to the design of the educational experience and facilitation of the learning process. Garrison and colleagues [23] speak of it as 'a means to an end', referring to the function of teaching presence – to support and enhance cognitive and social presence in the learning environment by promoting meaningful interaction [23, 24].

Combining the model of individual versus collective knowing development through discourse [5] with a types of knowledge specifications model [23] allows to frame the knowledge exchange processes in general terms yet with sufficient specificity that assessment and evaluation require and thus to define learning through interaction. Figure 1 visualizes a possible relation between the two models.

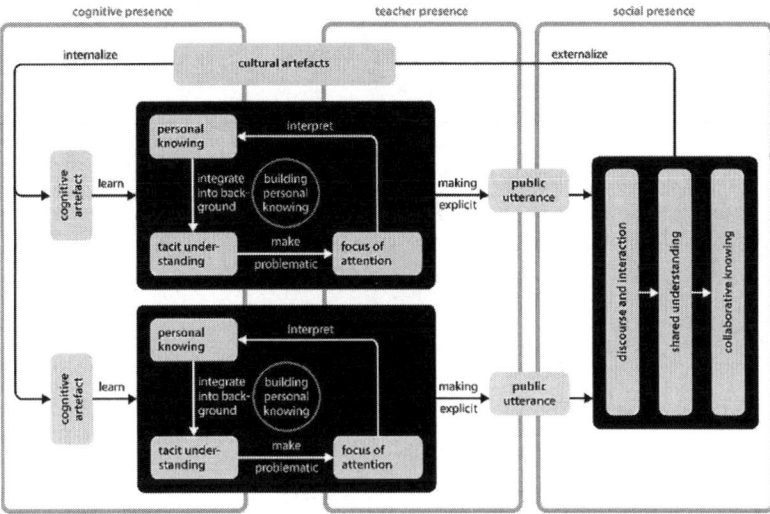

Fig. 1. Specifying the type of knowledge (and presence) involved according to Garrison [23] in the model of individual and shared cycle of knowledge exchange and construction according to Stahl [5]

The study described below applied this combined framework to analyze interactions between MOOC participants in order to assess MOOC learning. Given the benefits shown in other studies from combining quantitative and qualitative research [9, 25], a mixed-method approach was used to answer the formulated research questions.

2   Methodology

2.1   Context

The context of this study is a MOOC on the topic of blended learning. The MOOC targeted teachers interested in using blended learning principles and tooling in a course design using internet technologies. The MOOC was offered free of charge, an optional certified track required a fee and required participants to maintain a portfolio and submit a final assignment (a blueprint of course design or redesign).

The MOOC lasted eight weeks and covered five different topics related to the use of internet technology for course design, assessment, communication, individual and collaborative learning and the role of a teacher as designer of learning activities.

The first week combined an introduction to the topic with personal introductions as a way for learners to get to know each other. The final week included a reflection on own progress and on the general topic of the MOOC.

All topics followed the same structure. The week started with an orientation on a topic through self-study followed by an expert introduction of the topic presented in an interactive online video session. The expert also gave general feedback on the contributions to the orientation assignment, responded to questions and posts in the forum or posed in the chat during the online session and elaborated on subsequent tasks. Additional readings were available for those interested in in-depth learning.

Collaboration and exchanges between participants were stimulated by task design that anchored tasks in professional contexts relevant for participants and invited participants to share assignments with others participants, and give each other feedback. To streamline this process, 1181 participants were divided into 13 subgroups, each with access to a dedicated discussion forum next to the general forum. Group size varied between 64 and 119, with an average of 90 [15].

Participants were informed that the MOOC was part of ongoing research and that their participation and contributions in the MOOC would be tracked. By registering for and enrolling in the MOOC, participants agreed to their data being used for research. Participants were informed that participation remained voluntary and that they could withdraw at any time.

2.2   Data Analysis

Participant contributions to discussion forums were analyzed in two ways. First, a quantitative descriptive analysis was made of participation in the discussion forums of all 13 groups. This entailed a calculation of frequency of messages sent, number of threads, and thread length.

Because the quantitative analyses seemed to suggest difference in posting behavior between groups, a systematic text analysis method [26–28] was applied to determine whether this quantitative difference was also reflected in the type of messages posted. Therefore, a selection of groups was made to provide sufficient data for the required analyses. Selection was based on the total number of messages in the discussion forum and the number of messages related to each of the 16 different assignments.

Three groups with the least exchanges and three groups with the most exchanges were selected for the systematic text analysis. In the remainder of this paper, these are referred to as 'high activity' and 'low activity' groups.

NVivo10 (http://www.qsrinternational.com/) was used to analyze the forum messages. Before starting with coding an initial exploration of the forum messages was made based on word frequency and word clouds to inform the coding categories.

For text analysis purposes, messages of each of the discussion forums for the six groups were exported from the database in CSV format and imported into an Excel sheet. This Excel sheet was then imported into NVivo, marking the column containing the message text as NVivo codable. Fields that could identify individual persons were excluded from analysis. A complete individual post (text message) was used as the unit of analysis. More than one category could be used to code the message.

Table 1. Coding categories of the forum messages, type of presence and example of posts in the forum

Personal introduction	
Type of presence	Social presence triggered by instruction - teacher presence
Definition	Participants introduce themselves, provide some background and indicate their learning needs and goals for participating in the MOOC
Example	My name is E. A… and I participate in this MOOC out of curiosity about the possibilities of adapting education to the 21st century. …
Social interaction	
Type of presence	Social presence
Definition	Any message that was not related to content or assignments of the MOOC but consisted of social exchange
Example	… Nice to read your introduction, in which I see similarities with my own experiences. …
Knowledge telling	
Type of presence	Cognitive presence triggered by instruction - teacher presence
Definition	The participant presents facts, provides descriptions, reproducing information, knowledge without elaborating
Example	… . Within our faculty we use Blackboard, by many this VLE is only used to post slides and articles, but there is a small number of teachers who also use other available tools in education

(continued)

Table 1. (*continued*)

Elaborating on knowledge	
Type of presence	Cognitive presence
Definition	The participant not only reproduces facts, information, knowledge, but elaborates on it by providing: - examples from own experiences - examples from practice - personal view or view of others supported by theory
Example	When I consider my first learning experiences with MOOCs, I find this way of learning very powerful. Interesting reflection questions are asked (such as this assignment) and there is mutual feedback on each other's assignments. …
Invitation to respond	
Type of presence	Cognitive presence
Definition	The message is formulated to elicit response, by: - explicitly asking peers for feedback - explicitly asking for support, ideas, collaboration, or response - implicitly creating an opportunity for conversation, e.g. by asking stimulating questions, by providing questions that allow elicitation of solutions, etc., without explicitly asking the reader to respond or provide answers
Example	M…, I agree with many of your arguments… . I would also like to add that other guidance skills are also required from the teacher/tutor in online collaboration How should I guide 'my' teachers? What do they need and what will change for them if they move from 'contiguous' to a blend of contiguous and distributed? I wonder what you think of the example …?
Responding	
Type of presence	Cognitive presence
Definition	Responding by: - providing feedback to a previous message - answering posed questions - taking up earlier voiced ideas, concepts, thoughts etc. and clearly elaborating on it
Example	In response to W…, I think the rubric gives an answer to what 'insufficient, sufficient and good' means in practice. … It is a tool in the assessment process that always involves subjectivity. … However, it is indeed striking that terms such as 'relevant', 'essential', 'consistent' and 'reasonable' are mentioned, and that it is not yet immediately clear what these terms imply …
Rest	
Definition	Any off-topic message that could not be assigned to one of the other categories
Example	Hi C…, thank you for your feedback! May be the sound is not good enough. Unfortunately, I do not have a better headset, it is in the office. … Hello, K…., thanks for sending the article… E

Conceptual frameworks by Stahl [5] and Garrison et al. [23] and the grounded theory approach [29] were used to model learners' interactions. A coding scheme was developed in several iterations by the two researchers who performed the coding. The final model included the categories as shown in Table 1. The table provides the definition of the coding category and indicates between brackets the type of presence. Examples of coded utterances are provided to illustrate the categories that constitute the model.

Messages of three 'high activity' and three 'low activity' groups were analyzed to compare if groups that posted more messages also showed different interaction patterns and/or differed in the nature of their conversations. A chi-square analysis was performed to check if interaction level had an effect on the distribution of type of messages.

3   Results

3.1   Interaction in Group Forums: Visible Patterns

Participants of the six groups posted in total 1442 messages, grouped in 846 threads with an average thread length of 1.6. As shown in Fig. 2, by far the most messages (34%) were placed in week 1, while the number of messages for the other topics was lower but still consistent, although the number of messages seemed to decrease in week 6.

Overall, only half of participants engaged in the discussion forums. Moreover, two patterns could be observed in the activity in these forums. 'High activity' groups in which participants posted more messages (see Table 2) and remained active, i.e., kept posting messages for each of the assignments during the whole of the MOOC, and 'low activity' groups in which participants posted fewer messages and the number of messages declined with MOOC progression. Figure 2 illustrates the observed trend.

Table 2. Frequency of posting in high and low activity groups

	High activity	Low activity
Total number of participants	283	240
Total number unique participants posting	150	112
Total number of threads	555	291
Total number of messages	1049	393
Average number of threads per active poster	3.7	2.6
Average number of messages per active poster	7.1	3.6

Table 3 presents an overview of the type of interactions in both high and low activity groups. Although all types of messages are present in each group, the interaction patterns differ ($\chi2(6) = 96.14$, $p < .001$, Cramer V .243). In 'low activity' groups 'Knowledge telling' category is a dominant category and 'Personal introduction' is the second best represented category. Both these categories are associated with teacher presence as they represent contributions that result from instructional prompts.

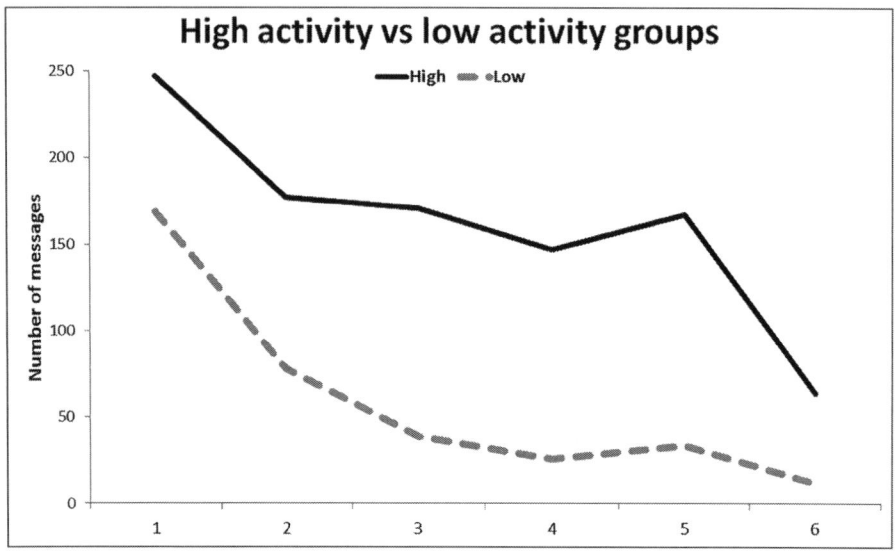

Fig. 2. Number of messages per topic/week for three 'high activity' groups (solid line) and three 'low activity' groups (dashed line)

These type of interactions are indicative of knowledge representation at best and do not instigate any learning or knowledge construction. In 'high activity' groups, statements from the categories 'Invitation to respond' and 'Responding' have the highest frequency. Both categories are associated with cognitive presence and are indicative of a participation metaphor or dialogical learning [17, 23]. These kinds of statements potentially elicit reactions and responses from others, thereby opening avenues for knowledge construction and thus learning.

Table 3. Distribution of type of messages in high and low activity groups (% within group)

Type of message	High activity %	Low activity %	Both groups %
Personal introduction	11.2	**21.8**	13.9
Social interaction	5.4	2.2	4.5
Knowledge telling	17.6	**33.0**	**21.6**
Elaborating on knowledge	13.3	7.9	11.9
Invitation to respond	**20.5**	15.1	15.1
Responding	**28.8**	16.7	**25.7**
Rest	3.1	3.3	3.2

The average number of words per message was similar in both groups (100 and 97 words for high and low respectively). However, in the 'low activity' groups, participants used almost twice as many words in 'Knowledge telling' messages compared to other type of messages. In 'high activity' groups, participants used more words per message to elaborate on knowledge and to invite interaction (Table 4).

Table 4. Distribution of the number of words used in the various types of messages, expressed as percentage of total number of words used within the group

Type of message	% in high activity	% in low activity
Personal introduction	14.0	**20.8**
Social interaction	2.3	0.9
Knowledge telling	22.1	**34.3**
Elaborating on knowledge	**30.7**	18.4
Invitation to respond	24.8	16.1
Responding	**30.1**	18.9
Rest	1.0	1.9

4   Conclusion

In this study, analysis of learners' interactions in group discussion forums was undertaken in order to define learning in a MOOC through these interactions and answer the question whether MOOC learning can be assessed based on the analysis of interactions between MOOC learners.

The approach taken - combining quantitative and qualitative methods [30] - proved valuable in defining an analytical framework and applying it to describe all interactions between MOOC participants that took place in the discussion forums.

According to these analyses, two distinct patterns could be discerned. These patterns can be described in line with the two theoretical frameworks applied - Stahl's model of individual and collective knowing [5] and Garrison's community of inquiry model [23]. Interactive learning environments (in this particular case: group discussion forums) may be both rich or poor in terms of visible individual and collaborative knowledge construction and in terms of social and cognitive presence.

Like in other studies, merely providing communication or collaboration tools does not guarantee that the participants will make use of them nor that they will engage in meaningful interaction. Recent studies showed that in MOOCs only a minor percentage of participants tend to use forums. On the other hand, whenever learners engage in interaction, through media as a part of the course activities, it can result in increased course completion as a proxy of learning [22, 31–33]. This study demonstrated that active forum use could also be seen as a proxy of learning when learning is associated with richer cognitive presence and social presence related to it.

This study confirmed that MOOC participants differ in the level of interaction. Social presence and cognitive presence were manifested in both the 'high activity' and 'low activity' groups. Both were triggered by prompts in the learning environment due to the design of the learning activity and assignments (teacher presence). However, in 'low activity' groups social presence was practically limited to the prompted activity of personal introductions while in 'high activity' groups social presence manifested itself in on-going exchanges throughout the course. In the latter, social interaction was related to cognitive presence that manifested itself in exchanges between learners, invitations to respond and responding. Cognitive presence in 'low activity' groups was limited to knowledge telling which in its turn was prompted by instruction (teacher presence). This kind of knowledge telling is merely indicative of knowledge representation and does not point towards more active knowledge attribution or even knowledge building. In 'high activity' groups, there was stronger and more explicit cognitive presence in the form of knowledge elaboration and interaction with others, providing means for active learning and thus opportunities for knowledge construction.

In terms of Stahl, we can assume that in 'high activity' groups both individual knowledge construction (individual knowing) resulting from knowledge elaboration and knowledge based exchanges with other learners, and collective knowledge construction (collective knowing) took place. The learning environment in these 'high activity' groups can be defined as learning-rich compared to the environment in the 'low activity' groups.

Based on the conducted analyses it can be assumed that the learning environment of a massive open online course that supports and stimulates knowledge exchange can make the knowledge-under-development of individual learners explicit. Instantiations of such knowledge exchanges provide insights in the quality of learning.

From MOOC design perspective, this study provided an argument in favor of active learning designs in which exchanges between learning are stimulated and orchestrated [22] as such interactions cannot be expected to emerge in open online environment by default [34] but result from a combination of factors, with learning design being an important one. As Laurillard [7, 22] explains, effective learning designs should stimulate learners to become active and engaged, not only by providing sufficient and stimulating learning activities and assignments but also by stimulating interaction through various roles a learner can take on.

From the MOOC learning assessment perspective, the quantity of exchanges and an easy-to-perform classification of these exchanges can be taken as a point of departure in designing learning analytics and (semi-) automated assessment modules to act as indicators that knowledge construction takes place and it is worthwhile to look further into its quality. The combination of quantitative and qualitative methodologies has been shown to be valuable and therefore it is advisable in future research to use this combination of methodology to provide sufficient quality of the measurements and provide meaningful feedback to teacher and learner [9, 26, 27, 35].

While learning in massive open online courses may remain less plannable and to a less extent predictable than other forms of learning, including online learning, understanding that designing and supporting interactions enhances learning and makes it visible and to a certain extent accountable, increases sustainability of open learning.

References

1. Henderikx, M., Kreijns, K., Kalz, M.: To change or not to change? That's the question… On MOOC-success, barriers and their implications. In: Delgado Kloos, C., Jermann, P., Pérez-Sanagustín, M., Seaton, Daniel T., White, S. (eds.) EMOOCs 2017. LNCS, vol. 10254, pp. 210–216. Springer, Cham (2017). https://doi.org/10.1007/978-3-319-59044-8_25
2. Henderikx, M.A., Kreijns, K., Kalz, M.: Refining success and dropout in massive open online courses based on the intention–behavior gap. Distance Educ. **38**, 353–368 (2017). https://doi.org/10.1080/01587919.2017.1369006

3. Dillenbourg, P.: What do you mean by collaborative learning? In: Dillenbourg, P. (ed.) Collaborative-Learning: Cognitive and Computational Approaches, pp. 1–19. Elsevier, Oxford (1999)
4. Stahl, G.: Collaborative information environments to support knowledge construction by communities. AI Soc. **14**, 71–97 (2000). https://doi.org/10.1007/bf01206129
5. Stahl, G.: Group Cognition: Computer Support for Building Collaborative Knowledge. MIT Press, Cambridge (2006)
6. Nijland, F.J.: Mirroring interaction: an exploratory study into student interaction in independent working. Tilburg University, The Netherlands (2011)
7. Laurillard, D.: Rethinking University Teaching: A Conversational Framework for the Effective Use of Learning Technologies. Routledge, London (2002)
8. Veldhuis-Diermanse, A.E., Biemans, H.J.A., Mulder, M., Mahdizadeh, H.: Analysing learning processes and quality of knowledge construction in networked learning. J. Agric. Educ. Ext. **12**, 41–57 (2006). https://doi.org/10.1080/13892240600740894
9. Schrire, S.: Knowledge building in asynchronous discussion groups: going beyond quantitative analysis. Comput. Educ. **46**, 49–70 (2006). https://doi.org/10.1016/j.compedu.2005.04.006
10. Strijbos, J.-W., Martens, R.L., Prins, F.J., Jochems, W.M.G.: Content analysis: what are they talking about? Comput. Educ. **46**, 29–48 (2006). https://doi.org/10.1016/j.compedu.2005.04.002
11. Weinberger, A., Fischer, F.: A framework to analyze argumentative knowledge construction in computer-supported collaborative learning. Comput. Educ. **46**, 71–95 (2006). https://doi.org/10.1016/j.compedu.2005.04.003
12. De Wever, B., Schellens, T., Valcke, M., Van Keer, H.: Content analysis schemes to analyze transcripts of online asynchronous discussion groups: a review. Comput. Educ. **46**, 6–28 (2006). https://doi.org/10.1016/j.compedu.2005.04.005
13. Kalz, M., Specht, M.: If MOOCS are the answer, did we ask the right questions? Implications for the design of large-scale online-courses. Maastricht School of Management (2013). http://hdl.handle.net/1820/5183
14. Berlanga, A.J., Kalz, M., Stoyanov, S., Van Rosmalen, P., Smithies, A., Braidman, I.: Using language technologies to diagnose learner's conceptual development. In: Proceedings of the 9th IEEE International Conference on Advanced Learning Technologies (ICALT 2009), pp. 669–673. IEEE (2009)
15. Rubens, W., Kalz, M., Koper, R.: Improving the learning design of massive open online courses. Turk Online J. Educ. Technol. **13**, 71–80 (2014)
16. Firssova, O., Brouns, F., Kalz, M.: Designing for open learning: design principles and scalability affordances in practice. In: L@S: Third Annual ACM Conference on Learning at Scale. ACM (2016). https://doi.org/10.1145/2876034.2893426
17. Paavola, S., Hakkarainen, K.: The knowledge creation metaphor – an emergent epistemological approach to learning. Sci. Educ. **14**, 535–557 (2005). https://doi.org/10.1007/s11191-004-5157-0
18. Scardamalia, M., Bereiter, C.: A brief history of knowledge building. Can. J. Learn. Technol. **36**(1) (2010). https://doi.org/10.21432/t2859m
19. Hewitt, J., Scardamalia, M.: Design principles for distributed knowledge building processes. Educ. Psychol. Rev. **10**, 75–96 (1998). https://doi.org/10.1023/a:1022810231840
20. Cacciamani, S., Perrucci, V., Khanlari, A.: Conversational functions for knowledge building communities: a coding scheme for online interactions. Educ. Technol. Res. Dev. **66**(6), 1529–1546 (2018). https://doi.org/10.1007/s11423-018-9621-y

21. Gunawardena, C.N., Lowe, C.A., Anderson, T.: Analysis of a global online debate and the development of an interaction analysis model for examining social construction of knowledge in computer conferencing. J. Educ. Comput. Res. **17**, 397–431 (1997). https://doi.org/10.2190/7MQV-X9UJ-C7Q3-NRAG

22. Laurillard, D.: The pedagogical challenges to collaborative technologies. J. Comput.-Support. Collab. Learn. **4**(1), 5–20 (2009). https://doi.org/10.1007/s11412-008-9056-2

23. Garrison, D.R., Anderson, T., Archer, W.: Critical thinking, cognitive presence, and computer conferencing in distance education. Am. J. Dist. Educ. **15**, 7–23 (2001). https://doi.org/10.1080/08923640109527071

24. Joksimović, S., Gašević, D., Kovanović, V., Riecke, B.E., Hatala, M.: Social presence in online discussions as a process predictor of academic performance. J. Comput. Assist. Learn. **31**, 638–654 (2015). https://doi.org/10.1111/jcal.12107

25. Pena-Shaff, J.B., Nicholls, C.: Analyzing student interactions and meaning construction in computer bulletin board discussions. Comput. Educ. **42**, 243–265 (2004). https://doi.org/10.1016/j.compedu.2003.08.003

26. Geisler, C.: Coding for language complexity: the interplay among methodological commitments, tools, and workflow in writing research. Writ. Commun. **35**, 215–249 (2018). https://doi.org/10.1177/0741088317748590

27. Geisler, C.: Analyzing Streams of Language: Twelve Steps to the Systematic Coding of Text, Talk, and Other Verbal Data. Pearson Longman, New York (2004)

28. Geisler, C.: Current and emerging methods in the rhetorical analysis of texts - introduction: toward an integrated approach. J. Writ. Res. **7**, 417–424 (2016). https://doi.org/10.17239/jowr-2016.07.03.05

29. Harry, B., Sturges, K.M., Klingner, J.K.: Mapping the process: an exemplar of process and challenge in grounded theory analysis. Educ. Res. **34**, 3–13 (2005)

30. Rourke, L., Anderson, T.: Validity in quantitative content analysis. Educ. Technol. Res. Dev. **52**, 5–18 (2004). https://doi.org/10.1007/bf02504769

31. Alario-Hoyos, C., Perez-Sanagustin, M., Delgado-Kloos, C., Parada G, H.A., Munoz-Organero, M.: Delving into participants' profiles and use of social tools in MOOCs. IEEE Trans. Learn. Technol. **7**, 260–266 (2014). https://doi.org/10.1109/tlt.2014.2311807

32. Huang, J., Dasgupta, A., Ghosh, A., Manning, J., Sanders, M.: Superposter behavior in MOOC forums. In: Proceedings of the First ACM Conference on Learning @ Scale Conference, pp. 117–126. ACM, Atlanta (2014). https://doi.org/10.1145/2556325.2566249

33. Kester, L., Sloep, P., Brouns, F., Van Rosmalen, P., De Vries, F., De Croock, M.: Enhancing social interaction and spreading tutor responsibilities in bottom-up organized learning networks. In: IADIS International Conference Web Based Communities 2006, p. 472. IADIS (2006)

34. Sloep, P., Kester, L.: From lurker to active participant. In: Koper, R. (ed.) Learning Network Services for Professional Development, pp. 17–25. Springer, Berlin (2009). https://doi.org/10.1007/978-3-642-00978-5_2

35. Rosé, C., et al.: Analyzing collaborative learning processes automatically: exploiting the advances of computational linguistics in computer-supported collaborative learning. Int. J. Comput.-Support. Collab. Learn. **3**, 237–271 (2008). https://doi.org/10.1007/s11412-007-9034-0

Corrective Feedback and Its Implications on Students' Confidence-Based Assessment

Rabia Maqsood[(✉)] and Paolo Ceravolo

Computer Science Department, Univeristà degli Studi di Milano, Milan, Italy
{rabia.maqsood,paolo.ceravolo}@unimi.it

Abstract. Students' confidence about their knowledge may yield high or low discrepancy in contrast to actual performance. Therefore, investigating students' behavior towards corrective feedback *(received after answering a question)* becomes of particular interest. We conducted three experimental sessions with 94 undergraduate students using a computer-based assessment system wherein students specified confidence level (as high or low) with each submitted response. This research study exploits their logged data to provide analyses of: (1) students' behaviors towards corrective feedback in relation to their confidence (about his/her answers), and, (2) impact of seeking corrective feedback on student's subsequent attempt. In conformance with previous studies, we determine that students tend to overestimate their abilities. Data analysis also shows a significant difference infv students' feedback seeking behavior with respect to distinct confidence-outcome categories. Interestingly, feedback seeking was predicted by (student) response's outcome irrespective of its related confidence level, whereas, feedback reading time shows dependency on the confidence level. Our most important finding is that feedback seeking behavior shows a positive impact on students' confidence-outcome category in the next attempt. Different possibilities for utilizing these results for future work and supporting adaptation based on students' needs are discussed in the conclusions.

Keywords: Confidence-based assessment · Certitude level · Confidence-outcome category · Feedback seeking · Feedback reading time · Computer-based assessment

1 Introduction

According to the life-long learning perspectives, one of the goals of a learning environment is to foster students' perseverance and determination. In this respect, 'feedback' (given to the students) offers a paramount opportunity to induce or inspire a positive continuation of the learning process. Computer Based Assessment (CBA) allows automating multiple types of feedback. Appropriate utilization of this feedback is indispensable for performing self-reflection which

© Springer Nature Switzerland AG 2019
S. Draaijer et al. (Eds.): TEA 2018, CCIS 1014, pp. 55–72, 2019.
https://doi.org/10.1007/978-3-030-25264-9_5

is an important ingredient for leveraging students self-assessment process [9]. In this respect, being able to identify students' varying behaviors towards the available "corrective feedback"[1] could be useful to determine student engagement during assessment and thus support adaptation in a confidence-based assessment system [8]; but the current literature do not offer an exhaustive investigation on the topic.

The current research aims to proceed a step forward towards analyzing students' behaviors to the feedback available after answering a question. Our focus is on *Confidence-based assessment*, which is a two-dimensional assessment paradigm that takes student's answer with a confidence level[2] (e.g. as *high* or *low*[3]). The confidence level specified about an answer reflects a student's expectations of his/her knowledge, therefore, investigating students' behaviors towards feedback becomes more informative in confidence-based assessment [13].

This additional "confidence" parameter is used primarily to ascertain actual knowledge in multiple-choice questions tests, which are more prone to be answered correctly by guessing [1]. Student's response outcomes (correct/incorrect) in combination with confidence levels (high/low) provide four knowledge regions. We will refer to these regions as *confidence-outcome* categories, and borrowed their names' abbreviations from [14]: high confidence - correct response (HCCR), high confidence - wrong response (HCWR), low confidence - correct response (LCCR) and low confidence - wrong response (LCWR)[4].

In other words, confidence-outcome categories capture a discrepancy between students' confidence (that reflects his/her expected performance) and the actual performance they achieved. This discrepancy or knowledge gap can be filled through correct information that is usually offered to the students through *task-level* feedback in a CBA system. We proposed that examining students' intention to fill this knowledge gap would serve as a key parameter in differentiating between *engaged* and *disengaged* behaviors of the students during assessment [8]. However, a preliminary step is to establish that feedback seeking is correlated with distinct confidence-outcome categories and it has a positive impact on students' learning. In this paper, we addressed these research issues in a detailed way with respect to a targeted population of higher education students taking an introductory programming course.

The remainder of this paper is structured in the following manner: after a discussion about the background literature used for preparing this work (Sect. 2), we framed our hypotheses in Sect. 3. Section 4 describes the experimental study

---

[1] *Task-level* feedback allowing students to fill knowledge gap(s) in one's understanding of subject material. Discussed in more detail in the next section.

[2] Also referred as certitude level in the literature (e.g. in [14]).

[3] We used binary measure in this work for simplicity. However, other measures may also be used to collect students' rating of their confidence level, e.g., a likert scale, percentages, etc.

[4] Alternative terminologies are available in the literature. For example, [3] distinguished these knowledge regions as: uninformed (wrong answer with low confidence); doubt (correct answer with low confidence); misinformed (wrong answer with high confidence); and, mastery (correct answer with high confidence).

including participants and materials (Sect. 4.1), the design (Sect. 4.2) and the collected dataset (Sect. 4.3). In Sect. 5, we present our data analyses and results; the paper concludes with our discussion in Sect. 6.

2   Background

In case of formative assessment, various types of *task-level* feedback are discussed in [12]. However, we consider the following three most commonly used feedback which are offered to enhance students' understanding of their knowledge level and misconceptions they may have in the subject matter.

– Knowledge of Result (KR): notifying if the student's answer is correct or incorrect.
– Knowledge of Correct Response (KCR): providing correct solution to the student.
– Elaborated Feedback (EF): a detailed explanation about the correct response that may additionally discuss merits of a wrong answer given by the student.

Several research studies conducted in the past have compared the usefulness of these feedback types from different perspectives. For example, findings of Van der Kleij et al. [4] showed that KCR and EF are more favorably perceived by the students when offered in an immediate context (i.e. implicitly given after each response submission) as compared to delayed settings (i.e. provided upon student's request). In addition to that, EF feedback has proved to have a higher impact on students' learning outcomes as compared to KR and KCR feedback types [5]. The experimental study conducted in [13] investigated the link between students' motivational beliefs, effort invested during assessment and students' behavior towards feedback provided by a CBA system. Their results indicate that feedback seeking is predicted by success expectancy, task-value beliefs and the student effort invested in the formative assessment. Readers are redirected to the work of Mory [11], Hattie et al. [2] and Shute [12] for a comprehensive discussion on designing appropriate feedback types in different assessment approaches.

In this work, we combined knowledge of correct response (KCR) and elaborated feedback (EF). We believe that a correct response along with brief explanation or comparison of the correct solution with a student's original response will serve the essential purpose of a feedback, that is, to fill knowledge gap(s). We refer to this combination of feedback as *corrective feedback (CF)*, which is originally defined by knowledge of result (KR) feedback in [2]. We further describe KR and CF feedback as they are used in this study in Sect. 4.2.

The role of feedback in confidence-based assessment has been studied for over 30 years [4–6, 10, 13, 14]. However, the confidence level considered in some of these studies is not related to each individual answer submitted by a student (e.g., [4, 5, 13]). The earliest study [6] reported students' different usage of feedback based on their confidence level and actual answer. In particular, students with high confidence and wrong answers spent more time on reading feedback, whereas, feedback gained less importance in case of correct answers given with high confidence. Similar results were found by [10] and [14] when compared feed-back reading time in relation to different confidence levels. These studies show that feedback has been perceived differently by students in distinct confidence-outcome categories and this information is being used to provide adaptive feedback to the students based on their needs (as determined by the respective confidence-outcome category) [10,14]. But, feedback usage is considered only in terms of "information processing" aspect (i.e. time spent on reading feedback), which is hard to predict accurately according to [13]. Furthermore, contrasting results are being reported in the literature about the accuracy of higher education students in specifying their confidence level. For example, [7] and [13] showed that students are poor estimators of their abilities while according to [14], students confidence accuracy was fairly well.

Thus, a study detailing different aspects of students' behaviors towards feedback (i.e. seeking/no-seeking and reading time) in confidence-based assessment and its impact on students' learning is still missing in the literature. In fact, this research direction is promising as it can contribute to highlight differences in students' (dis)engagement behaviors as they interact with a computer-based assessment system [8].

3   Objectives of This Study

The current study aims at providing analyses of students' behaviors towards corrective feedback in relation to distinct confidence-outcome categories. To be sure that we are producing solid conclusions, we first wanted to determine confidence judgment accuracy of the students participated in our study. The current literature offers conflicting results as mentioned in the previous section. We hence, state our first research question (RQ-1) for assessing students' ability in estimating their confidence in response's correctness. Moreover, to determine how distinct confidence-outcome category response(s) may affect a student's behavior towards available feedback in terms of seeking/no-seeking and its related time (i.e. time spent on reading feedback), we constructed two research questions RQ-2 and RQ-3, respectively. Finally, we will test if feedback seeking has any positive impact on students' confidence and/or response outcome in the subsequent attempt, RQ-4. As mentioned in Sect. 4.1, tasks given to the students in this study are "code tracing" problems which require a multiple-step solution and are not so easy for novice learners[5]. It is expected that seeking (corrective) feedback will help students in filling their knowledge gap(s) and answer later questions correctly from the same topic and consequently improve their confidence accuracy. In particular, this study was designed to answer the following research questions.

- RQ-1: To what extent are higher education students able to estimate their confidence judgement in response's correctness?

---

[5] This should not be confused with questions' difficulty levels.

– RQ-2: Does feedback seeking/no-seeking behavior varies with distinct confidence-outcome categories?
– RQ-3: Do students spend different amounts of effort on reading feedback with respect to distinct confidence-outcome categories?
– RQ-4: Does seeking feedback positively affect students' confidence and/or response outcome in the next attempt?

4   Experimental Study

4.1   Participants and the Computer-Based Assessment Environment

We conducted our experimental study with undergraduate Computer Science students of National University of Computer and Emerging Sciences (CFD campus), Pakistan. In total 94 first-year students taking introductory programming course participated in this study by using CodeMem (Code-to-Memory) tool; an existing computer-based assessment tool developed for evaluating code tracing skills of the students learning C/C++[6]. The tool facilitates students to test their knowledge by filling a trace-table for given code snippet(s)[7]. Each trace-table (solution) submitted by a student is then parsed and evaluated by comparing with the actual solution (that was auto-generated by the tool in assignment uploading phase).

4.2   Study Design

Three sessions of 40–45 min each were conducted in different weeks and students were given six (code tracing) problems per session in a self-assessment setting, that is, no time limit was specified for any question and there was no impact on students' course records based on their participation and/or performance in this study. Each session consisted of questions related to one topic, more specifically, questions were designed from the following three topics: basic operators *(variable initialization, arithmetic operators)*, selection statements *(if-else)* and repetition *(while loop)*, respectively. Whereas, questions were designed[8] carefully to maintain difficulty level from easy to medium.

Students were asked to specify their confidence level (as high or low) before submitting a solution. In fact, two submit buttons ('High confidence submit' and 'Low confidence submit') were available *(on student portal)* so that students can make a conscious choice of their confidence level for each answer. The tool provided knowledge of result (KR) feedback directly after submission of each answer *(i.e. notify if the submitted solution is correct or incorrect)*, whereas, corrective feedback (CF) was available upon student's explicit request *(i.e. provides correct solution along with student's submitted solution for mistakes identification*

---

[6] Developed by a team of three students from NUCES-CFD (Pakistan), under the supervision of the principal investigator of this research study.

[7] As uploaded by the instructor.

[8] By the principal investigator of this research study.

and filling knowledge gap). An example of CF[9] provided to a student is shown in Fig. 1. For the remainder of this paper, we will refer to students' behavior towards corrective feedback simply as feedback seeking/no-seeking. Moreover, students were allowed to freely navigate the system and attempt a question multiple times before making a final submission. Design and further details of the assessment model followed by the CBA tool are available in [8].

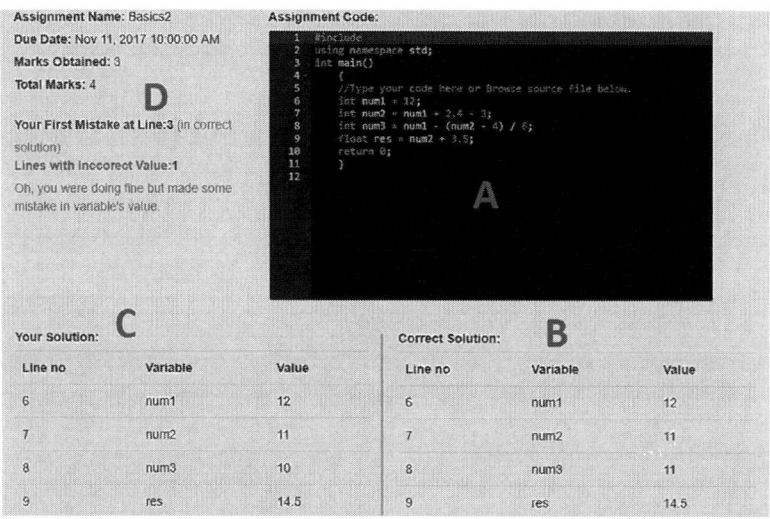

Fig. 1. An example (screen-shot) of corrective feedback provided to a students using the CBA tool, containing four labeled sections (A: shows code snippet; B: shows correct solution auto-generated by the tool; C: shows student's submitted solution; D: explanation/error(s) highlighting area)

4.3 Data Description

The collected dataset contains logged traces of student-system interactions along with a timestamp recorded for each activity. We treated each "Login-Logout" session as a new case to analyze students' multiple problem-solving traces. Sessions with zero problem submission were ignored as they reflect *exploratory behavior* of the students with the system (e.g. page navigation, check previous solutions and/or scores, etc.). The remaining dataset includes 231 logged sessions of 94 students, who submitted 1157 solutions in total[10]. Table 1 shows distribution of the number of problems solved with different confidence levels (in rows) and response outcome levels (in columns).

---

[9] We avoided textual explanation of the correct solution and instead highlighted student's error(s) for easy comparison with the correct solution.

[10] Note that some students did not submit solutions of all 18 problems.

Table 1. Number of problems solved with different confidence levels (in rows) and response outcome levels (in columns)

	Correct	Wrong	*Total*
High	452	564	*1016*
Low	38	103	*141*
Total	*490*	*667*	*1157*

5   Data Analyses and Results

5.1   Higher Education Student Confidence Judgment in Response's Correctness

In line with the existing observations of [7,10,13], data in the Table 1 show a relative majority of students giving wrong answers with high confidence (HCWR = 49%), in contrast to other confidence-outcome categories (HCCR = 39%, LCCR = 3%, LCWR = 9%). Also a big difference in the ratio of responses (both correct and incorrect) given with high and low confidence (i.e. 88% and 12%, respectively) shows that students rated their confidence level as high more often, out of which their judgments were inaccurate in 56% times (see data in the row labeled as 'High'). Without the need for a formal test we, therefore, conclude that higher education students are mostly wrong in their confidence judgments or tend to overestimate their abilities, and this answers our first research question (RQ-1).

5.2   Sessions of Variable Lengths

As students were free to solve as many questions as they could in the given time, the number of submitted problems in each session may not be equal. Also, we consider each "Login-Logout" as a new case, some students have multiple "Login-Logout" sessions. Therefore, we have sessions of different lengths based on the count of submitted problems, i.e. 1, 2, 3, 4, 5 and 6 (six being the maximum number of problems to be submitted in any session).

Table 2 shows the percentages of problems solved with different confidence-outcome category for each session length. We highlight a few interesting observations from this data in the following.

First, the percentage of problems solved with HCWR is much higher in all sessions as compared to other category responses; this supports our earlier observation that students overstate their confidence level. Second, the maximum number of correct responses given with high confidence (HCCR) appears to be in sessions with length 6; which shows that students having "mastery" or better knowledge tend to involve in longer problem-solving sessions. Furthermore, responses of LCCR category are visible in sessions of length 4 and above. This observation may be interpreted as students involved in longer sessions *do not*

Table 2. Problems solved per distinct confidence-outcome category in variable lengths sessions

Login-Logout session length	Confidence-Outcome category				Total problems solved
	LCCR count,(%)	LCWR count,(%)	HCCR count,(%)	HCWR count,(%)	
1	1,(7.1%)	1,(7.1%)	1,(7.1%)	11,(78.6%)	*14*
2	0,(0%)	6,(14.3%)	6,(14.3%)	30,(71.4%)	*42*
3	1,(2%)	9,(17.6%)	13,(25.5%)	28,(54.9%)	*51*
4	4,(14.3%)	2,(7.1%)	4,(14.3%)	18,(64.3%)	*28*
5	4,(8%)	13,(26%)	15,(30%)	18,(36%)	*50*
6	28,(2.9%)	72,(7.4%)	413,(42.5%)	459,(47.2%)	*972*

hesitate to admit their lower level of knowledge in some questions. Lastly, sessions of length 1 & 2 contain highest percentages of HCWRs; which reveals poor behavior of low performing students who may have quit earlier due to less motivational level. The support of these conclusions in terms of observed sessions is however quite low, hence, we believe that findings from a large dataset is required for confirmation.

5.3 Comparison of Feedback Seeking in Variable Lengths Sessions

Before moving towards the next research question, it is necessary to show that feedback seeking behavior of the students is not affected by sessions of different lengths. Therefore, we decided to compare feedback seeking frequencies and sessions of different lengths (as determined by count of problems solved in each Login-Logout session). A moderate positive correlation between the two will validate that it is appropriate to compare sessions of different lengths and sessions conducted during different weeks as the students' behaviors towards feedback remained persistent. A positive correlation is expected because naturally more problems solved will increase feedback seeking, a moderate positive correlation, however, indicates that session length is not a determinant.

We applied Spearman's rank correlation coefficient (non-parametric) test with $N = 205$ sessions[11] and the results show a significant positive relation ($r[205] = 0.40$, $p < 0.01$). It is thus appropriate to compare sessions of different lengths and feedback seeking behaviors for further analyses.

5.4 Feedback Seeking Behavior in Distinct Confidence-Outcome Categories

Comparison of feedback seek vs. no-seek per confidence-outcome category is shown in Fig. 2. We can see that feedback seeking behavior is prominent in case

---

[11] Total sessions - sessions with zero feedback seek ($231 - 26 = 205$).

of wrong answers given with high and low confidence (HCWR and LCWR), and feedback no-seeking in case of correct answers (HCCR and LCCR). Percentages of submitted solutions followed by feedback seeking activity for each distinct category are as follows: HCCR = 14%, HCWR = 74.8%, LCCR = 18.4%, and LCWR = 82.5%. These observations reveal that students sought feedback for some intended purpose and not just arbitrarily.

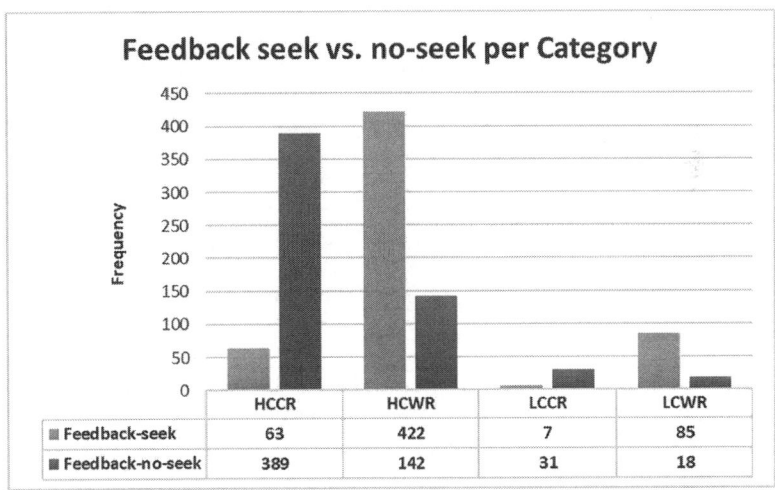

Fig. 2. Comparison of feedback seek vs. no-seek per confidence-outcome category

Next, we used Chi-square independence test and found a significantly positive correlation between confidence-outcome categories and feedback seeking, X^2 (3, N = 1157) = 432.87, p < 0.01. Based on the results of Chi-square, we reject the null hypothesis; and conclude that feedback seeking/no-seeking behavior is correlated with confidence-outcome categories, answering RQ-2.

However, Chi-square test did not provide us with a function for predicting feedback seeking behavior from confidence-outcome. We, therefore, ran a logistic regression using confidence-outcome categories and time taken to solve problems (in seconds), as our independent variables to predict feedback seeking. Our dataset contains 577 feedback seeking and 580 feedback no-seek observations; so there's clearly no class bias in the data. Both HCWR and LCWR were found to be positively related with feedback seeking at a significance probability of 0.001 (p < 0.001). With 75% train data, we achieved 80.28% prediction accuracy of the derived logistic model and area under ROC curve is 0.7974.

Based on these outcomes, we agree with [14] that students' feedback (seeking) behavior is attributed to response outcome irrespective of their confidence level. However, unlike [13], running a logistic regression we did not find "time taken to solve problems" (or effort) as a significant predictor variable for feedback seeking.

5.5 Feedback Reading Time in Distinct Confidence-Outcome Categories

Now we will present methods we used to study the impact of different confidence-outcome categories on feedback reading time (i.e. RQ-3). Table 3 shows descriptive statistics of feedback reading time associated with distinct categories (560 records in total, 17 records were eliminated with no time recorded due to abnormal termination of students' sessions).

Table 3. Statistics of feedback reading time per confidence-outcome category

Category	Count feedback seek (Cfs)	Total time spent (in Sec.)	Min.	Max.	Mean	Standard deviation
HCCR	61	5074	3	968	83.2	167
HCWR	408	33228	2	1716	81.4	131
LCCR	7	1003	6	532	143.3	230
LCWR	84	5487	5	1012	65.3	126

To visualize data normality, we drew a box plot chart which shows that feedback reading time is not normally distributed within different confidence-outcome categories. Hence, we took feedback reading time in logarithmic scale on the x-axis for better visualization, see Fig. 3; as there were huge differences in time spent per category.

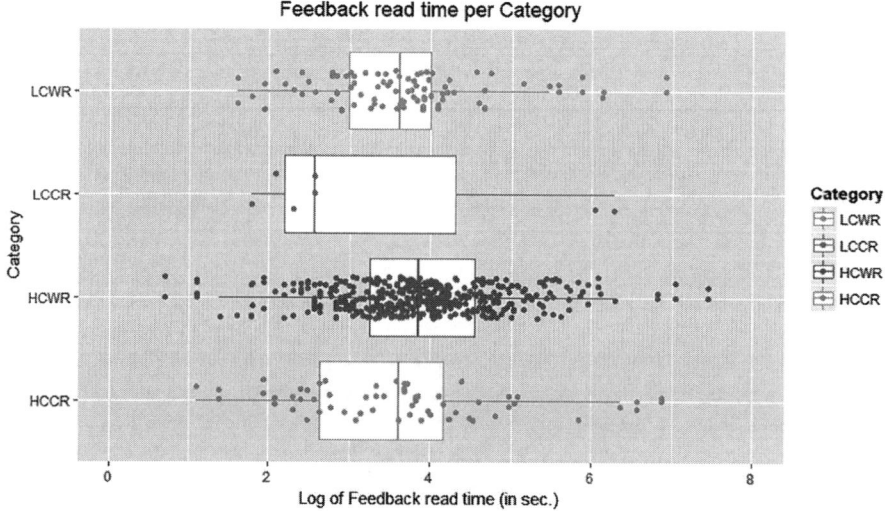

Fig. 3. Box plot chart: feedback reading time per confidence-outcome category

The chart shows that median, upper and lowers quartiles of HCWR is greater[12] than that of HCCR and LCWR (we ignored LCCR in our analysis due to insufficient number of instances: Cfs = 7). This observation confirms our intuition that students will take more time in filling knowledge gaps when the discrepancy is high between their expected and actual performance. Some prior works [6, 10] also revealed similar results, however, in our dataset the count of feedback seek with HCWR (Cfs = 408, from Table 3) is enormous than that of HCCR and LCWR (61 and 84, respectively); thus more evidence is required to support our results.

Next, feedback reading time was regressed on four confidence-outcome categories and time taken to solve problems; no variable showed a significant relation with feedback reading time except for "time taken to solve problems" ($p < 0.05$). Thus, we answer to our third research question (RQ-3) as 'no', because we did not find sufficient evidence to claim that students spend different time on reading feedback after distinct confidence-outcome category responses. We, in fact, agree in large with the views presented by Van der Kleij et al. [4] that feedback reading time is difficult to predict because of its dependence on multiple factors, for example, student's motivation to learn, his/her reading speed, information presented in the feedback, etc.

5.6 Impact of Feedback Seeking Behavior on Confidence-Outcome Category in Next Attempt

In this section, we enlighten on our findings on how feedback seeking behavior may impact a student's confidence level and response outcome in the subsequent attempt (RQ-4). To do this, we called the confidence-outcome category of the last submitted solution as "Original Category", and determined the impact of feedback seeking vs. no-seeking on: (1) confidence, (2) response outcome, and, (3) category (a combination of confidence and response outcome); in the next attempt[13]. Tables 4, 5 and 6 contain charts showing comparison of feedback seeking vs. no-seeking on students' confidence, response outcome and category, respectively; based on the original category. In the followings, we provide a precise description of our observations of the charts shown in all three tables, followed by concluding remarks.

Impact on Confidence Level in Next Attempt. Although a lesser number of students sought feedback with HCCR original category, a slight increase in the confidence levels of students is observed as compared to those with no

---

[12] As the data is shown in logarithmic scale for better visualization, thus, the slight increase in median of HCWR should not be ignored.

[13] To analyze the impact of feedback on performance attributes in the next attempt, we removed first problem solved per 'Login-Logout' session from the original dataset (N = 1157, total sessions = 231), as it has no ancestor variable to observe; this leaves us with 926 records.

feedback seeking, see charts shown in Table 4. Students with HCWR initial category showed a slight decrease in their confidence levels with feedback seek. This decrease in confidence level after seeking feedback may be interpreted as a realization of one's high estimation of his/her abilities (i.e. high confidence in a wrong response). A similar observation is reported in [14] although they presented a different reasoning. Further, we find an increase in high confidence in case of LCCR initial category after feedback seeking; while no change in the confidence is observed for students having LCWR initial category. In general, there is a positive impact of feedback seeking on students' confidence levels in the next attempt; confidence level increases in the case of correct responses and decreases minimally in case of wrong responses.

Impact on Response's Outcomes in Next Attempt. All charts in Table 5 show an increase in correct responses in the subsequent attempt for students who sought feedback irrespective of their original category. As mentioned earlier, questions were designed from the same topic for each experimental session and it was expected that seeking feedback will help students in answering later questions correctly. However, this might not be true for all students as only seeking feedback is not enough; it requires a positive attitude and willingness of a student to process the information presented [13].

Therefore, observations of Tables 4 and 5 answer our last research question RQ-4, that is, seeking feedback positively affected student confidence and response outcome in the next attempt.

Impact on Category in Next Attempt. To visualize the combined effect of a change in students' confidence and response outcome in the next attempt, Table 6 contains charts for confidence-outcome categories.

Students with HCCR initial category showed an increase in correct responses given with high confidence (HCCR) and a decrease in HCWR and LCCR responses after seeking feedback. A similar increasing trend is found in HCWR initial category cases, with an exception of a slight increase in responses (correct and incorrect, both) with low confidence. Again, we will interpret this behavior as a positive reflection of one's overestimation about his/her abilities in the previous attempt. Seeking feedback also helped students with LCCR initial category in giving more correct answers with high confidence and lesser wrong answers with either confidence level. While students with LCWR initial category showed increase in correct responses given with high confidence (HCCR) in the next attempt; ratio of LCCR and LCWR remained constant for answers followed by feedback seeking and no-seeking activity.

To conclude, feedback seeking has a positive impact on students' confidence level, response outcome and consequently on the confidence-outcome category in the subsequent attempt. Finally, to test the statistical significance of the relationship between feedback (seek/no-seek) and category in the next attempt, we used Chi-square independence test. The result shows sufficient evidence to reject the null hypothesis, X^2 (3, N = 926) = 27.44, p < 0.01; therefore, we conclude that

Table 4. Impact of feedback seek vs. no-seek on confidence level in next attempt

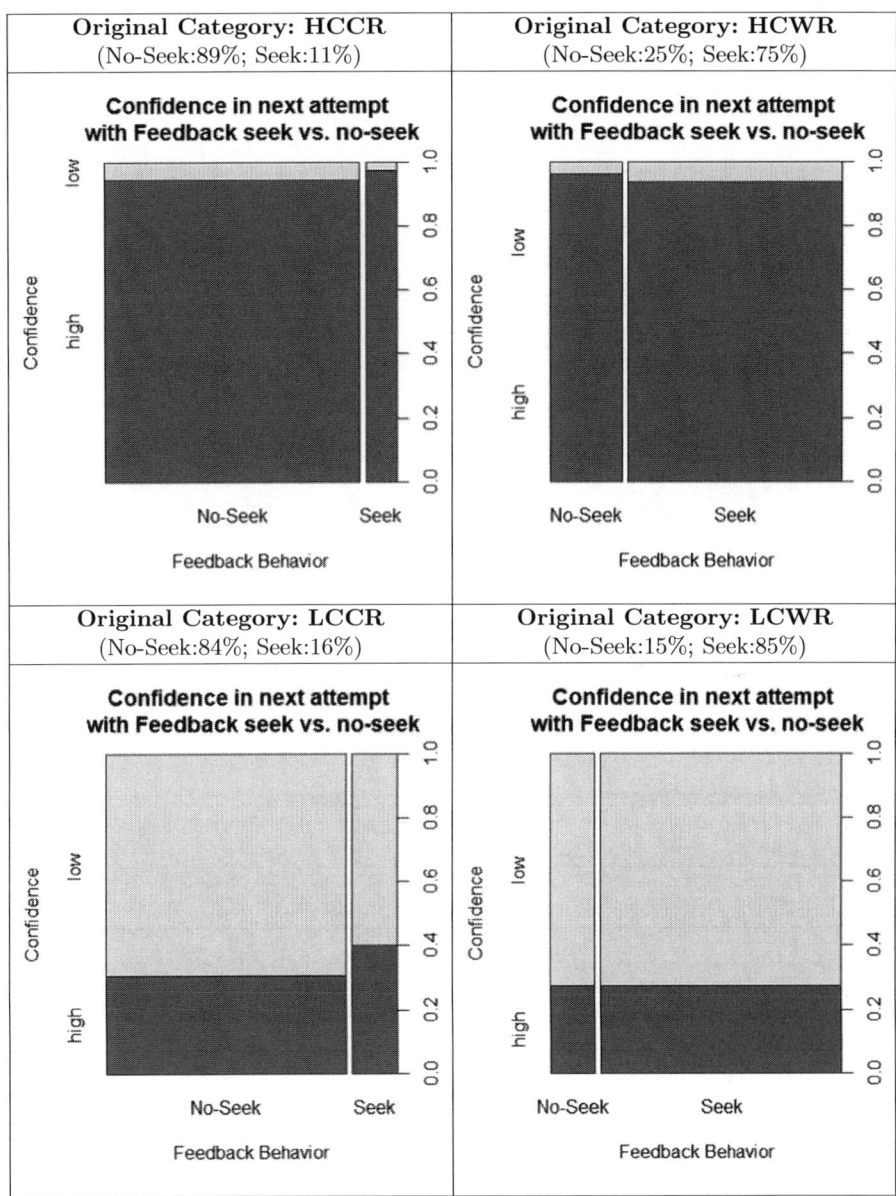

feedback (seek/no-seek) behavior and the confidence-outcome category in the next attempt are not independent.

Table 5. Impact of feedback seek vs. no-seek on response outcome in next attempt

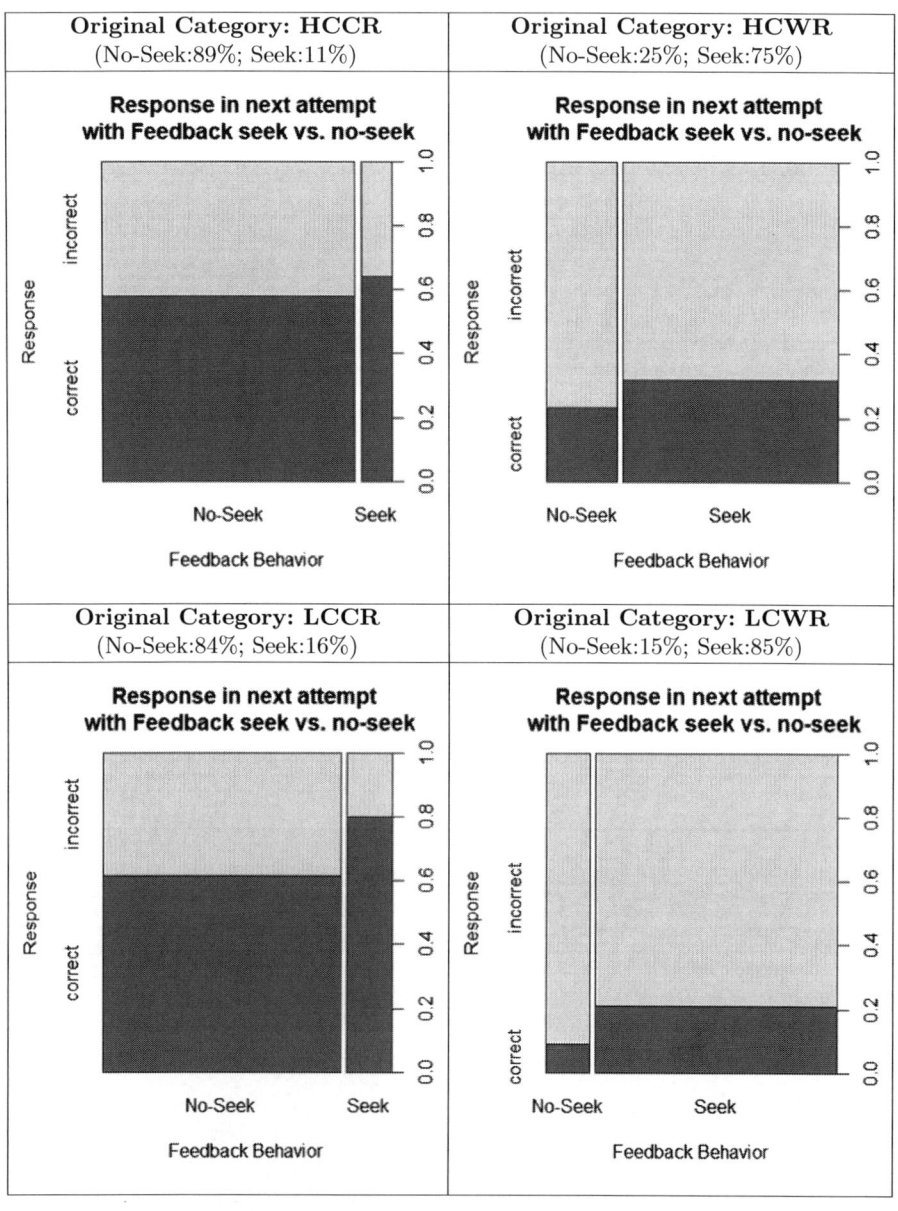

Table 6. Impact of feedback seek vs. no-seek on confidence-outcome category in next attempt

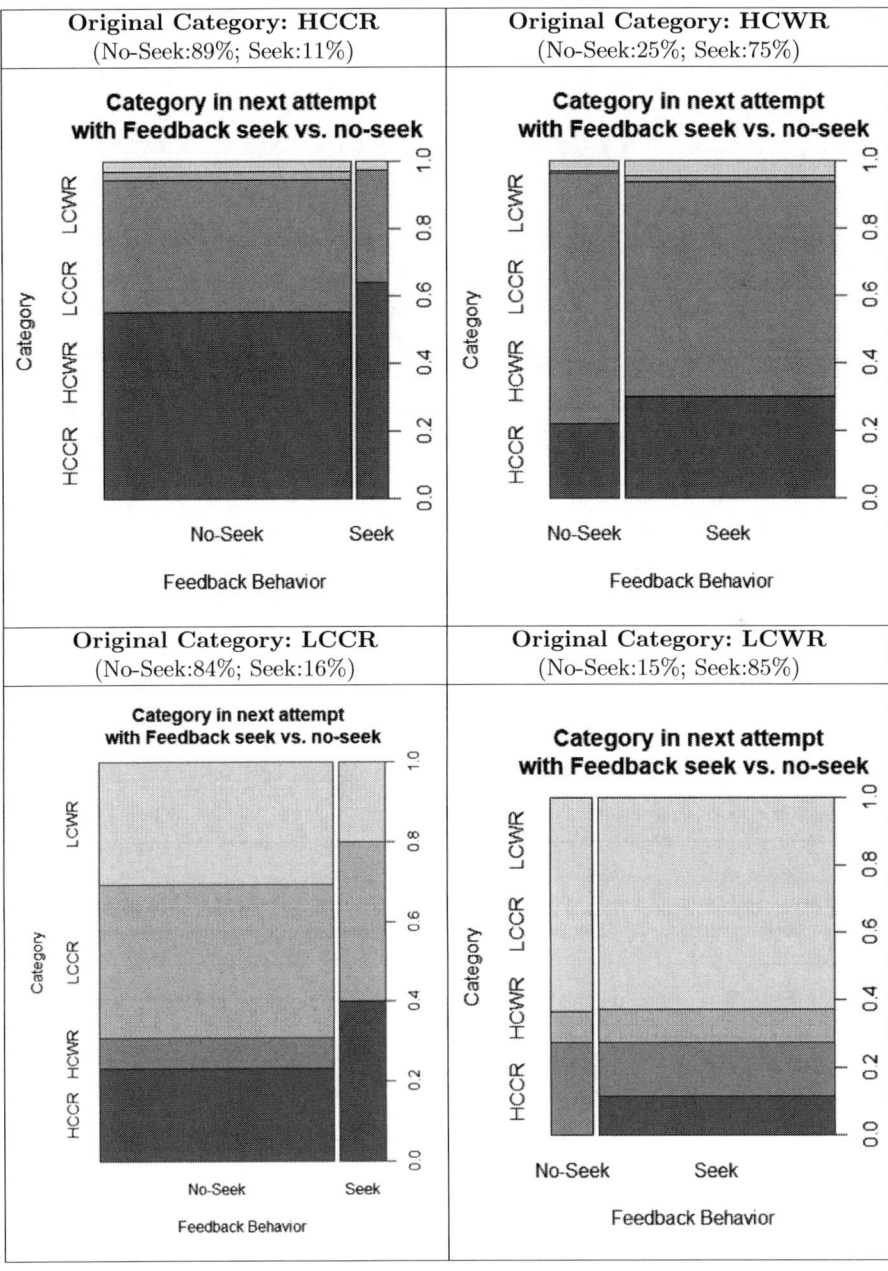

6   Discussion

Confidence-based assessment reveals a discrepancy between a student's confidence about an answer in contrast to the actual outcome. Feedback can play a central role in filling this *knowledge gap* provided that it contains the correct solution and allows students to make a comparison with their submitted solution [14] (i.e., through textual explanation or by highlighting errors; we adopted the latter approach). We called this combination of "knowledge of correct response" and "elaborated feedback" as *corrective feedback*. Students' positive attitudes towards different feedback types are reported by several researchers from varying perspectives, including their confidence (or certitude) level [4–6,10,13,14]. However, the confidence level considered in some of these studies is not related to each individual answer submitted by a student (e.g., [4,5,13]). Also, a detailed analysis of students' behaviors towards feedback in confidence-based assessment and its potential effect(s) were missing in the literature.

We conducted three experimental sessions with higher education students using a computer-based assessment system. This exploratory work analyzed logged data from different aspects which provide useful insights for our future work in particular, and supporting adaptation in a confidence-based assessment system, as discussed below.

First, our result shows that higher education students do not specify their confidence level accurately as identified by [7,10,13]. One approach to minimize this inaccuracy is by using some marking scheme, as done in [14], that assigns positive and negative scores based on distinct confidence-outcome category. However, this can impose internal pressure on the students to avoid penalization which may affect their performance as well. Hence, we propose to construct a prediction model which estimates the confidence accuracy of each student. And, utilize this information to generate personalized "feedback about self-regulation" (FR) that guides a learner on how to direct and regulate their actions towards learning goals [2]. In this case, FR feedback can help over- and under- confident students to improve their confidence accuracy and knowledge to achieve *mastery* in the subject domain.

Second, we compared feedback seeking behavior of students in sessions of variable lengths to analyze if this behavior is affected by the number of problems solved in a 'Login-Logout' session. This was also important as we conducted three experimental sessions in different weeks and we wanted to see if it is appropriate to compare them. Our results show a moderate positive relation between session lengths and feedback seeking behavior which confirms that students' behaviors towards feedback remained persistent.

Third, we find strong evidence that students' behaviors towards feedback vary with distinct confidence-outcome categories. More specifically, as the intuition suggests, we find that students' feedback seeking/no-seeking behavior is associated with their response's outcome (i.e. students read corrective feedback in case of wrong responses). Another important factor which has been associated with feedback seeking behavior is 'effort' (or time spent) in solving a problem [13]. However, we did not find any significant relation between the two in our study. Although, if proved, it could have been used to argument why all high discrepancy instances (i.e. wrong response given with high confidence) were not followed by a feedback seeking activity[14]. We can assume that students who spent less time answering a question, would rarely be interested in knowing correct response and/or their mistakes.

Next, we compared student feedback reading time with respect to distinct confidence-outcome categories. We observed that students took more time in reading feedback in case of wrong responses given with high confidence which is in line with prior results of [6,10]. However, we failed to find a significant difference in feedback reading times; hence, further investigation is required to study these time-specific behaviors in confidence-based assessment.

Another distinctive contribution of this work is that we determined the impact of seeking feedback on student's confidence level and response outcome in a subsequent attempt. We find a significantly positive effect of feedback seeking versus no-seeking on the confidence-outcome category. We remind that questions were designed from the same topic for each experimental session in this study. Therefore, it was expected that seeking corrective feedback will help students in answering a later question(s) correctly. However, our results show that feedback seeking also affected students' confidence level positively. For example, in case of *"low confidence-correct response"* approximately 10% of the students who sought feedback changed their confidence level as "high" in next question (see Table 4). We can assume hypothetically that seeking corrective feedback in case of a correct response helped a student in doubt (or low confident) to gain confidence about his/her knowledge. Positive change in students confidence level as an effect of seeking feedback was also observed by [14], but we provide detailed results which are proven statistically. To conclude, investigating students' behaviors towards feedback offer valuable information in case of confidence-based assessment as compared to traditional one-dimensional assessment approach.

Overall, we achieved very promising results which support our initial thoughts that capturing students' behaviors towards feedback in confidence-based assessment will serve as a useful parameter in determining their engagement/disengagement behaviors [8]. In this regard, our future work aims at defining various (dis)engagement behaviors using student's response outcome, confidence level and followed feedback seeking activity. Seeking and utilization of available feedback is much dependent on students' engagement level [11,13], which may vary within and across different sessions. We also plan to analyze these temporal traces at student level, that is, by constructing students' behavioral profiles for each Login-Logout session.

Acknowledgments. We are thankful for the support and contribution of Mr. Abdul Wahab (Instructor at NUCES CFD campus, Pakistan) and his students who participated in this experimental study.

---

[14] Leave aside students' personal characteristics for a moment; which may affect their feedback reading time: motivation, reading speed, etc., as discussed in [13].

References

1. Gardner-Medwin, A.R., Gahan, M.: Formative and summative confidence-based assessment (2003)
2. Hattie, J., Timperley, H.: The power of feedback. Rev. Educ. Res. **77**(1), 81–112 (2007). https://doi.org/10.3102/003465430298487
3. Hunt, D.P.: The concept of knowledge and how to measure it. J. Intellect. Cap. **4**(1), 100–113 (2003). https://doi.org/10.1108/14691930310455414
4. Van der Kleij, F.M., Eggen, T.J., Timmers, C.F., Veldkamp, B.P.: Effects of feedback in a computer-based assessment for learning. Comput. Educ. **58**(1), 263–272 (2012). https://doi.org/10.1016/j.compedu.2011.07.020
5. Van der Kleij, F.M., Feskens, R.C., Eggen, T.J.: Effects of feedback in a computer-based learning environment on students' learning outcomes: a meta-analysis. Rev. Educ. Res. **85**(4), 475–511 (2015). https://doi.org/10.3102/0034654314564881
6. Kulhavy, R.W., Stock, W.A.: Feedback in written instruction: the place of response certitude. Educ. Psychol. Rev. **1**(4), 279–308 (1989). https://doi.org/10.1007/bf01320096
7. Lang, C., Heffernan, N., Ostrow, K., Wang, Y.: The impact of incorporating student confidence items into an intelligent tutor: a randomized controlled trial. International Educational Data Mining Society (2015)
8. Maqsood, R., Ceravolo, P.: Modeling behavioral dynamics in confidence-based assessment. In: 2018 IEEE 18th International Conference on Advanced Learning Technologies (ICALT), pp. 452–454. IEEE (2018). https://doi.org/10.1109/icalt.2018.00112
9. McMillan, J.H., Hearn, J.: Student self-assessment: the key to stronger student motivation and higher achievement. Educ. Horiz. **87**(1), 40–49 (2008)
10. Mory, E.H.: Adaptive feedback in computer-based instruction: effects of response certitude on performance, feedback-study time, and efficiency. J. Educ. Comput. Res. **11**(3), 263–290 (1994). https://doi.org/10.2190/ym7u-g8un-8u5h-hd8n
11. Mory, E.H.: Feedback research revisited. Handb. Res. Educ. Commun. Technol. **2**, 745–783 (2004)
12. Shute, V.J.: Focus on formative feedback. Rev. Educ. Res. **78**(1), 153–189 (2008). https://doi.org/10.3102/0034654307313795
13. Timmers, C.F., Braber-Van Den Broek, J., Van Den Berg, S.M.: Motivational beliefs student effort and feedback behaviour in computer-based formative assessment. Comput. Educ. **60**(1), 25–31 (2013). https://doi.org/10.1016/j.compedu.2012.07.007
14. Vasilyeva, E., Pechenizkiy, M., De Bra, P.: Tailoring of feedback in web-based learning: the role of response certitude in the assessment. In: Woolf, B.P., Aïmeur, E., Nkambou, R., Lajoie, S. (eds.) ITS 2008. LNCS, vol. 5091, pp. 771–773. Springer, Heidelberg (2008). https://doi.org/10.1007/978-3-540-69132-7_104

Automated Feedback for Workplace Learning in Higher Education

Esther van der Stappen[(⊠)] and Liesbeth Baartman

Research Centre for Learning and Innovation, HU University of Applied
Sciences Utrecht, P.O. Box 14007, 3508 SB Utrecht, The Netherlands
{esther.vanderstappen,liesbeth.baartman}@hu.nl

Abstract. To cope with changing demands from society, higher education
institutes are developing adaptive curricula in which a suitable integration of
workplace learning is an important factor. Automated feedback can be used as
part of formative assessment strategies to enhance student learning in the
workplace. However due to the complex and diverse nature of workplace
learning processes, it is difficult to align automated feedback to the needs of the
individual student. The main research question we aim to answer in this design-
based study is: 'How can we support higher education students' reflective
learning in the workplace by providing automated feedback while learning in the
workplace?'. Iterative development yielded (1) a framework for automated
feedback in workplace learning, (2) design principles and guidelines and (3) an
application prototype implemented according to this framework and design
knowledge. In the near future, we plan to evaluate and improve these tentative
products in pilot studies.

Keywords: Automated feedback · Formative assessment ·
Technology-Enhanced Learning · Technology-Enhanced Assessment ·
Workplace learning · Learning analytics

1 Introduction

In higher education, institutions more and more aim for students to develop towards
reflective practitioners, combining a firm knowledge base with professional attitudes
and skills. To cope with changing demands from society, higher education institutes are
developing adaptive curricula in which a suitable integration of workplace learning
(WPL) is an important factor [1, 2]. Furthermore, learning at the workplace is crucial in
higher professional education, since it allows students to learn to act competently in
complex contexts and unpredictable situations.

While curricula in professional education are increasingly enhanced with different
kinds of technology, the use of technology to enhance WPL is lagging behind [3, 4].
Examples of developments in Technology-Enhanced Learning (TEL) are e-learning,
Massive Open Online Courses (MOOCs) and Computer-Supported Collaborative
Learning (CSCL). In general, technology can enhance learning in three different ways
[5]: (1) replicate existing teaching practices, (2) supplement existing teaching and
(3) transform teaching, learning processes and learning outcomes. When we explicitly

© Springer Nature Switzerland AG 2019
S. Draaijer et al. (Eds.): TEA 2018, CCIS 1014, pp. 73–90, 2019.
https://doi.org/10.1007/978-3-030-25264-9_6

use technology to support assessment, we speak of Technology-Enhanced Assessment (TEA). Supporting learning and assessment at the workplace is denoted by Technology-Enhanced Workplace Learning (TEWL).

A recent area of research in TEL is automated feedback, which can be used as part of formative assessment strategies to enhance student learning [6]. For example, automated feedback is available for MC-tests [7], short answer open question tests [8], (second language) writing [9, 10] and programming assignments [11]. For learning in the workplace, however, generating automated feedback is much more difficult. Students' learning processes at the workplace can be characterized as diverse and contextually specific [12, 13], making it more difficult to align automated feedback to the needs of the individual student. This paper focuses on formative assessment and feedback as important elements of TEL and on the enhancement of students' WPL processes specifically.

The main research question we aim to answer in this design-based study is: 'How can we support higher education students' reflective learning in the workplace by providing automated feedback while learning in the workplace?'. Iterative development yields (1) a framework for automated feedback in WPL, (2) design principles and guidelines for such automated feedback, and (3) an application prototype implemented according to this framework and design principles and guidelines.

2   Theoretical Background

In this section, we discuss theories on WPL, formative assessment and technology-enhanced (workplace) learning and assessment that inspired our study.

2.1   Workplace Learning in Higher Education

When students learn in diverse workplaces, their learning can be characterized as an implicit process often resulting in tacit knowledge development [13]. Especially in higher education, workplaces can be conceptualized as learning environments that afford specific learning opportunities in which the learner can choose to participate (learner agency) [12, 14]. Billett [12, p. 1] states 'the workplace as a learning environment must be understood as a complex negotiation about knowledge-use, roles and processes'. This makes it hard for learners to describe what is learned and to reflect on their learning. In an effort to overcome this, higher education institutes generally ask their students to formulate personal learning goals and to reflect specifically on those learning goals in order to assess WPL [15]. A more elaborate design and integration of WPL in educational programs has been studied the last decade [16, 17] and theories have been developed on the pedagogy of WPL in higher education [2, 18].

2.2   Formative Assessment in WPL

Research on formative assessment mainly focuses on school-based learning, for example teachers' roles in formative assessment in the classroom [19] or processes of feed up, feedback and feed forward [20]. Formative assessment is defined in many ways in different studies, generally referring to assessment that is specifically intended to generate feedback to improve learning (e.g. [21–23]). In this study, formative assessment is viewed as a continuous cyclic process, building on the core questions described by Hattie and Timperley [24]: where the learner is going (feed up) – where the learner is right now (feedback) and how to get there (feed forward). Also, we view formative assessment as both a planned process (for example a planned test) and a process happing "on the fly" [25]. To support student learning, the specific characteristics of WPL need to be taken into account, such as the often informal character of the learning process, the absence of teachers and the necessity for a highly iterative process of cycles of feed up, feedback and feed forward [19, 20]. Especially on the fly formative assessment may fit the character of these informal WPL processes.

Two concepts that are often used in research on formative assessment informed our study: data-based decision making (DBDM) and assessment for learning (AfL). Both approaches to formative assessment are geared towards optimizing student learning by using data. DBDM focuses on the collection, analysis and use of data to inform instructional decisions and mainly uses hard data such as test scores [20, 26]. DBDM has been used with teachers (teams) to guide their instructional decisions (e.g., adapt their teaching strategies) and empirical evidence supports the effects in terms of increasing test scores [27]. AfL strongly builds on teacher-student interaction in the classroom, focusing on an active role for students [20, 23]. It uses short feedback loops (often within one lesson) and uses informal data like student discussions or observations in the classroom. AfL often aims to stimulate learning processes like self-regulation or student autonomy, whereas DBDM tends to focus on increasing student test scores [19]. In a recent review on teacher activities in formative assessment, both approaches to formative assessment have been combined in a formative assessment cycle ([19]; see Fig. 1).

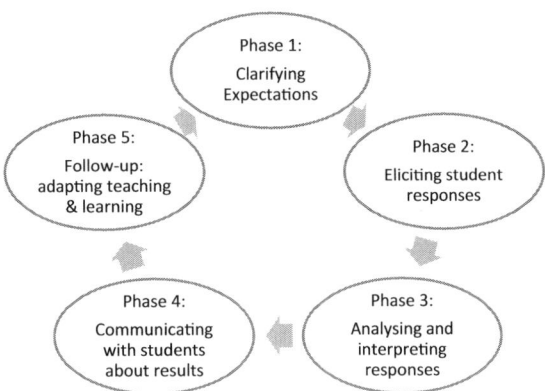

Fig. 1. Formative assessment cycle [19].

The formative assessment cycle represents formative assessment as a cyclic process consisting of five phases: (1) clarifying expectations, (2) eliciting student responses,

(3) analyzing and interpreting students' responses, (4) communicating with students, and (5) taking follow-up actions.

2.3 Principles of Good (Automated) Feedback

Feedback is an important element of almost all formative assessment strategies. In this study, we use the term feedback when we refer to information about the student's present state and feed forward to refer to tips (information) given to students to help them close the gap between the present state and the desired state [19, 20].

In this study, our aim was to increase students' reflective learning in the workplace by generating automated feedback. Nicol and MacFarlane-Dick [28] propose seven principles of good feedback in relation to the development of self-regulated learning, a learning process similar to what we intend to stimulate. Self-regulated learners actively interpret feedback and use feedback to regulate aspects of their thinking, motivation and behavior during learning [29]. Feedback is not just seen as the transmission of information, because students often experience difficulties in decoding and translating feedback into action [22]. Instead, students should be actively involved in the generation and interpretation of feedback, in order to stimulate self-regulated learning [30].

Nicol and MacFarlane-Dick [28] propose a model of feedback in which students continuously monitor their own performance against the goals (often unconsciously, e.g., in our case during WPL), and external feedback provided by the teacher or a system can augment, concur or conflict with the student's interpretation of the task and the learning progress. To realize an effect on learning, students must actively engage with this external feedback. Based on their model, Nicol and MacFarlane-Dick [28, p. 205] propose seven principles of good feedback to support self-regulated learning:

1. Clarify what good performance is, so students can take ownership;
2. Facilitate the development of reflection in learning;
3. Deliver high quality information to students about their learning;
4. Encourage dialogue around interpretation of feedback;
5. Encourage positive motivational beliefs and self-esteem;
6. Provide opportunities to work with the feedback and improve;
7. Provide information to teachers that can help shape teaching.

These principles and the underlying research on each of the principles were used to generate design guidelines for our automated feedback system.

2.4 Supporting WPL with Technology

Efforts to support or enhance WPL with the use of technology, is called Technology-Enhanced Workplace Learning (TEWL). Even though the number of studies in this area is increasing, only recently the design of such technology has been studied [3, 31]. An exploration of design principles for TEWL concluded such technologies should be of the type 'low effort – high impact' [3]. To be effective, learners should (want to) use TEWL on a regular basis.

In a later study, seven generic design propositions for TEWL were proposed [32]. These design propositions not only aim at more awareness of and insight into the learning process of the learner, but also aim to support the learner in 'knowing when to ask for support' and in gaining a broader repertoire of actions (interventions) to undertake. This set of design propositions states that TEWL solutions should offer learners a.o. data-driven feedforward and triggering questions and suggestions to stimulate reflection. These design principles were used as a starting point for our study.

Workplace Learning Analytics (WPLA)

Learning analytics (LA) is generally defined as "the measurement, collection, analysis and reporting of data about learners and their contexts, for purposes of understanding and optimizing learning and the environments in which it occurs" [33, p34]. LA applications that focus specifically on workplace settings are called Workplace Learning Analytics (WPLA) and are a specific form of TEWL.

Clow [34] introduced the Learning Analytics cycle, depicted in Fig. 2. Based on learning theories of Kolb [35] and Schön [36], Clow states that LA can only be effective by 'closing the loop', i.e. by feeding back the produced analytics to learners through one or more interventions.

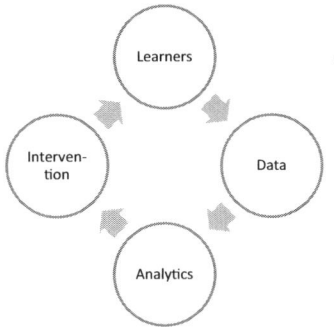

Fig. 2. The learning analytics cycle [34].

The third phase of the LA cycle - which Clow called 'metrics' - is the act of (automatically) processing learner data into metrics or analytics providing some insight into the learning process. Turning these metrics into a suitable intervention, especially in the workplace, is not at all straightforward and requires a learner to show initiative and to possess decision-making and reflective thinking abilities.

Recently, Ruiz-Calleja, Prieto, Ley, Rodríguez-Triana and Dennerlein [4] presented an extensive literature review of the field of learning analytics aimed at WPL. WPLA is still in an early stage of development and the number of contributions is relatively small. Ruiz-Calleja et al. [4] also mention several limitations of current WPLA applications. Firstly, the data collected in such systems is both incomplete as well as scarce (low number of users and interactions of those users with the system). Also, they state that the usability of WPLA tools have limitations and that it is often difficult for users to understand and interpret the visualizations and analytics in their own context.

Clow [34] argues that LA can only become effective if the cycle is completed, by which he means that metrics are used to drive one or more interventions that have some effect on learners. Key to the success of using an LA tool is allowing learners and/or teachers to perform such interventions based on these metrics. In WPL however, there is no teacher available to support learners in thinking about possible interventions and choosing which one to perform. Reflection on experiences in the workplace is essential to make such decisions. Automated feedback can support both reflection and interpretation of the analytics.

Technology Support for Reflective Learning

Reflective learning is a mechanism to learn from experiences and plays a key role in informal learning in the workplace [37, 38]. Reflective learning is viewed as learners' exploration of experiences in order to lead to new understandings, following definitions of Boud, Keogh and Walker [39], Boyd and Fales [40] and Schön [36]. It has been demonstrated that reflective learning can be supported by technology [41–45]. The CSRL-model by Krogstie, Prilla and Pammer [38] was developed to help design tool support for reflective learning, specifically in the workplace (see Fig. 3). The model represents reflective learning processes as intertwined learning cycles.

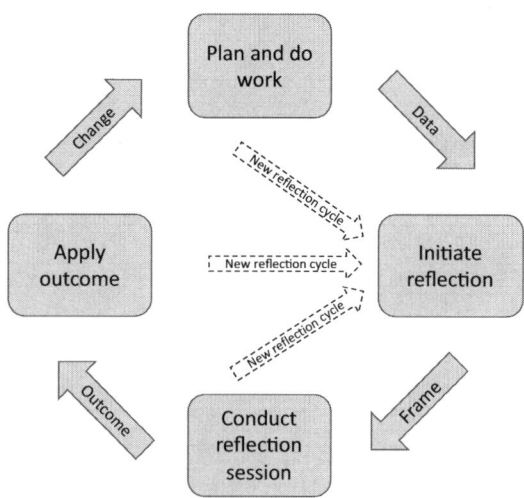

Fig. 3. Simplified version of the CSRL model by Krogstie, Prilla and Pammer [38].

Pammer, Krogstie and Prilla [37] only briefly mention the need for technology support for initiating reflection (phase 2). They state that there are three ways in which reflection in the workplace can be triggered. Only one of the three types of triggers they mention can trigger reflection in the workplace, originates in the phase 'Plan and do work' of the CSRL model and does not assume a previous reflection cycle has already been initiated before. Learners in higher education may not have reflective ability to the extent we expect from working professionals. The CSRL model of [38] does not consider the case in which the learner has low awareness of the learning process and thus rarely initiates reflection. However, this is quite common in higher education, when students are still developing their self-regulation and reflective learning skills.

2.5   Theory Gap and Research Question

We believe there is much to be gained by creating tool support aiming to initiate reflection and support decision-making for higher education students learning in the workplace. We propose that automated feedback in WPL can (1) stimulate learners to reflect more often on their learning process, and (2) support learners in their decision-making towards phase 5 of the formative assessment cycle (taking follow-up action), which is closely related to phase 4 of the learning analytics cycle (intervention).

This leads us to formulate the main research question for our study: *'How can we support higher education students' reflective learning in the workplace by providing automated feedback while learning in the workplace?'*.

3   Methodology

We answer the posed research question through a design-based study. We perform the first two phases of the Generic Design Research Model [46] (Problem Identification and Identification of Tentative Products and Design Principles). The objective of these two initial phases is to develop tentative products and design knowledge for automated feedback in WPL. We aim for the following three tentative products:

(1)   A framework for automated feedback in technology-enhanced WPL;
(2)   Design principles and guidelines for such automated feedback with corresponding examples;
(3)   A prototype showing the technical feasibility of a system based on this framework and guidelines.

We devised a framework for Automated Feedback in TEWL by combining the theories discussed in the previous sections. Simultaneously, we developed a prototype of an automated feedback system in an existing open source TEWL web application [31, 47]. We based the design and functionality of the automated feedback system on the developed framework. The target users for this system are students in higher professional education programs (Bachelor level). The app is generic in the sense that it has customization possibilities to contextualize the text and labels towards all possible education programs. At the start of our study, this application included functionality for learners to register their work and learning activities in an easy way (Fig. 4) as well as a dashboard with selected analytics visualizations (see Fig. 5). These screenshots give some insight into what (type of) data is being inputted by users of this app that can be used to generate automated feedback. The quality of this user-generated data cannot be guaranteed; students are expected to be responsible for their own data. Subsequent analytics and automated feedback will naturally reflect low quality or biased data (garbage in – garbage out).

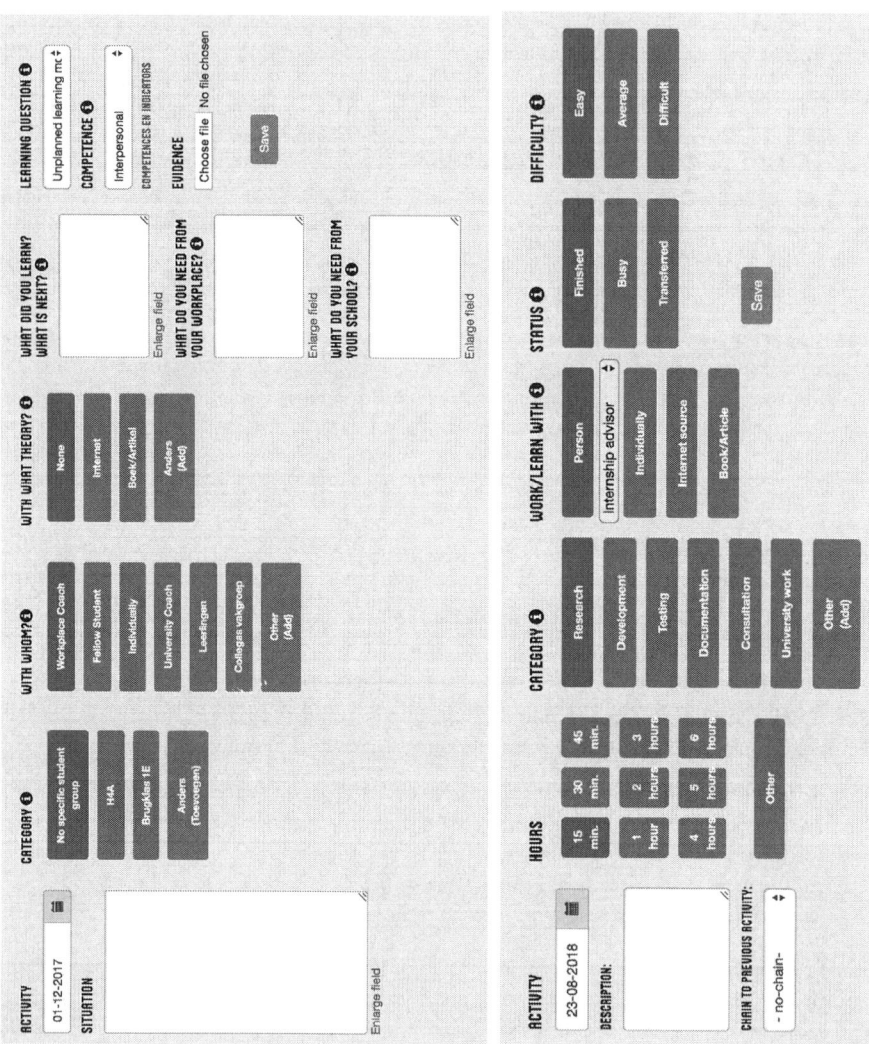

Fig. 4. Screenshots of the application: learning input functionality of the app contextualized for teacher training students (left) and learning input functionality contextualized for IT students (right).

ANALYSES AND STATISTICS

TIME PER CATEGORY

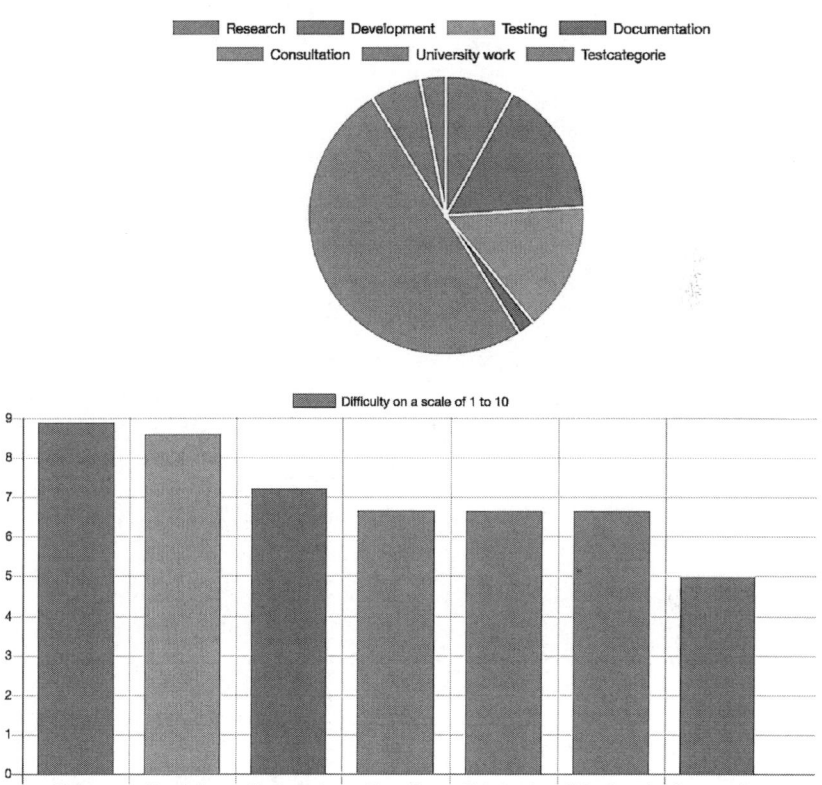

Fig. 5. Analytics dashboard contextualized for IT students.

4 Results

4.1 Framework for Automated Feedback in TEWL

By combining theories on formative assessment, WPL and learning analytics, we propose a new framework for automated feedback in (technology-enhanced) WPL. This framework is presented in Fig. 6. Our framework incorporates a cyclic process, matching the nature of the three models discussed in Sect. 2: (1) the formative assessment cycle, (2) the LA cycle and (3) the CSRL model.

In our framework, learners work and learn in an intertwined way. Starting point for the framework are the learning goals (and success criteria) set by the institution and/or the learner [19]. These learning goals determine what happens in the different phases of the model, for example data are gathered and analyzed in relation to these learning goals. In phase 2, the tool for WPL analytics gathers data comparable to the learning

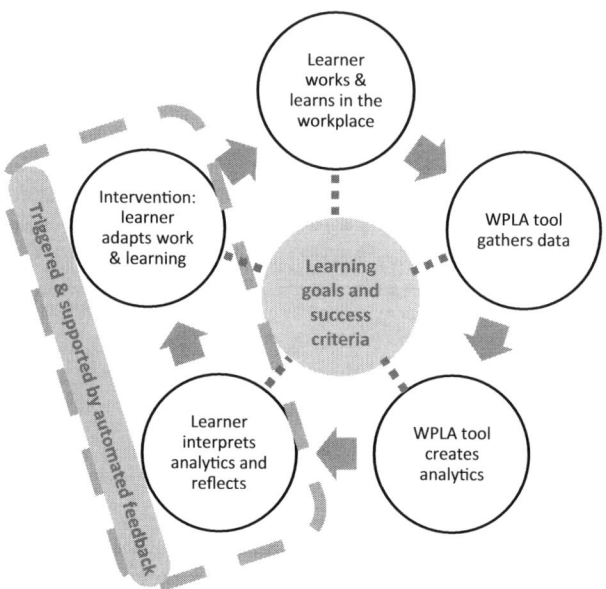

Fig. 6. Proposed framework for automated feedback in WPL.

analytics cycle [34] and the formative assessment cycle [19]. This data can be user- or system-generated (see Sect. 3), or a combination of both. Fitting the character of WPL processes, data can be gathered about both hard and soft data. In this case, quantitative data can be gathered about for example the number of tasks completed, but the often informal character of WPL also requires learner input such as experienced difficulties with a task and whether the learner asked for support. The WPLA tool then creates analytics such as dashboards or visualizations (comparable to [34] and [19]). In the LA cycle [34], the next phase is "interventions". From a WPL point of view, this model lacks the interpretation of the analytics by the learner (phase 3 in the formative assessment cycle) and the fact that interventions and decisions by the learner can be supported by feedback [19]. The idea that learners may lack reflective abilities and technology support might help is also supported by [38, 48, 49].

The novelty of our model is therefore that we propose that automated feedback can trigger and support the next two phases of the cycle, which are (1) interpreting and reflecting on these analytics - and the underlying experiences – and (2) performing an intervention in the learning process by proposing a specific adaption of work and learning. The character of WPL (as described in Sect. 2.1) makes it hard for learners to recognize the right moment or experience for reflection; automated feedback can support learners by giving suggestions on these aspects.

4.2   Automated Feedback: Conceptual Design and Design Principles

Figure 7 represents the conceptual design of our automated feedback system for WPL. Automated feedback will be triggered by the system in three different ways:

- Based on timing; e.g. general feedback that coaches give to (almost) all students at the start or just before finishing a work placement or internship;
- Based on analytics of the data gathered by the system (either system-generated or input by the student;
- A combination of both of the above.

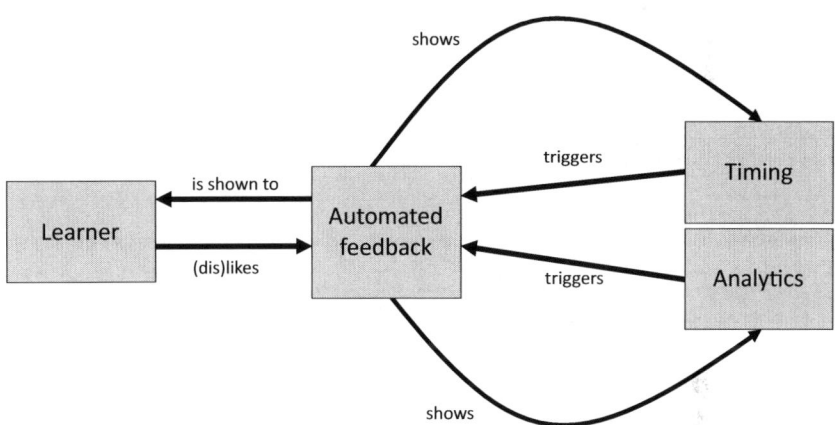

Fig. 7. Conceptual design of automated feedback system.

As an example of automated feedback triggered by both timing and analytics, the system could give feedback to a student that (*timing*) has started her WPL period three weeks ago, and (*analytics*) still has not registered any documenting activities (e.g. writing a project plan). The automated feedback can stimulate this student to start writing down her plans, e.g. by explaining it helps to (1) order your thoughts and (2) communicate your plans with others.

In the design of the automated feedback system, some guidelines/principles were used from the theories discussed in Sect. 2. The seven principles of good feedback (see Sect. 2.3 and [28]) proved valuable because of their focus on supporting self-regulated learning.

Not all principles of good feedback could be directly applied to automated feedback during WPL, but we tried to derive some guidelines/principles that could be incorporated in the system. The development of reflection is a key goal of our system. Nicol and MacFarlane-Dick [28] propose self-assessments and dialogues, in a class setting and between teachers and students. During WPL, teachers are absent, but our system pursues to *enhance the quality of dialogues* between students and workplace supervisors. Practical experiences show that students often do not know what to discuss in these meetings. Our system provides suggestions based on the analytics and automated feedback (e.g., seek help earlier). Also, the *interpretation of feedback* (in this case of the analytics) is deemed important. Though the system is not a dialogue per se, we tried to stimulate students' interpretation of the data by providing suggestions for interpretations (see Table 1). The *clarification of good performance*, comparable to feed up [20] or phase 1 in the FA-cycle [19] has been incorporated in our system by including feed up in the automated feedback (see Table 1). *High-quality information* is defined by Nicol and MacFarlane-Dick in terms of its effect on self-regulation: timely, when students still have opportunities to improve, provide corrective advice (and not just strengths and weaknesses), prioritized/limited in amount so that is can actually be used (see also [30]).

Considering the above insights, we propose a default structure for the content of automated feedback for WPL as shown in Table 1.

Table 1. Proposed structure of automated feedback for WPL.

Element	Example
Data	You work individually X% of the time, while you perceive Y% of your work as difficult
Interpretation	Maybe something is holding you back to ask for support?
Feed-up	Cooperation and knowing when to ask for help are essential skills for professionals
Feed-forward	You could discuss with your work coach why you tend to work individually and how you can try to reach out to others more easily

Altogether, the design principles that guided the development of an automated feedback system for WPL were:

- Automated feedback describes what good performance is, by referring to learning goals (feed up);
- Automated feedback is given regularly and when students are still working on their tasks and can improve;
- Automated feedback includes suggestions for dialogue with workplace supervisor;
- Automated feedback incorporates advice (feed forward).

In the next section, we describe the prototype application in which the above design principles have been incorporated. We also illustrate how the feedback content and triggering rules can be entered into the system.

4.3   Proof of Concept

Over the course of a semester we used an iterative approach to develop an automated feedback system within an existing TEWL application. In two-weekly meetings, the researchers and software developers discussed the (change in) requirements based on the concurrent development of the above framework and design knowledge.

There are two target user groups for the automated feedback system: (1) the learner and (2) educational program manager (administrator).

The system offers the administrator to add statistics, which are computed metrics based on the data available in the application (user- or system-generated). These statistics can then be used within a new 'tip' which is the term used in the application for automated feedback. When creating a new tip, the administrator can interactively couple statistics and adjust the threshold value for when to display a specific tip. Next, the content of the automated feedback – the text eventually displayed to the learner – can be edited. The value of the statistic can be included in this text by using a template parameter. This functionality for creating a tip is illustrated in Figs. 8 and 9.

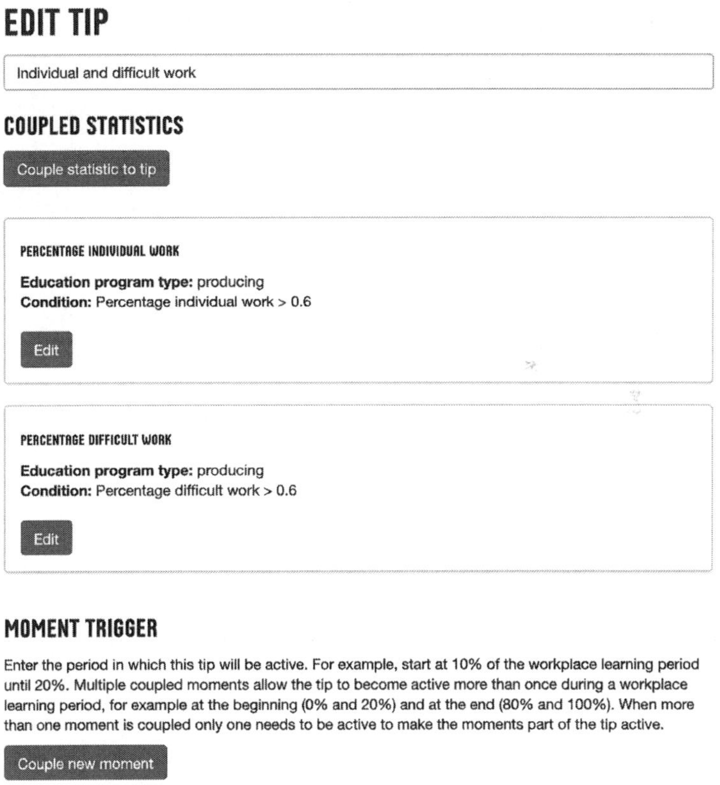

EDIT TIP

Individual and difficult work

COUPLED STATISTICS

Couple statistic to tip

PERCENTAGE INDIVIDUAL WORK

Education program type: producing
Condition: Percentage individual work > 0.6

Edit

PERCENTAGE DIFFICULT WORK

Education program type: producing
Condition: Percentage difficult work > 0.6

Edit

MOMENT TRIGGER

Enter the period in which this tip will be active. For example, start at 10% of the workplace learning period until 20%. Multiple coupled moments allow the tip to become active more than once during a workplace learning period, for example at the beginning (0% and 20%) and at the end (80% and 100%). When more than one moment is coupled only one needs to be active to make the moments part of the tip active.

Couple new moment

Fig. 8. Setting up new feedback.

Because it is important to ensure the automated feedback will have added value for learners, we recommend a monitoring system in which learners can register whether they like a specific tip, or not. If a learner dislikes a certain tip, this tip will not be displayed to that learner anymore. A monitoring system allows the administrators to customize, refine and expand the feedback entries in the system to raise the quality of the system content. It also facilitates the evaluation of our prototype and framework that is planned in the near future. We incorporated such this monitoring system in our prototype, which is illustrated in Fig. 10.

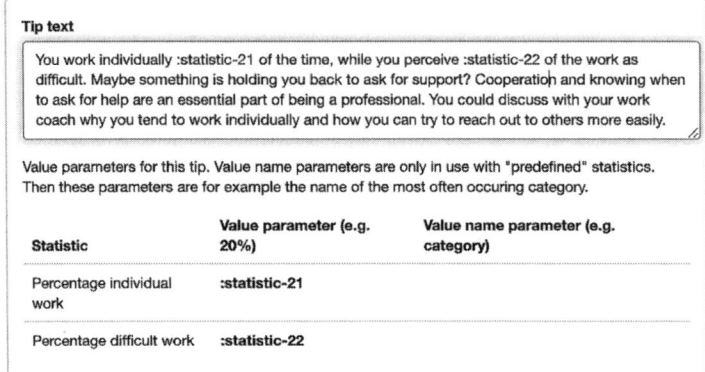

Fig. 9. Entering the feedback content based on data analytics values.

PERSONAL TIPS

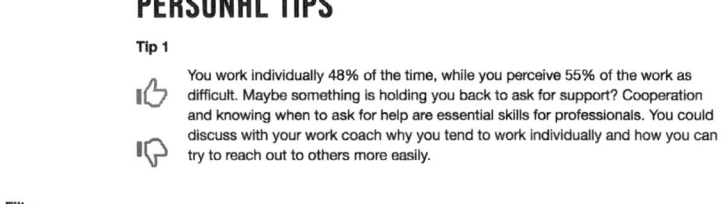

Fig. 10. Display of automated personalized feedback as shown to a student (top) and monitoring systems for views and likes (bottom).

5   Conclusion and Discussion

5.1   Conclusion

In this study, we developed two tentative products for automated feedback in WPL. Firstly, we developed a framework (Fig. 9) based on theories from formative assessment, WPL, learning analytics and (computer-supported) reflective learning. This framework adds to the current knowledge base by combining these theories and illustrating how automated feedback can be used to support (reflective) learning processes in the workplace.

Secondly, we developed a proof of concept application based on design principles and guidelines on the form and content of automated feedback for WPL. This design knowledge can both offer inspiration for future research as well as guide the design of new technology aiming to support WPL with automated feedback. The proof of concept application shows the (technical) feasibility of an automated feedback system for WPL. The source code of this automated feedback system (integrated into a larger

TEWL application) is published as an open source repository for future use by both researchers and practitioners.

5.2 Discussion and Future Work

As described in Sect. 3, this is a design-based study yielding tentative products. We plan to evaluate the proof of concept application with users and experts in the near future, thereby executing the next phases of the methodology proposed in [46].

During this study, one extra design principle for automated feedback for WPL was distilled from the theory in Sect. 2: automated feedback should prioritize what is most important to work on for the learner. However, due to technical issues we were unable to implement this functionality in the application.

Models of feedback often assume that students are able to compare their actual performance to a standards and take action [22]. Reflective skills are assumed, but this is not always realistic and depends on the educational program. For example, in teacher education, reflection skills are much more embedded in the curriculum (and the profession) than in programs in the engineering domain. It would be interesting to study differences in reflective skills of learners and their usage, adoption and satisfaction with the automated feedback system.

Given the nature of the application and the effort it takes for students to enter data on their learning process, we are currently undertaking research projects to analyze factors influencing the acceptation of the application by students and the potential impact of gamification on the adoption of technology supporting workplace learning.

Finally, the goal of generating analytics and providing automated feedback is to stimulate students towards becoming reflective learners. Researchers like Nicol and MacFarlane-Dick [28] and Boud [30] strongly emphasize the importance of dialogues to support students' interpretation of the feedback. Our system aims to enhance dialogues by providing topics to discuss with workplace supervisors. In that sense, our system provides external feedback. Further research is needed to evaluate whether this external feedback, combined with interpretation tips and feed forward can indeed enhance students' interpretation and understanding of feedback and the quality of dialogues between students and workplace supervisors.

Acknowledgements. We would like to thank Ellen Schuurink for her inspiration and support for this research, and Rogier Knoester and Roel Veldhuizen for their technical insights and efforts in developing the proof of concept.

References

1. Tynjälä, P., Slotte, V., Nieminen, J., et al.: From university to working life: graduates' workplace skills in practice. In: Higher Education and Working Life: Collaborations, Confrontations and Challenges, pp. 73–88 (2006)
2. Zitter, I., Hoeve, A., de Bruijn, E.: A design perspective on the school-work boundary: a hybrid curriculum model. Vocat. Learn. **9**, 111–131 (2016). https://doi.org/10.1007/s12186-016-9150-y

3. van der Stappen, E., Zitter, I.: Exploring design principles for technology-enhanced workplace learning. In: 29th Bled eConference: Digital Economy, Bled, Slovenia, pp. 472–478 (2016)
4. Ruiz-Calleja, A., Prieto, L.P., Ley, T., Rodríguez-Triana, M.J., Dennerlein, S.: Learning analytics for professional and workplace learning: a literature review. In: Lavoué, É., Drachsler, H., Verbert, K., Broisin, J., Pérez-Sanagustín, M. (eds.) EC-TEL 2017. LNCS, vol. 10474, pp. 164–178. Springer, Cham (2017). https://doi.org/10.1007/978-3-319-66610-5_13
5. Kirkwood, A., Price, L.: Technology-enhanced learning and teaching in higher education: what is 'enhanced' and how do we know? A critical literature review. Learn. Media Technol. **39**, 6–36 (2014). https://doi.org/10.1080/17439884.2013.770404
6. Redecker, C., Johannessen, Ø.: Changing assessment - towards a new assessment paradigm using ICT. Eur. J. Educ. **48**, 79–96 (2013). https://doi.org/10.1111/ejed.12018
7. Krause, U.-M., Stark, R., Mandl, H.: The effects of cooperative learning and feedback on e-learning in statistics. Learn. Instr. **19**, 158–170 (2009). https://doi.org/10.1016/J.LEARNINSTRUC.2008.03.003
8. Attali, Y., Powers, D.: Effect of immediate feedback and revision on psychometric properties of open-ended GRE® subject test items. ETS Res. Rep. Ser. **2008**, i–23 (2008). https://doi.org/10.1002/j.2333-8504.2008.tb02107.x
9. Ware, P.D., Warschauer, M.: Electronic feedback and second language writing. In: Hyland, K., Hyland, F. (eds.) Feedback in Second Language Writing: Contexts and Issues, pp. 105–122. Cambridge University Press, Cambridge (2006)
10. Whitelock, D., Twiner, A., Richardson, J.T.E., et al.: OpenEssayist: a supply and demand learning analytics tool for drafting academic essays. In: Fifth International Conference on Learning Analytics and Knowledge (LAK 2015), pp. 208–212. ACM, Poughkeepsie (2015)
11. Ala-Mutka, K.M.: A survey of automated assessment approaches for programming assignments. Comput. Sci. Educ. **15**, 83–102 (2005)
12. Billett, S.: Workplace participatory practices: conceptualising workplaces as learning environments. J. Work. Learn. **16**, 312–324 (2004). https://doi.org/10.1108/13665620410550295
13. Eraut, M.: Non-formal learning and tacit knowledge in professional work. Br. J. Educ. Psychol. **70**(Pt 1), 113–136 (2000). https://doi.org/10.1348/000709900158001
14. Billett, S.: Learning through work: workplace affordances and individual engagement. J. Work. Learn. **13**, 209–214 (2001)
15. Tynjälä, P.: Perspectives into learning at the workplace. Educ. Res. Rev. **3**, 130–154 (2008). https://doi.org/10.1016/j.edurev.2007.12.001
16. Billett, S.: Realising the educational worth of integrating work experiences in higher education. Stud. High. Educ. **34**, 827–843 (2009). https://doi.org/10.1080/03075070802706561
17. Nieuwenhuis, L., Hoeve, A., Nijman, D.-J., van Vlokhoven, H.: Pedagogisch-didactische vormgeving van werkplekleren in het initieel beroepsonderwijs: een internationale reviewstudie (2017)
18. Tynjälä, P.: Toward a 3-P model of workplace learning: a literature review. Vocat. Learn. **6**, 11–36 (2013)
19. Gulikers, J., Baartman, L.: Doelgericht professionaliseren: formatieve toetspraktijken met effect! Wat DOET de docent in de klas? (2017)
20. Wiliam, D.: What is assessment for learning? Stud. Educ. Eval. **37**, 3–14 (2011). https://doi.org/10.1016/J.STUEDUC.2011.03.001
21. Bennett, R.E.: Formative assessment: a critical review. Assess. Educ. Princ. Policy Pract. **18**, 5–25 (2011). https://doi.org/10.1080/0969594X.2010.513678

22. Sadler, D.R.: Formative Assessment: revisiting the territory. Assess. Educ. Princ. Policy Pract. **5**, 77–84 (1998). https://doi.org/10.1080/0969595980050104
23. Sluijsmans, D., Joosten-ten Brinke, D., van der Vleuten, C.: Toetsen met leerwaarde: Een reviewstudie naar de effectieve kenmerken van formatief toetsen. Den Haag (2013)
24. Hattie, J., Timperley, H.: The power of feedback. Rev. Educ. Res. **77**, 81–112 (2007). https://doi.org/10.3102/003465430298487
25. Shavelson, R.J., Young, D.B., Ayala, C.C., et al.: On the impact of curriculum-embedded formative assessment on learning: a collaboration between curriculum and assessment developers. Appl. Meas. Educ. **21**, 295–314 (2008). https://doi.org/10.1080/089573 40802347647
26. Van der Kleij, F.M., Vermeulen, J.A., Schildkamp, K., Eggen, T.J.H.M.: Integrating data-based decision making, Assessment for Learning and diagnostic testing in formative assessment. Assess. Educ. Princ. Policy Pract. **22**, 324–343 (2015). https://doi.org/10.1080/0969594X.2014.999024
27. Lai, M.K., Schildkamp, K.: Data-based decision making: an overview. In: Schildkamp, K., Lai, M., Earl, L. (eds.) Data-Based Decision Making in Education - Challenges and Opportunities. SIEL, vol. 17, pp. 9–21. Springer, Dordrecht (2013). https://doi.org/10.1007/978-94-007-4816-3_2
28. Nicol, D., MacFarlane-Dick, D.: Formative assessment and self-regulated learning: a model and seven principles of good feedback practice. Stud. High. Educ. **31**, 199–218 (2006). https://doi.org/10.1080/03075070600572090
29. Pintrich, P.R., Zusho, A.: Student motivation and self-regulated learning in the college classroom. In: Smart, J.C., Tierney, W.G. (eds.) The Scholarship of Teaching and Learning in Higher Education: An Evidence-Based Perspective, pp. 731–810. Agathon Press, New York (2007)
30. Boud, D.: Sustainable assessment: rethinking assessment for the learning society. Stud. Contin. Educ. **22**, 151–167 (2000). https://doi.org/10.1080/713695728
31. van der Stappen, E., Zitter, I.: Design propositions for technology-enhanced workplace learning. In: Proceedings of EAPRIL, Hämeenlinna, Finland, pp. 37–51 (2017)
32. Denyer, D., Tranfield, D., van Aken, J.E.: Developing design propositions through research synthesis. Organ. Stud. **29**, 393–413 (2008). https://doi.org/10.1177/0170840607088020
33. Siemens, G., Long, P.: Penetrating the fog: analytics in learning and education. Educ. Rev. **46**, 30–32 (2011)
34. Clow, D.: The learning analytics cycle: closing the loop effectively. In: 2nd International Conference on Learning Analytics and Knowledge – LAK 2012, p. 134 (2012)
35. Kolb, D.A.: Experiential learning: experience as the source of learning and development. Prentice-Hall, Englewood Cliffs (1984)
36. Schön, D.A.: The Reflective Practitioner: How Professionals Think In Action, 1st edn. Basic Books, New York (1984)
37. Pammer, V., Krogstie, B., Prilla, M.: Let's talk about reflection at work. Int. J. Technol. Enhanc. Learn. **9**, 151–168 (2017)
38. Krogstie, Birgit R., Prilla, M., Pammer, V.: Understanding and supporting reflective learning processes in the workplace: the CSRL model. In: Hernández-Leo, D., Ley, T., Klamma, R., Harrer, A. (eds.) EC-TEL 2013. LNCS, vol. 8095, pp. 151–164. Springer, Heidelberg (2013). https://doi.org/10.1007/978-3-642-40814-4_13
39. Boud, D., Keogh, R., Walker, D.: Reflection, turning experience into learning. Routledge, Abingdon (1985)
40. Boyd, E.M., Fales, A.W.: Reflective learning. J. Humanist Psychol. **23**, 99–117 (1983). https://doi.org/10.1177/0022167883232011

41. Kori, K., Pedaste, M., Leijen, Ä., Mäeots, M.: Supporting reflection in technology-enhanced learning. Educ. Res. Rev. **11**, 45–55 (2014). https://doi.org/10.1016/J.EDUREV.2013.11.003

42. Chen, N.-S., Kinshuk, W.C.-W., Liu, C.-C.: Effects of matching teaching strategy to thinking style on learner's quality of reflection in an online learning environment. Comput. Educ. **56**, 53–64 (2011). https://doi.org/10.1016/J.COMPEDU.2010.08.021

43. Chen, N.-S., Wei, C.-W., Wu, K.-T., Uden, L.: Effects of high level prompts and peer assessment on online learners' reflection levels. Comput. Educ. **52**, 283–291 (2009). https://doi.org/10.1016/J.COMPEDU.2008.08.007

44. Hsieh, S.-W., Jang, Y.-R., Hwang, G.-J., Chen, N.-S.: Effects of teaching and learning styles on students' reflection levels for ubiquitous learning. Comput. Educ. **57**, 1194–1201 (2011). https://doi.org/10.1016/J.COMPEDU.2011.01.004

45. Leijen, Ä., Valtna, K., Leijen, D.A.J., Pedaste, M.: How to determine the quality of students' reflections? Stud. High. Educ. **37**, 203–217 (2012). https://doi.org/10.1080/03075079.2010.504814

46. van den Akker, J., Bannan, B., Kelly, A.E., et al.: An introduction to educational design research. In: Plomp, T., Nieveen, N. (eds.) Proceedings of the Seminar Conducted at the East China Normal University. SLO (Netherlands institute for curriculum development), Shanghai, China (2007)

47. HU Institute for ICT: GitHub Repository Prototype App. In: GitHub (2018). https://github.com/HUInstituteForICT/workplacelearning

48. Duke, S., Appleton, J.: The use of reflection in a palliative care programme: a quantitative study of the development of reflective skills over an academic year. J. Adv. Nurs. **32**, 1557–1568 (2000). https://doi.org/10.1046/j.1365-2648.2000.01604.x

49. Scott, S.G.: Enhancing reflection skills through learning portfolios: an empirical test. J. Manag. Educ. **34**, 430–457 (2010)

Formative Assessment of Inquiry Skills for Responsible Research and Innovation Using 3D Virtual Reality Glasses and Face Recognition

Alexandra Okada[1](✉) [ID], Ana Karine Loula Torres Rocha[2],
Simone Keller Fuchter[3], Sangar Zucchi[3], and David Wortley[4]

[1] The Open University, Milton Keynes, UK
ale.okada@open.ac.uk
[2] University of the State of Bahia, Salvador, Brazil
anakarineltrocha@gmail.com
[3] Centro Universitário Estacio de Sá, Florianópolis, Brazil
simonekf.2011@gmail.com, sangarzucchi89@gmail.com
[4] 360 in 360, Alderton, UK
david@davidwortley.com

Abstract. This exploratory study examines the experience and views of students about 3D Virtual Reality Glasses (3DVRG) and e-authentication systems. The authors developed the "Virtual Reality Classroom" App, which is an Open Educational Resource based on 360 photos of the renowned "Bletchley Park". Participants were 2 groups of students from the UK and Brazil who explored in pairs this App using a 3DVRG in the classroom and also completed a formative assessment activity using the TeSLA face recognition system. Our research question focuses on whether the students' interactions through the 3DVRG enhance learning and assessment of inquiry skills for Responsible Research and Innovation (RRI). Findings suggested that the combination of authentic scenario, interactive tasks and assessment-in-context helped students acquire new information and connect with their existing knowledge and practice the inquiry skills together. These interactions enhanced their immersion, particularly for those who found the activities fun as they did not experience motion sickness. Three types of interactions were identified between students with: the virtual space (1), their peer (2) and the topic (3). These three interactions propitiated, respectively, students virtual, social and cognitive presence, which supported their experiential learning.

Keywords: 3D virtual reality · Authentic scenarios ·
Interactive tasks in pairs and assessment-in-context · Fun · RRI ·
Face recognition

© Springer Nature Switzerland AG 2019
S. Draaijer et al. (Eds.): TEA 2018, CCIS 1014, pp. 91–101, 2019.
https://doi.org/10.1007/978-3-030-25264-9_7

1 Introduction

This study considers the importance of effective and inclusive approaches for engaging students with technologies that can help them to acquire knowledge, develop skills and extend their learn-to-learn strategies in online learning environments. Due to the fast development of technology, open access and authoring tools, educators and learners have far more educational resources than ever before. However, there is the lack of inclusive and fun approaches to foster scientific literacy [1] such as inquiry skills for Responsible Research and Innovation - RRI (Table 1).

Table 1. Inquiry skills for RRI OKADA [2]

Inquiry skills for RRI	Description
Devise questions (?)	Refers to a socio-scientific issue
Communicate Ideas (💡)	Presents (informed) ideas related to the issue
Critique claims (−)	Highlights counter-argument that refutes an idea
Justify opinions (+)	Explain opinions linked to knowledge, facts or data
Examine consequences (±)	Shows benefits or risks for society or environment
Interrogate Sources (🔍)	Shows details about reliable evidence

To address this gap, this study investigates immersive learning with easy-to-use VR technologies that include authentic scenarios, peer-to-peer interaction and assessment-in-context. Assessment-in-context refers to modes of formative assessment based on situated scenarios, designed to better support the learning goals [2]. This study considers the proposition that learners and educators must be prepared to make sense of real-world issues, scientific developments and technological innovations related to the past, present and future [3]. This qualitative pilot study based on Responsible Research and Innovation (RRI) approach [4] examines the experience and views of learners about technological innovations such as 3D Virtual Reality Glasses (3DVRG) and e-authentication systems to enhance peer-learning and assessment in context. RRI which was coined by the European Commission to highlight the importance of a "*transparent, interactive process by which societal actors and innovators become mutually responsive to each other with a view on the (ethical) acceptability, sustainability and societal desirability of the innovation process and its marketable products in order to allow a proper embedding of scientific and technological advances in our society*" [5].

Although VR literature has been published since the 1960s [6], studies with immersive glasses only emerged at the end of the 1990s with the first widespread commercial releases of consumer headsets. However, there has been few examples of empirical research developed about the effective use of virtual reality for educational purposes [7]. Immersive learning practices [8] have been emerging recently with cheaper immersive glasses and free Virtual Reality resources for mobile devices and authoring systems such as the Unity 3D. The VR experience enables people who can't be physically in specific learning places (e.g. museums) experience and learn together as if they were actually there.

This qualitative study focuses on the app "virtual classroom" created in the Unity 3D with 360-degree photos and videoclips of the famous "Bletchley Park" created by the authors and the TeSLA e-authentication instruments for voice and face recognition. TeSLA is an Adaptive Trust-based e-Assessment System that combines biometric, textual analysis and security instruments, which is funded by the European Commission.

The museum Bletchley Park, located in the town of Bletchley in England was selected for our study due to its relevant socio-cultural history, which attracts the interest of many learners across the globe, particularly those who watched the film "The Imitation Game". Bletchley park was once a secret military installation in which the German codes were decrypted during the Second World War, a project coordinated by Alan Turing who developed the first computer known as "Turing Machine".

2 Methodology

The research questions focused on examining the use of virtual reality resources to enhance peer-learning with assessment-in-context. Our research questions were:

1. How do peers interact with each other and with the 3DVRG?
2. Do these interactions enhance peer-learning and assessment-in-context of inquiry skills for RRI?
3. What are the key recommendations for teaching staff and technology teams interested in virtual reality and e-authentication assessment systems?

This pilot study was developed based on qualitative exploratory approach including various types of data, such as: pre-pilot and post-pilot questionnaires, video recording of the experience, and observations to reflect on the outcomes with all participants.

Four pairs of students from the area of Computing and Educational Technology were invited from the Open University-UK, Estácio de Sá University and from the Virtual University UNISUL in Brazil as well as two facilitators. Each pair comprised students from the same university and each student used immersive glasses (3DVRG) with an Android smartphone and the Virtual classroom app (available in Google Play Store) to visit the Bletchley Museum simultaneously. They completed seven activities:

1. Watch a short video about the aims of this study on virtual reality with 3D immersive glasses and assessment-in-context with e-authentication.
2. Fill out the participation consent about the project to authorise open anonymised data.
3. Read the orientations about the usage of the glasses and the installation of VR app, including how to adjust the lens and how to navigate in the app.
4. Answer the pre-questionnaire for sharing their interests, views and experiences (Laptop with access to TeSLA system).
5. Use 3DRVG to visit the Bletchley museum at their study or working place (e.g.at home or university). Participants could sit down or stand up, turn around, move their head up or down, talk naturally about the room, sensations, memories, questions and surprises. For this purpose, they should be together in the same virtual room, interacting and helping each other.

6. Complete the assessment-in-context activity by using the same app to answer a few questions about technology, art history and culture related to the Bletchley park museum and socio scientific and ethical issues about code breaking, security and privacy.
7. Fill out the post-questionnaire to reflect and share their views about peer learning, assessment-in-context and e-authentication. (laptop with access to TeSLA system).

The data was analysed considering different types of interactions grouped on three categories: virtual, social and cognitive. It observed peers, roles, duration, description, feelings, shared information, pre-knowledge, questions and comments. In addition, data from the pre-pilot questionnaire were examined in terms of learning interests, preferences on assessment resources and reasons for visiting the Bletchley Park museum. Data from the post- pilot questionnaire was used for triangulation to identify their reflections about peer-learning, assessment-in-context during the Virtual Reality experience and views on e-authentication.

3   Findings

The results of this qualitative exploratory pilot study revealed that the immersive experience with 3DVRG can enhance (and be enhanced by) peer-learning, assessment-in-content and features inherent in Virtual Reality such as engagement, interaction and visual realism [9].

In this study, the data revealed that a sense of immersion was created through visual interaction in the virtual environment and also via the verbal interaction with their real peer.

The snapshot below (snapshot 1) illustrates that participants were engaged with the virtual environment due to their freedom to move, spin, observe and visualize their surroundings according to their interests. They shared positive and negative sensations and technical comments that emerged from the use of 3DVRG. Although the students in Snapshot 1 found that the experience was not pleasant, they were engaged also with the topic and willing to interact more with the objects of the environment, read more information and see more interactive components [10].

Snapshot 1: VIRTUAL PRESENCE

Peer Student:	For me it wasn't a very pleasant sensation, it is not very comfortable, I feel a bit dizzy in this 3D reality.
Student:	It looks like a picture, static.
Peer Student:	Yes.
Student:	It is a still photo. And because of it, is static, so is boring; it ends up being a bit boring because is static, if it was more dynamic, if you could move around the room, it would be closer to the real life.
Peer Student:	Or maybe, like for example in this… if we could, when we are close to these pictures on the wall, if we stared at them and could make it closer so we could be able to read it maybe it would better too.
Student:	Yes. As well as if the people that are standing could move.

Student: I found a thing which approximates and decreases at least on these glasses. I can pull forward or back places, but it doesn't pull much, it doesn't go much.

Student: It also causes a dizziness sensation if you move too much.

Peer Student: Yeah, Humm, if you move too much. For me specially if you move too much down, look down, or spin around too much gives me a dizziness sensation.

Data shows various interactions that enabled social presence activating participants' curiosity on the social-historical cultural context through the feeling of being together (Let's go, Wait,..We are in,…). Participants shared questions (Is him Turing?, Is it actually him?, Have you ever watched the movie The Imitation Game?) comments (I did, it's very good, I recommend to watch the film again… on the cinema) including their interests and previous knowledge (There are some replicas of the Enigma… the original… it's there in the museum). They also talked about issues that they faced (Can we walk forward here?) and new features to improve their experience with the 3DVRG (Were you able to approximate anything?).

Snapshot 2: SOCIAL PRESENCE

Student: Do you want to go to another room?

Peer Student: Let's go. Wait, the "next" button is here, right?!

Student: Yeah, just fix your eyes on it… there.

Peer Student: We are in!

Student: There, the man is here. Is him Turing? Is it actually him?

Peer Student: Yeah, that's him. Have you ever watched the movie The Imitation Game?

Peer Student: I did, it was fun! …very good, I recommend watching the film again… on the cinema.

Student: There are some replicas of the Enigma, but on the original one, actually original that was used for the film; It was used for the film and it's there in the museum.

Student: Can we walk forward here? I'm just sideways. If I stand up and walk forwards, I will go forwards?

Peer Student: Did you go forwards?

Student: No, you just stand in the same place.

Peer Student: Yeah, in this room that we are, I am trying to fix my eye in some places, but it's not approximating. Were you able to approximate anything?

In this study, it was evident that the interaction between peers [11] had an important role in activating previous knowledge (at the university, we learn, Turing machine is the origin of everything, right) to connect it with visual information from the virtual space (The most interesting thing to see is the size right?! From the machine, which was needed to process all this)? This enabled learners to connect knowledge on social-cultural historical context through visual and verbal interactions about objects, space and people from the past). Participants' social, virtual and cognitive experiences supported their successful learning outcomes. Assessment-in-context through questions connected to their experience helped them consolidate their learning experience and reflections about the technological innovations from the past comparing to the present (What objects Alan Turing had in his office?… that's obvious, right? What cultural object of the time was used, mainly by women?… Sewing machine, I know this is the answer).

Snapshot 3: COGNITIVE PRESENCE

Peer Student:	At the university, we learn, Turing machine is the origin of everything, right?
Peer Student:	The most interesting thing to see is the size, right?! From the machine, which was needed to process all this.
Student:	It is considered the first computer.
Peer Student:	Yes, yes. In college we learn, Turing machine is the beginning of everything, right.
Peer Student:	What objects did Alan Turing have in his office?
Student:	Mobile phone, computer, ha-ha. Honestly, that's obvious, right?! Typewriter and phone, someone received a message here on the cell phone, here vibrated.
Peer Student:	Yeah, it's mine, it must be my class.
Student:	Now for the next question. What object of the culture of the time was used, especially by women (hee-hee) This one the feminists will not like it!
Peer Student:	Do not go!
Student:	Sewing machine, I know this is the answer.

It was possible to observe from the extracts above important indicators of the interaction that facilitated an immersive experience when participants recalled previous knowledge to make sense and connect their experience in a different period of time and location offered by the Bletchley Park museum. This connection between visual information, reflection in pairs and previous experiences supported their performance through the assessment-in-context.

In terms of supporting teaching staff with the use of 3DVRG for peer-learning, the data provided some insights into creating pedagogical activities which might support peer-learning:

- Guide participants to explore together the same virtual room to expand social, virtual and cognitive interactions.
- Identify and find ways to solve problems, such as check if they were visiting the same place, and if not, how they could find each other
- Describe rooms, objects, features, familiar and unfamiliar sensations to identify what was already observed or not.
- Relate their virtual experience with current facts or past events as well as connecting previous knowledge with their visual information.

- Encourage peers to share question, relevant aspects, topics, doubts, techniques to create opportunity to acquire new knowledge, hook curiosity, develop inquiry, co-learn and co-assess together.
- Share observations and feedback during the process to extend their experience and views considering different peer's opinions and experiences.
- Assess the acquired knowledge and the process of learning as well as evaluate the whole experience including the immersive resources.

In relation to the aspects highlighted by the participants for technical teams and technology developers of virtual reality apps, the recommendations are:

- Include extra links to text that might help them to read information and expand cognitive interactions.
- Allow them to experience the approximation with objects and people in the virtual space (zoom in and Zoom out) to enrich their virtual interactions within the environment.
- Enable participants to go forward and backward, with [start, exit] next and return options to navigate in the space with more flexibility as well as strengthening the social interaction arising from being together in the same area.
- Include a mini-map to facilitate an overview of the place, for planning the navigation and encouraging different experiences through virtual, social, and cognitive presence.
- Include a video clip to expand interactive areas to highlight topics and expand their immersive experience.
- update the App by enhance the locations or objects that are special with sound and video) to offer different experiences and possibilities for participants.
- Include extra information for novice students about virtual reality and an option to sit down and use a 3D VR with a tablet instead of glasses.

In relation to the authenticated evaluation, although it was not possible to use the TeSLA face and voice recognition instruments in this pilot, the pairs of students discussed the possibilities based on the project TeSLA video clip [12] and the current environment. Previous studies about TeSLA examined students' acceptance of e-authentication [13]. The participants' views and comments were:

- VR technologies and assessment with e-authentication might facilitate users' identification by naturally sharing their faces and voices during their immersive experiences without having to login using passwords.
- the recognition of students' voices and faces might enable adaptive and personalized learning with Virtual Reality.
- Authentication and new ways of assessment through voice and face recognition might enable new ways of co-learning by moving from the traditional exams and written assignments to more engaging and immersive assessment-in-context connected to peer-learning experiences.

In terms of participants comments from the post-questionnaire about Face Recognition, there was a diversity of opinions. Students shared various issues.

Theme: Technical persistence
Initially I had problems with the face recognition tool because the system was not in Chrome browser. After changing it, I did not have any technical problem

Theme: Trust
I found the whole process longer than traditional assessment without e-authentication, however, I do believe that the face recognition will increase trust of participants with online assessment. Students who are committed to study will benefit with the e-authentication system.

Theme: Quality of e-assessment
To ensure quality of the e-assessment activities, I think that various tools should be integrated (e.g. voice and face recognition as well as plagiarism and forensic analysis).

Theme: Disabled students with special needs
Disabled students might have problems in the face recognition system and might need extract support from the TeSLA team.

4   Discussion and Conclusion

This study revealed possibilities and recommendations on how students in pairs interact with the 3DVRG to enhance immersive learning. The results showed the value of virtual, social and cognitive interactions mediated by VR artefacts, peer-interaction and assessment-in-context with Face recognition. Students did not have significant difficulties and they received prompt support for their technical issues about e-authentication.

The study investigated experiential activities [14] through 3DVRG between pairs that interact virtually with the artefacts, socially through verbal dialog mediated by technologies and cognitively with the studied object and visual information. This initial exploratory study offers educators- instructors, tutors, course-designers and learner the possibility of using Virtual Reality with pedagogical activities in pairs including contextualized assessment [15] with authentication.

It also provides important guidelines for technologists interested in creating apps about real remote places with 360° pictures and videos which can be connected with engaging topics and fun activities. The limitation of this exploratory study was a small number of participants. However, our next step is a mixed method study with more institutions in the area of computing and data science, as Bletchley Park provides authentic and engaging learning scenarios.

5 Display Items

See Figs. 1, 2, 3 and 4.

Fig. 1. Virtual classroom app - 360-degree interactive white board https://play.google.com/store/apps/details?id=com.SangarZucchi.VRClassroom&hl=en

Fig. 2. 360 Photo of the Bletchley Park museum https://bletchleypark.org.uk/

Fig. 3. Example of a student with a Peer Student using Virtual Classroom App and Virtual Glasses https://www.rridata.com/vrclassroom

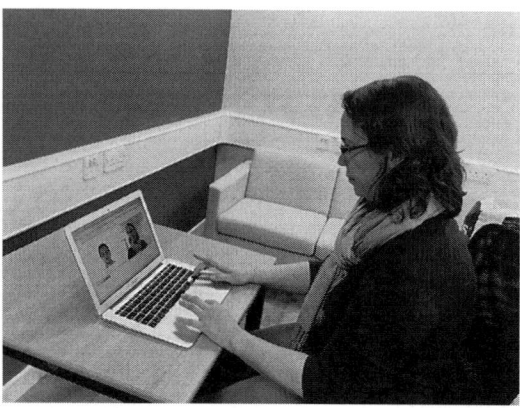

Fig. 4. Example of a student using e-authentication with face recognition through TeSLA–adaptive trust e-assessment system https://tesla-project.eu/

Acknowledgments. This work is supported by the European Commission (H2020-ICT-2015/H2020-ICT-2015), Number 688520 and collaborators who developed the artefacts were supported by CAPES Brazil Government.

References

1. Hodson, D.: Looking to the Future: Building a Curriculum for Social Activism. Sense, Rotterdam (2011)
2. Okada, A.: Engaging Science with Virtual Reality (2016). engagingscience.eu
3. Ryan, C.: Science education for responsible citizenship (2015). http://ec.europa.eu/research/swafs/pdf/pub_science_education/KI-NA-26-893-EN-N.pdf
4. EC, European Commission: Responsible research and innovation (2014). https://ec.europa.eu/programmes/horizon2020/en/h2020-section/responsible-research-innovation
5. Von Schomberg, R.: Prospects for technology assessment in a framework of responsible research and innovation. In: Dusseldorp, M., Beecroft, R. (eds.) Technikfolgen abschatzen lehren. Bildungspotenziale transdisziplinarer Methoden, pp. 39–61. Springer, Wiesbaden (2011). https://doi.org/10.1007/978-3-531-93468-6_2
6. Artaud, A.: The Theater and its Double. Grove Press Inc., New York (1958)
7. Whitelock, D., Brna, P., Holland, S.: What is the value of virtual reality for conceptual learning? Towards a theoretical framework. In: Proceedings of EuroAIED, Lisbon (1996)
8. Goetz, E.T., Merchant, Z., Cifuentes, L., Keeney-Kennicutt, W., Davis, T.J.: Effectiveness of virtual reality-based instruction on students' learning outcomes in K-12 and higher education: a meta-analysis. Comput. Educ. **70**, 29–40 (2014). https://doi.org/10.1016/j.compedu.2013.07.033
9. Rosemblum, L.J., Cross, R.A.: The challenge of virtual reality. In: Earnshaw, W.R., Vince, J., Jones, H. (eds.) Visualization & Modeling, pp. 325–399. Academic Press, San Diego (1997)

10. Wu, F., Liu, Z., Wang, J., Zhao, Y.: Establishment virtual maintenance environment based on VIRTOOLS to effectively enhance the sense of immersion of teaching equipment. In: Proceedings of the 2015 International Conference on Education Technology, Management and Humanities Science (ETMHS 2015). Atlantis Press (2015). https://doi.org/10.2991/etmhs-15.2015.93
11. Gwee, M.C.E. Successful learning: peer learning: enhancing student learning outcomes (2003)
12. TeSLA Project: TeSLA - Adaptive Trust-based e-Assessment System video clip. https://www.youtube.com/watch?v=bJDFkrbPir0&t=3s
13. Okada, A., Whitelock, D., Holmes, W., Edwards, C.: Student acceptance of online assessment with e-authentication in the UK. In: Ras, E., Guerrero Roldán, A.E. (eds.) TEA 2017. CCIS, vol. 829, pp. 109–122. Springer, Cham (2018). https://doi.org/10.1007/978-3-319-97807-9_9
14. Le, Q.T., Pedro, A., Park, C.S.: A social virtual reality based construction safety education system for experiential learning. J. Intell. Rob. Syst. **79**(3–4), 487–506 (2015)
15. Kearney, S.: Improving engagement: the use of Authentic self-and peer-assessment for learning to enhance the student learning experience. Assess. Eval. High. Educ. **38**(7), 875–891 (2013)

Quizbot: Exploring Formative Feedback with Conversational Interfaces

Bharathi Vijayakumar[1], Sviatlana Höhn[2]([⊠]), and Christoph Schommer[3]

[1] University of Luxembourg, Esch-sur-Alzette, Luxembourg
bharu19@gmail.com
[2] Artificial Companions and Chatbots Lab, University of Luxembourg,
6, Avenue de la Fonte, 4364 Esch-sur-Alzette, Luxembourg
sviatlana.hoehn@uni.lu
[3] Interdisciplinary Lab for Intelligent and Adaptive Systems,
University of Luxembourg, 6, Avenue de la Fonte, 4364 Esch-sur-Alzette, Luxembourg
christoph.schommer@uni.lu
https://acc.uni.lu

Abstract. Conversational interfaces (also called chatbots) have recently disrupted the Internet and opened up endless opportunities for assessment and learning. Formative feedback that provides learners with practical instructions for improvement is one of the challenging tasks in self-assessment settings and self-directed learning. This becomes even more challenging if a user's personal information such as learning history and previous achievements cannot be exploited for data protection reasons or are simply not available. This study seeks to explore the opportunities of providing formative feedback in chatbot-based self-assessment. Two main challenges were faced: the limitations of the messenger as an interface that restricts visual representation of the quiz questions, and zero information about the user to generate adaptive feedback. Two types of feedback were investigated regarding their formative effect: *immediate feedback*, which was given after answering a question, and *cumulative feedback* detailing strengths and weaknesses of the user in each of the topics covered along with the directives for improvement. A chatbot called SQL Quizbot was deployed on Facebook Messenger for the purposes of this study (Try out the prototype at https://www.messenger.com/t/2076690849324267). A survey conducted to disclose users' perception of the feedback reveals that more than 80% of the users find immediate feedback helpful. Overall this study shows that chatbots have a great potential as an aiding tool for e-learning systems to include an interactive component into feedback in order to increase user motivation and retention.

Keywords: Formative feedback · Educational chatbot · Quizbot

1 Introduction

Although online education revolutionised the conventional style of learning, many of the e-learning implementations only reproduce textbooks and do not

© Springer Nature Switzerland AG 2019
S. Draaijer et al. (Eds.): TEA 2018, CCIS 1014, pp. 102–120, 2019.
https://doi.org/10.1007/978-3-030-25264-9_8

offer interactive feedback, in contrast to teacher-student communication. In addition, online education suffers from a large number of drop-outs, which is a consequence of insufficient interaction, according to the study by Muirhead and Juwah [1]. The authors recommend to develop strategies that will enhance guidance for online students, such as creating a timeline for feedback and having a specific feedback. Previous academic publications show that student retention is higher when Facebook is used for course interaction [2]. MOOC (Massive Open Online Course) students were more engaged in Facebook groups, and they preferred interacting in social media, which they use anyway, rather than through the course tools dedicated to course-related communication.

However, in 2015, the preferred way of communication was no longer social networks. At this time, big social media companies realised that more users are active in instant messengers than in social networks[1]. The messenger providers opened their APIs (Application Programming Interfaces) to facilitate the development of a special sort of interfaces to services - chat robots.

A conversational interface, a chat robot, or simply a *chatbot* is a software program that usually interacts with the users in instant messengers and understands input in human languages, but also may use buttons and predefined replies to facilitate language understanding. The first chatbot was created in the 1960s by Weizenbaum [3]. After being very unpopular for many decades, chatbots disrupted the Internet in 2015 and keep growing. Intuitively, a chatbot in a commonly used messenger has good chances to be used actively by students who are accustomed to using messengers in their daily communication. The chatbot could help the students in self-directed learning and, most importantly, provide meaningful feedback in an interactive way.

The traditional view on chatbots is still very dominant, saying that a chatbot needs to possess extraordinary conversational abilities in order to be useful. However, if used for computer-based assessment and feedback, the questions of usability and user experience combined with the opportunities to provide meaningful feedback in the dialogical setting need to be clarified. For instance, how to present various types of tasks to the learner and how to deal with the tasks that cannot be presented in a messenger for some reasons?

Prior to providing feedback, some form of evaluation of a learner's performance is needed, and assessment is one possible form of a systematic evaluation. Shute defines *formative feedback* as information communicated to the learner and intended to modify their thinking or behaviour to improve learning [4]. Formative assessment implies obtaining the best possible evidence about what is learned, and then using this information to decide what to do next.

Assessment methods can be classified as short-term and long-term methods. Short-term methods only assess the learner's state of proficiency in a particular subject at a specific time point without the need to capture the learning process or the intermediate milestones in learning. In contrast, long-term methods would continuously monitor the learner's progress at various levels and can be

---

[1] http://uk.businessinsider.com/the-messaging-app-report-2015-11?r=US&IR=T, last checked 22.11.2018.

associated with multiple tasks. Consequently, there is no need to store any kind of information about the learner in the short-term setting.

Short-term settings for chatbot-based assessment are especially interesting in the context of the new General Data Protection Regulation (GDPR) that provides a legal framework for the collection and processing of personal information of individuals within the European Union (EU). Despite the exclusion of assessment data from the closed list of sensitive data provided by Article 9.1 of the GDPR, this type of information has an intrinsic 'sensitiveness' due to the potential discriminatory outcomes against the learner that can emerge from a wrongful evaluation, in addition to the potential use of personal data by chatbots. These issues need to be considered in the design of chatbot-based assessment solutions.

Objective. With the motivation in the preceding paragraphs, the objective of this study is to *explore how formative feedback can be implemented for an educational chatbot in a short-term assessment setting.*

Method. A chatbot can be made available in various chat platforms such as Facebook Messenger, Slack, Viber, Telegram, Kik and Snapchat. However, legacy platforms, such as email and SMS, or voice-based platforms, such as Alexa and Google Assistant, can be used for chatbot development, too. For the purposes of this study we chose Facebook Messenger for the implementation because of the availability of multiple tools that facilitate deployment of a Messenger chatbot. We chose the topic of SQL database query language because of its popularity and a high number of learners. The chatbot was named SQL Quizbot. It can be easily found in Messenger using the keyword *quiz*. Test items of the SQL Quizbot were designed as two-step questions: in the first step, a question related to SQL is presented to the user; in the second step, the user needs to score their own confidence in the answer. Section 3 explains the details of the design, the implementation and the methodological and technological challenges. To evaluate the feedback effectiveness we set up a user survey focusing on the user's perception of feedback usefulness. Section 4 explains the results of the evaluation. Finally, Sect. 5 makes conclusions based on the findings of this work and formulates suggestions for future development of the formative chatbot-based assessment.

Contribution. This research has two main contributions: first, it shows that simple feedback, such as presentation of a correct answer, motivated the students to continue learning, if presented at the right moment. This was achieved through the additional requirement for the learners to self-assess their confidence level; and second, it shows that for education and assessment practitioners, there is a fast and affordable way to create working chatbots for assessment using only free-of-charge cloud-based libraries and APIs.

2   Setting up the Frame

We see the research objective of this work as linked to mainly three domains:

1. Assessment research related to the interplay between learning, feedback and assessment methods;
2. Psychology helping to understand mutual dependencies between task properties, learner skills and confidence, and test validity;
3. Use of instant messengers and chatbots in educational settings.

The following sections discuss previous academic publications in these domains and place the research work of this paper in relation to the state of the art.

2.1   Formative Feedback, Assessment and Learning

Feedback in general has one of the most persuasive influences on learning and performance, but this impact can both positive and negative [5]. Education research disclosed dependencies between variables such as learner level of competencies, learner motivation, task properties and feedback effectiveness [6]. In addition, adaptive feedback was found more helpful for the learner than generic feedback. Feedback is called *formative* if the information provided to the learner by means of feedback is used by the learner as an instruction for action with the purpose to improve performance [7]. Although formative feedback research emphasises the importance of including information about the learner in the feedback generation, it is not possible to use or access knowledge about the learner in some settings. One attempt to overcome these limitations was described in [8] where a user's insufficient confidence in the answer had been captured through mouse movements during the tests runtime.

Feedback in general can be provided at several conceptually different points (after or during a test/exam or during the work process) and by different actors (teacher, peers or learners themselves). If provided by an automated system, the system still takes a role of one of the listed actors: it acts as an expert, or a co-learner, or the learner uses the system for self-feedback. Prior research shows that automated feedback may be very appreciated by the students if it is well-structured and meaningful, and may be even preferred as compared to a teacher's feedback [9]. The target of the feedback may be correcting inappropriate task strategies, procedural errors, or misconceptions. Any of these feedback types can be formative or not. Strong criticism of assessment for its inability to reflect e.g. the actual state of learners' proficiency level in a particular subject or skill due to such issues as test validity, resulted in the development of the theory of *formative assessment* [10]. Formative feedback in this context will be provided to the learner before, during or after a sort of assessment. The feedback needs then to be tailored to the user, task and environment in a way that facilitates the learner's improvement in a subject or a skill.

The information provided in a feedback message may contain more or less details on the error and the correct answer. The types of feedback from this perspective include presentation of the correct answer, verification (correct/incorrect), error flagging and elaborated feedback. The latter may contain hints or prompts, and the learner may have a possibility to try again or even to continue trying until a correct answer is given [4]. Goal-directed feedback provides learners with information about their progress towards the desired goal (or set of goals) rather than providing feedback on discrete responses.

Wiggins defines 7 key characteristics of effective feedback: goal-related, tangible and transparent, actionable, user-friendly (specific and personalized), timely, ongoing and consistent [11]. Furthermore, [12] shows that a dialogic perspective of feedback potentially promotes learning. The components of such feedback are (1) providing feedback before the task is completed, (2) incorporating peer feedback into the process, and (3) allowing resubmission once the feedback has been received. Thus, feedback needs to be subject to rebuttal rather than being a final verdict in order to be effective. In line with this need, Narciss [13] argues that feedback messages can only have a formative effect if students have occasions to use the feedback information for regulating their learning process.

Types of feedback regarding timing that can be found in literature are immediate, delayed and postponed. Butler and Roediger show that the immediate feedback makes a positive impact when presented immediately after an incorrect response [14]. Bälter et al. investigate the effect of correct/incorrect feedback as part of generic quizzes [15]. The study shows that simple quizzes combined with simple feedback are effective in the first weeks of a course. This gives an idea about the ideal placement of this type of activity.

In line with these findings, we chose a multiple-choice quiz as an activity type and decided to provide feedback immediately after each test item. Evaluative feedback will be provided after correct answers and correct answer will be provided immediately after incorrect answers. However, the quiz will not be part of a course but an independent activity. The details are discussed in Sect. 4.

Novel forms of assessment always set new challenges in evaluation; see, for instance, [16] on psychometric multimedia-based assessment. Because of complex mutual dependencies and multiple feature combinations, it is difficult to evaluate the formative effect of automated feedback in a chatbot. A simple evaluation framework applicable for the technological proof of concept described in this article is needed. As Hattie and Timperley [5] suggest, feedback that enhances learning needs to answer three questions:

(1) Where am I going? (Feed Up);
(2) How I am going? (Feed Back);
(3) Where to go next? (Feed Forward).

We use this three-dimensional framework as the baseline for feedback evaluation in the set of user tests with the SQL Quizbot.

2.2 Quizzes, Feedback and Confidence

The validity of test results is an important prerequisite for meaningful feedback. In addition to the issue of test validity (did we test what we wanted to test?), assessment based on multiple-choice questions makes it easy for the students to guess the right answer. For instance, the study by Novacek shows how multiple-choice questions can be passed if the students are simply guessing the answers [17]. Consequently, the success of such a form of assessment depends on the honesty of the learner, and therefore is suitable as a self-feedback tool without any consequences for official exam grades or course scores. In such cases, an opportunity to reflect on their own confidence may create an environment for the learners in which they develop a deeper level of self-regulation.

The learner's confidence helps to assess the meta-cognitive level of the learner's knowledge. It provides an insight into what learners think they know and what they think they do not know, as opposed to performance-based assessment. For instance, Hench highlights the use of confidence and performance details of a learner to provide feedback by first demonstrating the data on a simple linear model [18]. The model is used to provide feedback that allows students to infer either the difficulty or the degree of under- or overconfidence associated with a specific question. The findings show that confidence indicators encourage students to reflect on their knowledge and rethink their choices.

However, there are differences in confidence judgments in students of different genders and proficiency levels. The study presented in [19] investigates gender differences in item-specific confidence judgments. The students had to judge their confidence in the answer correctness after each item. The study shows that undergraduate males were especially overconfident when their answers were incorrect. In contrast, female subjects tend to judge their confidence more precisely. A more recent study [20, p. 562], however, argues in the discussion of the state-of-the-art literature, that previous results on gender-specific differences in confidence judgment accuracy are mixed and not able to resolve the issue. The study itself [20] does not find any clear support for gender differences, either. The authors conclude that "gender differences with respect to realism in confidence judgments are unstable" and "dependent on the knowledge domain and/or on the cognitive processes activated by the task given in a knowledge domain" [20, p. 562].

Confidence can be measured at different time points related to the task: as a self-report or "online" as a post-question immediately after the task [21]. As suggested in [19], confidence judgments are more accurate if the students need to estimate their abilities immediately after answering the respective item. The "online" confidence judgment is more closely related to measuring the ability in contrast to personality, for which self-reports suit better [21].

With regard to the scales for confidence measurements, multiple approaches can be found in the academic literature: binary (high vs. low), discrete multi-class (a small number of discrete classes), such as a scale from 20 (guessing) to 100% (absolutely sure) [20, 22], and continuous (e.g. the student needs to mark a point on a line without any scale on it, which represents the infinite number of points between 0 and 1), which then is also mapped to a number of discrete classes, but the classes are defined after the measurement.

Gardner-Medwin suggests using a simple three-value scale (1, 2, 3 or low, medium, high) and assign higher scores for correct answers with higher confidence or give higher penalties for incorrect answers with increasing confidence (e.g. -6 points for incorrect answers and high confidence, but only -2 pints for incorrect answers and medium confidence) [23,24]. We use the same scoring principles in our approach described in detail in Sect. 3.1, Table 1.

The study by Ericsson et al. [25] suggests that we have to keep practicing in order to remember what we have learned. This finding is confirmed by [26] arguing that every topic or subject requires a set of core skills and knowledge that will be used repeatedly, and this forms the basis for any kind of expert knowledge a person can acquire. Because multiple-choice questions offer the learners an easy way to practice while testing their own knowledge, we see this kind of quizzes as a possible implementation of a chatbot-based self-assessment to support learning.

The study presented in [27] shows that quizzing helps learners grasp more information than re-reading. This is also called the "testing effect" or "retrieval practice". The authors considered the concepts of dynamic testing and formative assessment useful to improve learning.

Based on the discussion above, this research builds on the concept of confidence to capture at least some additional information about the user's knowledge during the test run-time. The "online" measurement was chosen because of the need to measure specific technical knowledge and will be performed in the form of a post-item question. The measurement scale was chosen to be *low* for *not sure*, *high* for *absolutely sure* and *medium* for *not sure whether I know this*. Section 3.1 explains the details.

2.3   Chatbots in Education

Contemporary intelligent tutoring systems and e-learning platforms providing automated feedback to the user are grounded in education research [13]. Automated feedback in different learning contexts has been investigated for traditional e-learning systems and artificial agents acting on websites (see, for instance Petersen [28] and Wilske [29]). In addition, the use of chatbots in educational settings is subject of multiple academic publications (see, for example Kerly et al. [30] and Kane [31]). Multiple different classes of chatbots in education have been introduced during recent decades, such as agent, virtual character, intelligent agent, pedagogical agent, avatar, and a so-called guidebot; see for example Soliman and Guetl [32] for a review. A more broader term of *conversational interfaces* is used today to describe all more or less complex types of software that communicates with human users by means of some kind of human language [33].

Because chatbots were seen in the beginning as software that mainly has to engage in conversations with a user, a large part of all educational chatbots focuses on second-language acquisition [34–37]. In this context, feedback mainly concerns correction of linguistic errors, is usually grounded in Second Language Acquisition theory and is called *corrective feedback* [38,39]. Providing feedback based on linguistic features, learner information and activity information is seen as one of the major challenges for Intelligent Computer-Assisted Language Learning [40].

Another popular domain of educational chatbots is related to programming and technical skill acquisition. For instance, Gross and Pinkwart [41] introduce an intelligent, adaptive learning environment for Java programming called FIT Java Tutor. It provides feedback to learners in the form of a solution for the programs whenever the learners request it. A system which assists students in converting natural language phrases to First Order Logics is discussed in [42]. After submission of the answer in the end, the system characterises the answer in terms of completeness and accuracy to determine the level of incorrectness, based on a template. In this way, the system provides elaborated feedback to the users. Both [41] and [42] use some history information about the student to provide adaptive feedback.

Despite the huge landscape of tools that support chatbot development for messengers (rapid prototyping, natural language understanding libraries, connectors and messenger native APIs), the majority of research publications after 2015 still report about chatbots based on custom solutions (usually own university prototypes). In this work, we explore how a set of state-of-the-art tools for chatbot development can be used to implement an educational chatbot that provides formative feedback with limited information about the user. The next section explains the details.

3   Designing Formative Feedback for the SQL Quizbot

This section explains the design decisions regarding an implementation of a formative feedback component for an educational chatbot acting in Facebook Messenger without using personal user information or interaction history. Section 3.1 provides details of the quiz structure and the features used for feedback generation. Further, Sect. 3.2 describes the overall software architecture of the SQL Quizbot and the tools used.

3.1   Quiz and Feedback Design

For the purposes of this research we chose the quiz to be composed of 25 multiple-choice questions randomly combined to a sequence of 25 test items presented to the user one by one. It is mandatory for the user to answer every question. The user can go to the next question only after they answered the preceding one. The quiz questions will be distributed across five different technical topics: SQL Basics, Functions, Joins, Index, and Stored Procedures. Every question will be bound to only one topic. As argued in Sect. 2, the level of learner's confidence can be used as an additional source of information to provide relevant feedback. For our solution, we chose to let the users decide and self-assess their confidence on each test question. Following this design decision, every test item consists of two parts:

1. Multiple-choice question related to one of the five topics;
2. Self-assessment scoring of the confidence level related to the answer.

The user will be informed about the requirement to judge their own confidence regarding every answer. We expect this feature to have a double effect: first, the user would be more conscious in answering questions (internal feedback), and second, in case of a mismatch between the confidence level and the correctness level (low confidence and correct answer or high confidence and incorrect answer) the user would be made more sensitive to feedback and more perceptive for corrections.

The user is not allowed to go back to the preceding questions because the impact of revisiting the question and immediate feedback is not studied in this work. Also, proceeding to the next question is currently controlled by the bot. Whenever the user is away from the system, or active in another window, the quiz is automatically paused and can be continued later as per the preference of the user. This pausing is allowed because time spent on a question is not considered for the assessment and feedback. There is also an option to restart the quiz, but it is only to facilitate the user to restart when there are technical glitches.

As we argued in Sect. 2.2, the concept of *confidence* can be exploited for filling the gap in information about the user in order to make the feedback adaptive. We chose a grading scheme based on confidence at three levels: low, medium and high. Depending on the correctness of the answer, a joint score reflecting confidence and correctness will be assigned to the user for the respective test item Table 1 summarises the differences in scoring for all six cases.

Table 1. Scores assigned to learner per test item in case of correct and incorrect answers based on the reported confidence level

Confidence	Low	Medium	High
Correct answer	1	2	3
Incorrect answer	0	−2	−6

Because of the expected double-effect of the confidence judgment, the feedback based on the confidence/correctness score will consist of two parts:

1. Immediate feedback provided immediately after each test item.
2. Cumulative feedback over all test items provided at the end of the quiz.

Immediate feedback will be generated from a template and contain a message with content depending on the confidence/correctness level. The feedback message will contain two parts: a didactic part and a social part. The didactic part will address the correctness of the answer and may be as short as "Correct!" statement if the user's answer is correct. The system will present the solution, if the user's answer is incorrect. The social part of the message will address the confidence level of the user combined with the correctness of the answer. Especially for the incorrect answers, the chatbot will show empathy using emoticons and encourage the user to learn from mistakes. Figure 1 provides an example of a test item and some immediate feedback. In this example, the user chose a wrong answer, and the specified confidence level is low. The feedback message that SQL Quizbot provides to the user contains a correct answer and encouragement to continue learning.

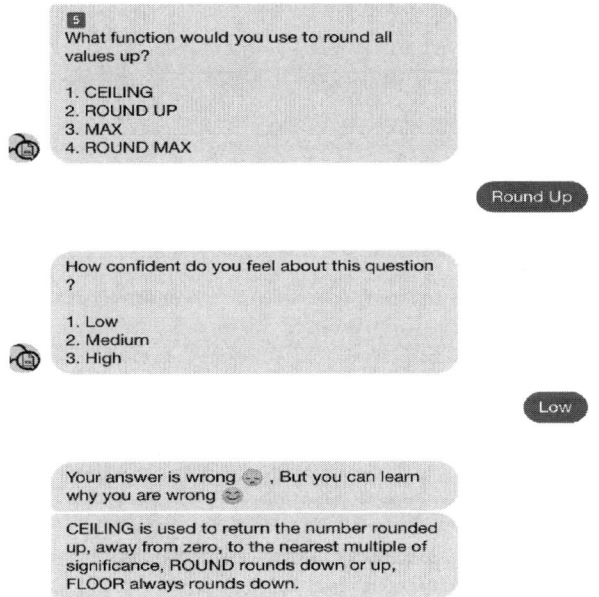

Fig. 1. An example of a test item and immediate feedback

Cumulative feedback generated and presented to the user at the end of the quiz contains two types of information:

1. Conventional total correctness score with one point per each correct answer and zero points for each incorrect answer. The total score indicates overall performance.
2. Total score based on the confidence level. Table 1 summarizes the recommendations shown to the user to address user's overconfidence and underconfidence on specific topics of the quiz.

The cumulative feedback design is based on the confidence level that the user enters after answering every question. A total score based on confidence is calculated, and it can range from -150 (if all 25 questions are answered wrong with high confidence) and a maximum score of 75 (if all answers are correct with high confidence). A total confidence score greater than the normal score indicates that the user has performed really well overall in the SQL quiz with a genuine exhibition of confidence, leading to a positive feedback or appreciation. A total confidence score lower than the medium score indicates that the user has misjudged the level of confidence in most of the questions which were answered wrongly, leading to feedback encouraging improvement. This feedback suggests the scope for improvement in the knowledge regarding the subject and also clearly distinguishes what the user knows and what he/she was guessing. The summary about how a feedback message is generated using confidence level is specified in Table 2.

Table 2. The interpretation of the confidence scores providing a basis for different feedback messages

Confidence level	Correct answer	Incorrect answer
Low	Good score but the user underestimates her/his abilities	The user did not score well but identified correctly that there is scope of improvement
Medium	Good score but there is a lack of meta-knowledge	The user did not score well and did not identify correctly that there is a need for improvement
High	Good score and judged appropriately that he knows the answer	The user did not score well and is overconfident

In both the above discussed scenarios (i.e positive feedback and feedback for improvement), there may be some questions in specific subtopic/competency performed well compared to another subtopic. Because every question is mapped to a topic, the user is informed about the performance in every topic.

After finishing the quiz, the user had to participate in a survey targeting the effect of the feedback that had been presented to her/him. Table 3 presents the survey questions and the results.

The credibility of the system providing feedback might be a matter of discussions. If a chatbot is involved in the assessment process, the users need to trust it to accept the feedback. Therefore by asking the user to enter the confidence level, we involve them in the feedback design. Whenever negative feedback is presented to a user, the user may perceive it as partly based on her/his own decision and is less likely to experience negative emotions (compare to [43]). In order to reduce the negativity during the quiz, if the user gives three consecutive incorrect answers, the SQL Quizbot sends the user a message encouraging and cheering her/him up. The user is provided with sufficient time to read the feedback before proceeding to the next question.

3.2 Implementation

We used Chatfuel[2] for designing conversational interactions for the Quizbot. The entire interaction with the user takes place in Facebook Messenger, since Chatfuel allows easy connection to Facebook. However, Chatfuel does not store any data and cannot do complex manipulations using the data. Back-end processing such as storing the quiz summary after answering a question and generating the cumulative feedback based on confidence is done using Firebase[3]. Simple tasks like navigating to the next question and storing the survey results in Google sheets are done using Integromat[4].

Every question in the quiz is composed as a flow of static text cards for the question along with the choices in a vertical arrangement. The Chatfuel generates dynamic blocks or cards based on the JSON response using the API links connected to Chatfuel platform.

We chose Firebase for managing user answers and scores because of its flexibility, scalability, possibility to store data in JSON format, its simplicity of integration with Chatfuel and its popularity in small-scale development. In addition, it is not required in Firebase to create database schema prior to development, therefore it allows changes to the schema during the phase of development. Cloud functions run back end code in response to events triggered by Firebase features and HTTPS requests. The code is stored in Google cloud and runs in a managed environment. The integration of Admin SDK together with Cloud Functions provides a webhook for the Chatfuel.

The Integromat is used in the SQL Quizbot for two scenarios: first, for navigating from one question block to another in Chatfuel; and second, for saving the survey results from every user to Google Sheets.

4 Evaluation

This section describes the evaluation of the SQL Quizbot with regard to the participants' perception of the usefulness of the feedback. As mentioned in Sect. 3.1, every user was asked to participate in a survey at the end of the quiz. Section 4.1 explains the details of the experimental setup and the population. In Sect. 4.2 we discuss the findings.

4.1 Experiment Design and Main Findings

The participants of the study were acquired through researchers' personal channels. The population included representatives from diverse backgrounds (students, IT professionals, academic staff, and business analysts) with a gender ratio close to 1:1. The participants received a personal invitation to join the SQL Quizbot on Facebook Messenger upon their prior agreement to participate

---

[2] https://chatfuel.com.

[3] https://Firebase.google.com.

[4] https://www.Integromat.com/.

in the study. The participants were allowed to use the Messenger on any device and at any time they prefer. Although the chatbot offers the option to rerun the quiz, only the first fully accomplished attempt counts for this study. One important observation is that none of the users required any demonstration or explanation on how to use the chatbot, the technology adoption happened on the fly because of the familiarity with messengers and quizzes.

Overall 47 persons agreed to participate in the study. Out of these 47, seven persons quit the quiz either in the beginning or in the middle of the quiz. Out of these seven persons, two persons could not continue because of technical problems, and the remaining five did not show interest in finishing the quiz. In total, more than 90% of the users completed the quiz and were then asked the questions presented in Table 3.

The results show a high grade of acceptance and a positive attitude towards a chatbot-based assessment from all the users. In all the survey questions, either "very helpful" or "helpful" was selected as survey answers by over 80% of the users. Overall, only less than 4 users had felt that the bot was either "unhelpful" or "none" leading to negative feedback. Table 3 shows the distribution of the answers to each survey question.

Table 3. Survey questions

Survey question	Very helpful	Helpful	Unhelpful	None
How would you rate the quiz in chat format?	47%	41%	9%	3%
How would you rate the feedback based on confidence?	39%	49%	9%	3%
How would you rate the immediate explanation on wrong answers?	47%	41%	9%	3%
How would you rate the Confidence Indicators in making you rethink or reflect on your answers?	37%	47%	9%	6%
How would you rate the overall experience with the Quizbot?	64%	30%	0%	6%

In addition to these scored questions, the users had a possibility to leave an open comment and share their experience with the developer. About 30% of the users (13 out of 40) chose to do this. The content of the comments confirms a high grade of user acceptance of this kind of technology: 7 of the 13 qualitative answers were praising. Six remaining comments provide meaningful directions for further development and include suggestions such as providing the correct answer in the feedback even if the user's answer is correct but the confidence level is low; providing a final overview of all question numbers and the correctness of the response; making the length of the quiz variable. Overall, the SQL Quizbot was perceived as "cool" and "fun", which also shows positive attitude towards artificial learning companions.

4.2   Results and Discussion

As was announced in Sect. 2.1, we use the three feedback criteria to evaluate the SQL Quizbot (Feed Up, Feed Back, Feed Forward). In addition, we address the issues of technology adoption and novelty, and technical advantages and limitations.

Feed Up. Although goal setting was not the purpose of the SQL Quizbot, it needs to be taken into consideration that the same feedback has different effect for users with different goals in using the Quizbot. Factors such as professional relevance and assessment purpose can be captured in a pre-quiz in order to make feedback more helpful. However, it was a design decision in the beginning of the study not to use any personal information.

Feed Back. The need to reflect on their own confidence after each answer was expected to make the users reflect on their own knowledge of SQL. The findings confirm this hypothesis: the users were made sensitive towards the presentation of correct answers when they were overconfident or underconfident. In this way, the feedback generated by the chatbot was only effective in connection to the self-feedback based on this meta-knowledge. However, as discussed in Sect. 2.2, complex relationships between confidence and different personality features do exist and need to be investigated in a separate study.

Feed Forward. This research confirms an earlier finding that making a mistake can feel rewarding when the brain is given the opportunity to learn from its mistakes and assess its options [44]. Although users who made multiple errors reported that they felt frustrated and would prefer to get a bit of encouragement from the chatbot, they also reported that they found the immediate feedback helpful. This subjective perception of the feedback's helpfulness may not be confirmed in a post-test. However, the subjective perception of the helpfulness is a great motivator to learn and to keep using the tool. In addition, the cumulative feedback in the end of the quiz provides explicit instructions on topics to be revised.

Although the novelty effect might be one of the reasons for the users' positive perception of the SQL Quizbot, a sustainable adoption may be very likely for this kind of assessment for the following reasons: first, the learners are familiar with the concept of the quiz, there is nothing conceptually new for them in a quiz; second, a quiz has by itself a game principle, and earning a higher score may motivate the users to use the chatbot again and again; third, users' expectations towards the Quizbot's conversational capabilities are managed in a way that the user would normally not expect extraordinary language understanding from the bot, and therefore not become disappointed; and finally, the interactive feedback component of the bot in a messenger showed a motivating effect and positively influenced users' intention to learn. Nevertheless it needs to be investigated in a separate long-term study whether this forecast is true.

The biggest challenge in implementation of the quiz questions was determined by the limitations of the messenger as interface. Although instant messengers provide their own widgets (e.g. carousel) that can be used for creating new types of questions, sometimes they make it difficult to transfer commonly known question types into messenger window. More specifically, long texts in task descriptions are not appropriate in a messenger window, and automatically generated short replies are not well-displayed if their number is higher than three. Therefore, the question of user experience in chatbot-based assessment may be worth a more detailed study.

The existing implementation of the Quizbot has the advantage that even persons without coding skills can create such quizbots. However, the implementation is not flexible because it has a fixed number of test items. All the questions are added as static text cards along with answer options in the form of quick replies in Chatfuel. Therefore there will be 25 blocks for accommodating the quiz questions alone in the dashboard of this project. This makes the project in the Chatfuel dashboard difficult to interpret for a person without an explanation. Firebase cloud function is used only for storing the quiz results and getting the immediate and cumulative feedback. If we plan to do any changes to the number of questions, introduce a new subtopic, or display the choice as a list of images, it requires changes in both Chatfuel and Firebase, which is not well maintainable. In addition, any change to the Firebase function needs to be built and deployed again to make the changes come into effect. A more flexible and scalable approach would be an advantage.

Although elaborated feedback may be helpful in many settings, instant messenger interface requires concise information presentation and short text messages. This adds a new challenge to the feedback and formative assessment research requiring that formative feedback, which is elaborated, adaptive and personalised, needs to be in addition very concise and interactive.

Because knowing what one knows and what one does not know has certain implications for the learning behaviour, confidence judgment in chatbot-based quizzes is one of the options how we can help students to achieve an appropriate confidence calibration and optimise their studies.

This implementation of multiple-choice tests is different from current computer-based assessment platforms or quiz functions in "regular" learning management systems. First, the users do not need to have a separate account for the system, they simply add a new contact to their messenger, which makes the onboarding easier. The students learn 'where they are' (i.e. in a messenger). Second, the entire history can be viewed in the messenger window by a simple scrolling up at any point of interaction. Third, messenger and NLP APIs make it easy to use resent NLP technology for free-text responses, that were not part of this study, but can be included in the next step. And finally, the interaction with an artificial intelligence makes the experience of quiz-based learning less boring and more motivating, as our test persons reported.

5   Conclusions and Future Work

This paper presented a research study focusing on the design and implementation of formative feedback in a chatbot acting in an instant messenger. Although prior research states that elaborated feedback is usually more effective, our study shows that simple feedback such as presentation of a correct solution has a formative effect if presented at the right time, namely, when the students are made sensitive to their mismatch in confidence and correctness results. This also shows the effectiveness of a reflection on meta-knowledge.

The use of artificial teaching assistants such as SQL Quizbot was difficult in the past because of the implementation effort that was needed for the custom solution. It was argued in this study that on the practical level it is quite fast and easy to implement a working prototype for a proof of concept using only free-of-charge cloud services without the need to write complex program code. This result may encourage other researchers in the education and assessment field to continue these investigations.

This study generated more open questions than answers. We make a short outline of possible future research directions based on the presented findings.

Because existing question databases such as Moodle already contain a huge number of potential test items for chatbot-based assessment, it needs to be tested in practice which of them can be transferred into messenger with which effort. In this way, guidelines for user experience for chatbot-based assessment can be formulated. As a continuation, automated test-item generation from text books and open learning resources similar to [45] can be adapted to be presented in a messenger.

To make the quiz more interactive and competitive, the Quizbot can be implemented in a team-work environment such as Slack. Team members may play with the bot against each other or against the bot and compete in their expert skills. Deployment of the same Quizbot on multiple messengers is possible and easy with the current tool support.

Although the SQL Quizbot explicitly excluded the use of the learner's personal information, future personalisation can help in providing more effective feedback. If implemented as a long-term learning companion that assists the learner for many weeks of a course, the chatbot can store intermediate quiz results and track learning progress. In addition, long-term data capturing and personalised user modelling in the educational context may help to get deeper insights in the process of learning, which in turn may initiate new and modify traditional psychology and learning theories.

References

1. Muirhead, B., Juwah, C.: Interactivity in computer-mediated college and university education: a recent review of the literature. J. Educ. Technol. Soc. **7**(1), 12–20 (2004)

2. Zheng, S., Rosson, M.B., Shih, P.C., Carroll, J.M.: Understanding student motivation, behaviors and perceptions in MOOCs. In: Proceedings of the 18th ACM Conference on Computer Supported Cooperative Work & #38; Social Computing, CSCW 2015, pp. 1882–1895. ACM, New York (2015)

3. Weizenbaum, J.: ELIZA - a computer program for the study of natural language communication between man and machine. Commun. ACM **9**, 36–45 (1966)

4. Shute, V.J.: Focus on formative feedback. Rev. Educ. Res. **78**(1), 153–189 (2008)

5. Hattie, J., Timperley, H.: The power of feedback. Rev. Educ. Res. **77**(1), 81–112 (2007)

6. Lipowsky, F.: Unterricht. In: Wild, E., Möller, J. (eds.) Pädagogische Psychologie. SLB, pp. 69–105. Springer, Heidelberg (2015). https://doi.org/10.1007/978-3-642-41291-2_4

7. Wiliam, D.: Embedded Formative Assessment. Solution Tree Press, Bloomington (2011)

8. Höhn, S., Ras, E.: Designing formative and adaptive feedback using incremental user models. In: Chiu, D.K.W., Marenzi, I., Nanni, U., Spaniol, M., Temperini, M. (eds.) ICWL 2016. LNCS, vol. 10013, pp. 172–177. Springer, Cham (2016). https://doi.org/10.1007/978-3-319-47440-3_19

9. Denton, P., Madden, J., Roberts, M., Rowe, P.: Students' response to traditional and computer-assisted formative feedback: a comparative case study. Br. J. Educ. Technol. **39**(3), 486–500 (2008)

10. Black, P., Wiliam, D.: Developing the theory of formative assessment. Educ. Assess. Eval. Account. (Former.: J. Pers. Eval. Educ.) **21**(1), 5 (2009)

11. Wiggins, G.: Seven keys to effective feedback. Educ. Leadersh. **70**(1), 10–16 (2012)

12. Espasa, A., Guasch, T., Mayordomo, R., Martínez-Melo, M., Carless, D.: A dialogic feedback index measuring key aspects of feedback processes in online learning environments. High. Educ. Res. Dev. **37**(3), 499–513 (2018)

13. Narciss, S.: Designing and evaluating tutoring feedback strategies for digital learning. Digit. Educ. Rev. **23**, 7–26 (2013)

14. Butler, A.C., Roediger, H.L.: Feedback enhances the positive effects and reduces the negative effects of multiple-choice testing. Mem. Cogn. **36**(3), 604–616 (2008)

15. Bälter, O., Enström, E., Klingenberg, B.: The effect of short formative diagnostic web quizzes with minimal feedback. Comput. Educ. **60**(1), 234–242 (2013)

16. De Klerk, S., Veldkamp, B.P., Eggen, T.: The psychometric evaluation of a summative multimedia-based performance assessment. In: Ras, E., Joosten-ten Brinke, D. (eds.) CAA 2015. CCIS, vol. 571, pp. 1–11. Springer, Cham (2015). https://doi.org/10.1007/978-3-319-27704-2_1

17. Novacek, P.: Confidence-based assessments within an adult learning environment. In: International Association for Development of the Information Society, pp. 403–406 (2013)

18. Hench, T.L.: Using confidence as feedback in multi-sized learning environments. In: Kalz, M., Ras, E. (eds.) CAA 2014. CCIS, vol. 439, pp. 88–99. Springer, Cham (2014). https://doi.org/10.1007/978-3-319-08657-6_9

19. Lundeberg, M.A., Fox, P.W., Punćcohaí, J.: Highly confident but wrong: gender differences and similarities in confidence judgments. J. Educ. Psychol. **86**(1), 114 (1994)

20. Jonsson, A.C., Allwood, C.M.: Stability and variability in the realism of confidence judgments over time, content domain, and gender. Pers. Individ. Differ. **34**(4), 559–574 (2003)

21. Burns, K.M., Burns, N.R., Ward, L.: Confidence–more a personality or ability trait? It depends on how it is measured: a comparison of young and older adults. Front. Psychol. **7**, 518 (2016)
22. West, R.F., Stanovich, K.E.: The domain specificity and generality of overconfidence: individual differences in performance estimation bias. Psychon. Bull. Rev. **4**(3), 387–392 (1997)
23. Gardner-Medwin, A.: Confidence assessment in the teaching of basic science. ALT-J **3**(1), 80–85 (1995)
24. Gardner-Medwin, A.: 12 confidence-based marking. In: Innovative Assessment in Higher Education, p. 141 (2006)
25. Ericsson, K.A., Krampe, R.T., Tesch-Römer, C.: The role of deliberate practice in the acquisition of expert performance. Psychol. Rev. **100**(3), 363–406 (1993)
26. Christodoulou, D., Wiliam, D.: Making Good Progress?: The Future of Assessment for Learning. Oxford University Press, Oxford (2017)
27. Roediger, H.L., Karpicke, J.D.: The power of testing memory: basic research and implications for educational practice. Perspect. Psychol. Sci. **1**(3), 181–210 (2006). PMID: 26151629
28. Petersen, K.A.: Implicit corrective feedback in computer-guided interaction: does mode matter? Ph.D. thesis, Georgetown University (2010)
29. Wilske, S.: Form and meaning in dialog-based computer-assisted language learning. Ph.D. thesis, University of Saarland (2014)
30. Kerly, A., Hall, P., Bull, S.: Bringing chatbots into education: towards natural language negotiation of open learner models. Knowl.-Based Syst. **20**(2), 177–185 (2007)
31. Kane, D.A.: The role of chatbots in teaching and learning. In: E-Learning and the Academic Library: Essays on Innovative Initiatives, UC Irvine, pp. 1–26 (2016)
32. Soliman, M., Guetl, C.: Intelligent pedagogical agents in immersive virtual learning environments: a review. In: MIPRO 2010 Proceedings of the 33rd International Convention, pp. 827–832. IEEE (2010)
33. MacTear, M., Callejas, Z., Griol, D.: The Conversational Interface: Talking to Smart Devices. Springer, Cham (2016). https://doi.org/10.1007/978-3-319-32967-3
34. DeSmedt, W.H.: Herr Kommissar: an ICALL conversation simulator for intermediate German. In: Holland, V.M., Sams, M.R., Kaplan, J.D. (eds.) Intelligent Language Tutors: Theory Shaping Technology. Routledge, New York (1995)
35. Lu, C.-H., Chiou, G.-F., Day, M.-Y., Ong, C.-S., Hsu, W.-L.: Using instant messaging to provide an intelligent learning environment. In: Ikeda, M., Ashley, K.D., Chan, T.-W. (eds.) ITS 2006. LNCS, vol. 4053, pp. 575–583. Springer, Heidelberg (2006). https://doi.org/10.1007/11774303_57
36. Jia, J.: CSIEC: a computer assisted english learning chatbot based on textual knowledge and reasoning. Knowl.-Based Syst. **22**(4), 249–255 (2009)
37. Höhn, S.: A data-driven model of explanations for a chatbot that helps to practice conversation in a foreign language. In: Proceedings of SIGDIAL 2017 Conference. ACM (2017)
38. Lyster, R., Ranta, L.: Corrective feedback and learner uptake. Stud. Second Lang. Acquis. **19**(01), 37–66 (1997)
39. Lyster, R., Saito, K., Sato, M.: Oral corrective feedback in second language classrooms. Lang. Teach. **46**, 1–40 (2013)
40. Amaral, L.A., Meurers, D.: On using intelligent computer-assisted language learning in real-life foreign language teaching and learning. ReCALL **23**(01), 4–24 (2011)

41. Gross, S., Pinkwart, N.: Towards an integrative learning environment for Java programming. In: 2015 IEEE 15th International Conference on Advanced Learning Technologies (ICALT), pp. 24–28, July 2015
42. Perikos, I., Grivokostopoulou, F., Hatzilygeroudis, I.: Assistance and feedback mechanism in an intelligent tutoring system for teaching conversion of natural language into logic. Int. J. Artif. Intell. Educ. **27**(3), 475–514 (2017)
43. Ryan, T., Henderson, M.: Feeling feedback: students' emotional responses to educator feedback. Assess. Eval. High. Educ. **43**(6), 880–892 (2018)
44. Palminteri, S., Khamassi, M., Joffily, M., Coricelli, G.: Contextual modulation of value signals in reward and punishment learning. Nat. Commun. **6**, 8096 (2015). https://doi.org/10.1038/ncomms9096
45. Ras, E., Baudet, A., Foulonneau, M.: A hybrid engineering process for semi-automatic item generation. In: Joosten-ten Brinke, D., Laanpere, M. (eds.) TEA 2016. CCIS, vol. 653, pp. 105–116. Springer, Cham (2017). https://doi.org/10.1007/978-3-319-57744-9_10

Best of Two Worlds: Using Two Assessment Tools in One Course

Raoul Deuss[1], Christine Lippens[2], and Michael Striewe[3(✉)]

[1] Antwerp University, Campus Middelheim,
Middelheimlaan 1, 2020 Antwerp, Belgium
raoul.deuss@uantwerpen.be
[2] Antwerp University, Stadscampus, Prinsstraat 13, 2000 Antwerp, Belgium
christine.lippens@uantwerpen.be
[3] University of Duisburg-Essen, Gerlingstraße 16, 45127 Essen, Germany
michael.striewe@paluno.uni-due.de

Abstract. This paper reports on practical experiences with the two e-assessment tools AlephQ and JACK, explains their key features and sketches usage scenarios from two different universities. Using a lecture in accountancy as a concrete example, the paper then presents a successful concept for improving a lecture by introducing both e-assessment systems. Conclusions are drawn on how to improve a lecture by selecting and combining the most suitable features from different tools.

Keywords: E-Assessment · Practice report · Item types · Usage scenarios

1 Introduction

Using e-assessment systems for formative and summative assessments can facilitate the task of the lecturer in a variety of ways: reducing the effort for grading exams (e.g. [1]) but also improving the learning outcomes through a more timely and sophisticated feedback (see e.g. [2, 3]). As the optimization of the learning experience will vary greatly on the course content and learning requirements, choosing the right e-assessment system is not an easy task. Some desired features may be not available within a single system or even not available at all. Using a freshman's year Accountancy course as a concrete example, this paper presents a successful e-assessment deployment by using two different systems in two steps. In a first step, the lecturers chose to develop and use their own e-assessment system. Later, another system (also developed by lecturers but at a different university) augmented the set up to overcome some known shortcomings.

This paper is organized as follows: Sect. 2 presents the e-assessment system AlephQ, its usage at Antwerp University and its key features. Section 3 does the same for the e-assessment system JACK from the University of Duisburg-Essen. Section 4 discusses the freshman's year Accountancy course from Antwerp University as a case in point where the learning experience was improved by combining both tools. Section 5 presents the lessons learned and conclusions from this case study.

S. Draaijer et al. (Eds.): TEA 2018, CCIS 1014, pp. 121–139, 2019.
https://doi.org/10.1007/978-3-030-25264-9_9

2   The E-Assessment System AlephQ

The e-assessment tool AlephQ was developed by and is used at Antwerp University. It originated out of a need to assess answers of which the constituent parts could be given in an arbitrary order (such as accounting entries) and thus provided lecturers a solution which most question type based e-assessment tools like Questionmark Perception, Respondus and e-assessment tools in Blackboard, Brightspace, Canvas or Moodle did not address. With modular building blocks, AlephQ offers the lecturer a user-friendly interface to implement its own questions with ordering and grading schemes for the answers.

This section describes the main features and the philosophy behind the software AlephQ, its implementation and reach at Antwerp University and the benefits for teachers and students. The section ends with some practical examples depicting some of the core features of AlephQ.

2.1   AlephQ as a User Friendly Building Block Based System

AlephQ originated from an Excel based macro prototype and hence retains some typical spreadsheet features in its basic features. The AlephQ building blocks consist of "pages", "rows" within these pages, and "elements" in these rows. Two supplementary objects are "clusters" and "rules". The final building blocks, constituting a complete exam or assignment are called "Versions".

Pages – Rows – Elements. To build a question, the teacher starts from a number of empty rows on a page. She then creates the required number of elements on each row. Each element has a specific format to distinguish between types of question related input and display: read-only text, input – short text, input – essay, input – numeric, check box, drop down menu, LaTeX, image, etc.… Elements can be organized in a table-structure across several rows. At the level of each input-element, a grading scheme can be defined at any time during the process of building or grading.

Clusters – Rules. AlephQ allows for students to enter their answers in a different but equally correct sequence of elements or rows (for example when asked for an enumeration of symptoms, features, …). These interchangeable elements or rows are then grouped in a cluster during the question building phase and a rule (one of four possible sorting and grading algorithms) is linked to this cluster. Clustering can also be used when defining rules setting a required minimum score or a pass mark on a set of elements.

Versions. Different versions of the same answer sheet relate to different sets of marking rules which are applied to the same exam question lay-out. The lecturer can use different versions to honor a variety of different but equally valid solution method-ologies, each with their own marking rules. It can also be used when a student completes a whole page in an unexpected but possibly coherent way, potentially meriting a partial mark or even full marks. AlephQ then allows for a supplementary version of this page with a dedicated grading scheme, thus allowing the teacher more flexibility while ensuring consistency in grading.

The building block system of AlephQ offers the lecturer more implementation possibilities for questions with respect to the chosen format, the content and the grading algorithm. Although intuitive to use, it can take a lecturer up to 3 h of tutorial work or direct instruction before mastering how to build a complete exam in AlephQ without help. The university schedules regular training sessions for lecturers interested in adoption. Once a level of proficiency is acquired AlephQ offers users a limited number of additional editing functionalities such as 'copy and paste', and compatibility of Text-fields with MS Word which facilitate exam building.

2.2   Usage and Benefits of AlephQ Within the Antwerp University

In the second term of 2014–2015 AlephQ was tested on a few pilot courses. The roll out of the software package started in the academic year 2015–2016 and it quickly became be the most popular e-assessment tool (see Table 1).

Table 1. Number of electronic exam copies by application at Antwerp University

	Total	AlephQ		Blackboard*	
2015–2016	20594	12780	62%	7814	38%
2016–2017	24137	15657	65%	8480	35%
2017–2018	31922	23884	75%	8038	25%

*Blackboard examination consists of online tests and assignments

In the latest academic year 2017–2018 AlephQ was used in 92 courses in 9 different faculties of the Antwerp University. 75% of all electronic exam copies were AlephQ files, compared to 25% of Blackboard* online tests or assignments. Moreover, the total number of electronic exam copies has increased by 50% in just 3 years.

The introduction of AlephQ at Antwerp University has brought the following benefits for lecturers, support staff and students:

- The time teachers spend on grading exams has reduced significantly (by up to a factor 10). It is no surprise that the biggest gains were realized in the Accountancy course where the manual grading of about 750 exam copies (each containing answers to around 30 questions in which some 250 items are quizzed) was reduced from three weeks to two days, which was the main motivation for developing the application. But new users experience similar efficiency gains: in most cases several days of manual grading is reduced to half a day.
- The diversity and complexity of traditional (e-)assessments can be increased: there is no longer a need to design the questions in a format that makes them 'easy to mark'. AlephQ allows for question formats that quiz in depth methodological understanding by grading alternative solution paths with different "Versions".
- AlephQ can free up time for staff to organize mid-term or other intermediate e-assessments and home assignments to provide students with more timely feed-back on their progress. This is especially useful in freshman's courses as it can motivate students to increase their study effort. Some lecturers use the intermediate

AlephQ assessments and assignments as a way to offer students a look and feel of the actual final exams.

- It follows that students also benefit from the software AlephQ. Annual evaluation surveys suggest that students perceive AlephQ home assignments as a good preparation for the final exams.
- In some courses, lecturers have been able to increase the depth of their course learning outcomes by increasing the level of difficulty of exams without affecting pass grades. In total, 92 courses have changed their exam content when adopting AlephQ as the primary assessment tool.

2.3   AlephQ: Practical Examples

Figure 1 shows a Chemistry exam question. In question 4a the teacher wishes to assign a score only if all of the four answers by the student (i.e. 2, 2, 4, 1) are correct (because the answers are the result of a single stoichiometric computation). Therefore, the four fields of question 4a are grouped in a cluster and a proper grading rule is defined accordingly.

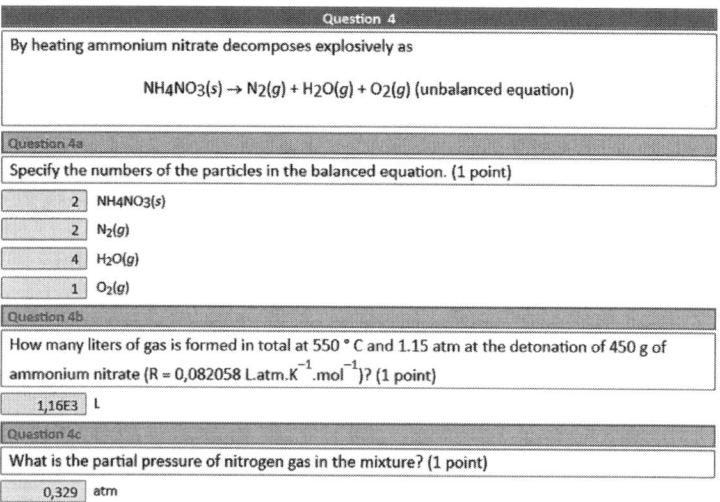

Fig. 1. Clustering numeric elements – grading

The answer of question 4b relates to the answers of question 4a by the formula: $1,16E3 = 5,62 \times (1 + \mathbf{4/2} + \mathbf{1/2}) \times 0,082058 \times 823/1,15$. When grading by hand, most teachers would prefer to assign a partial mark for a correct use of the formula, even if the absolute value of the student's answer in 4b were incorrect, due to a student's mistake in 4a. AlephQ offers this partial grading functionality: The teacher defines for answer field 4b the dependency and the appropriate partial mark as a marking rule. In addition, AlephQ offers the possibility to use acceptable ranges on calculated outcomes (e.g. to allow for rounding errors), alternative answers and alternative dependencies.

A different application of AlephQ is shown in Fig. 2. As part of a Spanish vocabulary test, students need to complete the Spanish sentences by translating the bold faced word groups from their mother tongue Dutch.

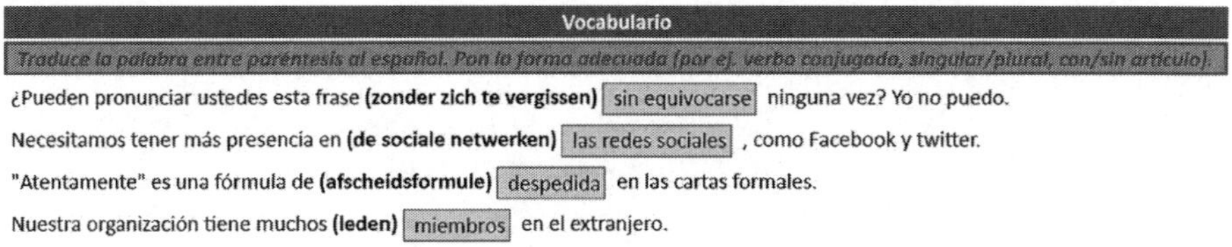

Vocabulario
Traduce la palabra entre paréntesis al español. Pon la forma adecuada (por ej. verbo conjugado, singular/plural, con/sin artículo).

¿Pueden pronunciar ustedes esta frase **(zonder zich te vergissen)** sin equivocarse ninguna vez? Yo no puedo.

Necesitamos tener más presencia en **(de sociale netwerken)** las redes sociales , como Facebook y twitter.

"Atentamente" es una fórmula de **(afscheidsformule)** despedida en las cartas formales.

Nuestra organización tiene muchos **(leden)** miembros en el extranjero.

Fig. 2. Question with text elements

While AlephQ is not linked to a language interpreter, it can easily produce a sorted overview of all answers that the students have given and the frequency of each answer, thus offering the lecturer a fast way of marking each unique answer through a tabulated input screen that defines the marking rule for that element (or cluster).

While this method is not fully automated (as it requires ex-post input from the lecturer), lecturers have given feed-back that this greatly reduces the time spent on grading whilst offering them the comfort of mind of grading consistency.

In Fig. 3, the sorted list of unique answers for the text element "miembros" from the Spanish vocabulary test (see Fig. 2) is shown. The frequency of each answer is indicated. For each text element in the exam, teachers can go through the corresponding list and add partial marks for partially correct or alternative answers.

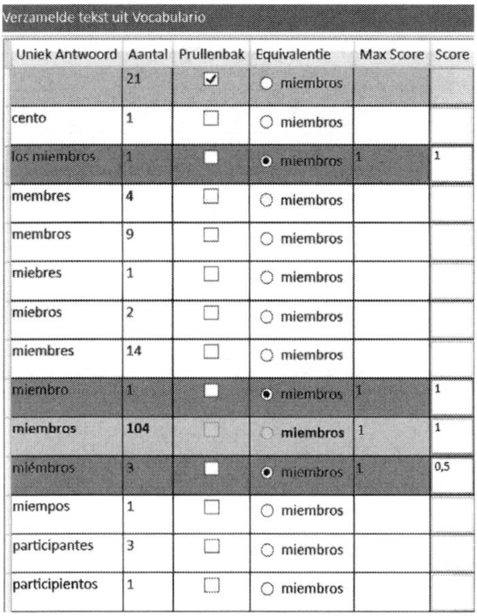

Verzamelde tekst uit Vocabulario					
Uniek Antwoord	Aantal	Prullenbak	Equivalentie	Max Score	Score
	21	☑	◉ miembros		
cento	1	☐	○ miembros		
los miembros	1	■	◉ miembros	1	1
membres	4	☐	○ miembros		
membros	9	☐	○ miembros		
miebres	1	☐	○ miembros		
miebros	2	☐	○ miembros		
miembres	14	☐	○ miembros		
miembro	1	■	◉ miembros	1	1
miembros	104	☐	◯ miembros	1	1
mièmbros	3	■	◉ miembros	1	0,5
miempos	1	☐	○ miembros		
participantes	3	☐	○ miembros		
participientos	1	☐	○ miembros		

Fig. 3. Collection of unique given answers for the text element "miembros"

Lists can be compressed as appropriate by providing specific parsing preferences, such as deleting white space, ignore punctuation or case sensitivity during the aggregation of the list which the lecturer might deem less important.

Surveying the lecturers on the necessary grading time for text elements, even in this semi-automated way, we observed an average reduction by 70% (Q1 = 65%; Q3 = 83%; Average = 72%; Median = 74%; based on data of 50 different exam papers).

Figure 4 shows a Family Law course question (at the Law faculty). In this example, the teacher asks the student to summarize two legal grounds ("Grond 1" and "Grond 2" in Dutch) together with the corresponding law paragraph number ("Artikel") for a given legal situation.

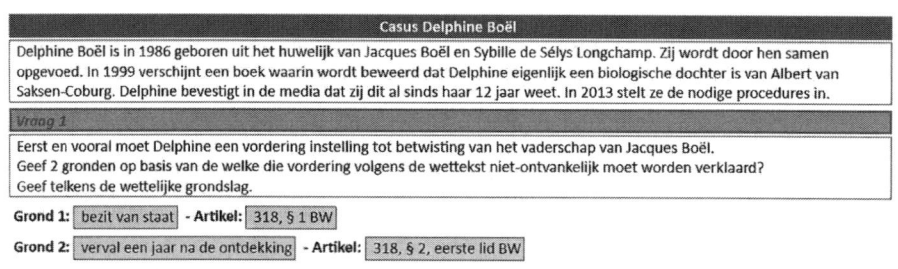

Fig. 4. Clustering interchangeable rows

The student is allowed to choose the order in which the two grounds are entered. Use of synonyms or equivalent legal wordings are permitted. Spelling errors are to be ignored. The student is not allowed to combine "grond 1" (legal basis 1) with the law paragraph of "grond 2" (legal basis 2) or vice versa. The student is not allowed to enter the same legal basis twice.

As with the Spanish vocabulary example, AlephQ is able to grade this question in a semi-automated process. In the question building phase (prior to the exam), the lecturer will have grouped the two rows with the answer fields in an interchangeable cluster and will have defined a rule penalizing duplicate answers (none or only one ground will be graded). After the exam, the lecturer will be presented a list of unique answers where synonyms or good answers with spelling errors can be selected from the list of unique answers. Because the lecturer indicates whether a validated answer belongs to a unique legal ground, the AlephQ rule will eliminate synonym duplicate answers.

If during the grading process a third ground should emerge as a possible valid answer, this supplementary answer can be added to the grading scheme in back-up rows ("reserve draden") as shown in Fig. 5. As a result, a correct answer will consist of two out of the three possible legal bases.

Fig. 5. A supplementary answer on a back-up row

2.4   AlephQ: Limitations

While the examples above illustrate the versality of potential applications, the system has its drawbacks:

First, as the application interface is not web-integrated with its correction engine, students do not receive immediate feedback. This would require adding a web-service and a central database to the current set up.

Further, any produced question in the design engine is unique in its numerical features. While this is not necessarily a disadvantage, as it allows for an open student discussion and sharing of the learning experience, it does open the possibility for students to copy numerical results from their peers when submitting home assignments, thus potentially defeating the educational benefit. A way to solve this could be to introduce a question generating engine that would produce essentially the same question but with slight numerical alterations in the given data. This would require the possibility to parametrize given input values of a question.

Finally, AlephQ does not contain a system to pool questions from a larger database, which could be an impediment to create randomized tests. However, some lecturers warn of the need to maintain a balance in question content and difficulty, which would then require additional forms of parametrization.

3   The E-Assessment System JACK

At the University of Duisburg-Essen, the e-assessment system JACK is used. It offers simple exercise types like multiple choice or multiple response questions, cloze texts as well as complex exercise types like code submission for programming exercises. In this paper, we focus on the simple exercise types. An important feature for the simple exercise types are JACK's capabilities to use placeholders within exercise texts that JACK can fill dynamically and individually for each student [4]. It is possible to use placeholders for simple elements like numbers and texts, but also for complex elements like images. Content can be assigned to these placeholders by random selection, by calculations via computer algebra systems (CAS) or via an image generation mechanism (such as plotting a graph via a CAS). As it is possible to use placeholders in many parts of an item (such as item stem, answer options or feedback texts) this feature goes beyond the capabilities of current standardized item formats such as QTI [5] or the proprietary formats of many learning management systems (e.g. Moodle, Blackboard) as well as commercial systems like MapleTA. However, using a CAS within an e-assessment system is a rather common feature for many systems and not unique to JACK.

Another core feature for simple exercise types is the possibility to split an exercise into several stages that have to be solved one after another. The sequence of stages does not have to be linear, but the choice of the next stage may depend on the input in previous stages or on random selection [6]. Similar features are available in other e-assessment systems (e.g. [7] and also commercial ones like MapleTA) as well as in some learning management systems (e.g. the "learning path" feature in Moodle), but the degree of possible complexity in designing paths and branching rules may be different.

The following sections provide an overview on the usage scenarios of JACK at the University of Duisburg-Essen (Sect. 3.1), demonstrate and discuss some sample exercises (Sect. 3.2), and discuss benefits for teachers (Sect. 3.3) as well as for students (Sect. 3.4).

3.1   Usage Scenarios

The University of Duisburg-Essen uses JACK in various domains of study and in different usage scenarios covering diagnostic, formative and summative assessments.

Table 2 provides an overview of the size of several scenarios in recent years.

Table 2. Numbers of different lectures and courses using JACK at the University of Duisburg-Essen in recent years.

Assessment type	Number of different lectures/courses (approx. sum of participants)				
	Summer term 2016	Winter term 2016/17	Summer term 2017	Winter term 2017/18	Summer term 2018
Diagnostic	–	5 (570)	3 (1670)	6 (1740)	3 (2000)
Formative	7 (1450)	9 (3800)	9 (1770)	10 (2100)	8 (2200)
Summative	5 (1230)	5 (1430)	5 (1000)	1 (230)	5 (1440)

Diagnostic assessments are performed for placements tests for language courses for foreign students. Different tests exist that can be taken either from at home or from a computer pool at the university. Each test can only be taken once. These placement tests solely use C-tests with a single stage per exercise. None of the specific features of JACK regarding dynamic replacement of placeholders are needed in this scenario, as calibrated tests are used which need to be the same for all participants.

Formative assessments are offered to support a wide range of lectures across several institutes of the university, including economics, computer science, mathematics, mechanics, biology, pedagogy, psychology, and language studies. In most of these cases, homework exercises are offered and students may take an unlimited number of attempts to each of them. Most assessments make use of fill-in exercises or cloze texts with numerical or textual input. Particularly in economics, mathematics, and mechanics many exercises with numerical input are used that rely on dynamic creation of exercise contents via computer algebra systems.

Summative assessments are offered in two different ways: Mid-term assessments every few weeks during the term are used in the institutes of economics and mechanics.

In most cases, these assessments are conducted in a computer room of the university, but there are also some cases of assessments that can be taken from at home. End-term assessments via JACK are used in the institutes of economics and language studies. In summative assessments, the same exercise types and features are used as in formative assessments, with a lower share of exercises using dynamically generated content. In particular, the institute of language studies uses similar exercises for all participants in their summative assessments.

3.2   Sample Exercises

This section demonstrates and discusses some system features that exercise authors commonly use in various lectures and domains of study. The demonstration of each feature include a sample exercise from an actual course.

The first sample exercise is shown in Fig. 6. It is taken from a first-year course in the institute of economics. The exercise item presents a small table with some randomly generated integer numbers and asks students to enter the result for a specific sum operation on that data in an input field. In this case, not only the numbers in the table are selected randomly within certain bounds, but also the various elements of the sum operation. In particular, the sum does not necessarily run from 1 to 5 (as shown in Fig. 6) and may refer to x_i in one case and y_i in another case. Consequently, the correct answer also differs for each instance of this item. Hence, a computer-algebra-system is used to evaluate the correctness of the input by performing the same calculation and comparing the result to the input.

Frage 1

Gegeben sind:

i	1	2	3	4	5	6
x_i	7	9	7	7	7	1
y_i	5	8	9	1	6	2

Berechnen Sie: $\displaystyle\sum_{i=1}^{5} x_i = \boxed{}$

Fig. 6. Sample exercise on mathematics with random elements. Both the numbers in the table at the top of the exercise as well as the elements arrange around the sum symbol are selected randomly within certain bounds for each instance of this exercise.

The second sample exercise is shown in Fig. 7. It is taken from an introductory course on botanics at the institute of biology. The exercise item presents five formal descriptions of blossoms and asks students to tick the one that fits to a particular family of flowers named by their scientific name. As in the previous example, the item content is generated randomly. However, the mechanisms for content generation are different. Obviously, the scientific name of the family of flowers needs to be chosen from a list of

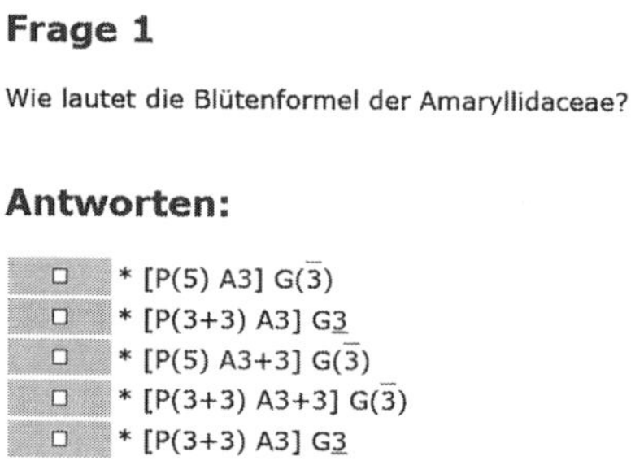

Frage 1

Wie lautet die Blütenformel der Amaryllidaceae?

Antworten:

☐ * [P(5) A3] G($\bar{3}$)
☐ * [P(3+3) A3] G3
☐ * [P(5) A3+3] G($\bar{3}$)
☐ * [P(3+3) A3+3] G($\bar{3}$)
☐ * [P(3+3) A3] G3

Fig. 7. Sample exercise on botanics with random answer options. The answer options are created randomly based on rules that assure each answer option to be almost similar but not equal to the correct one.

names that matches the contents of the introductory course. For each of these names, one correct answer option exists that needs to be listed. The other answer options are generated by replacing one or more small segments of the correct answer by wrong elements. An exercise author can design precise rules on what to replace and how to replace individually for each family of flowers. This way, the answer options can cover typical mistakes. At the same time, wrong answer options are not too easy to identify, as they do not contain segments that are obviously wrong as it could occur with plain random generation.

The third sample exercise is shown in Fig. 8. It is again taken from a first-year course in the institute of economics and is part of the exercise pool for homework exercises. The exercise item consists of six stages that must be answered one after another. The first stage of the item introduces a small scenario about two farmers and their products. The text also contains some numbers that are crucial for the calculations to be performed throughout the whole item. However, also the names of the products, the names of the farmers and even their gender are generated randomly to make the exercise more vivid. All random choices are applied to all six stages of the item, but user input may be considered as an additional parameter for content generation later on. Hence, the content of one stage can also depend on input from previous stages, which allows to account for subsequent faults or to allow students to choose one of several appropriate methods for solving a particular problem.

3.3 Benefits for Teachers

Items as the ones shown in Sect. 3.2 can be used both for formative and summative assessments. In formative assessments, it is sufficient to define one item template with carefully designed rules for random content generation to produce a virtually unlimited amount of item instances for practice. In summative assessment, this amount of different but similar item instances can help to avoid plagiarism. Consequently, one of the main benefits for teachers and exercise authors is the relatively low amount of time they need to create a large amount of items. Although it consumes significantly more time to design an item with dynamic content generation than to design a static item this is outweighed by the reduced need to produce several items. As a downside, JACK

Frage 1

Die beiden Landwirte Franzi (F) und Margarete (M) leben und arbeiten in einem kleinen Dorf. Die Bewohner des Dorfes haben eine spezielle Diät für sich entdeckt und ernähren sich seitdem nur von zwei Gütern: Erdbeeren und Käse. Den beiden Landwirten bleibt also nichts mehr anderes übrig als sich auf die Produktion von diesen beiden Gütern zu spezialisieren.

Franzi kann entweder 2 Kilogramm Erdbeeren oder 6 Kilogramm Käse pro Stunde produzieren.
Margarete kann 5 Kilogramm Erdbeeren oder 8 Kilogramm Käse pro Stunde produzieren.

Die möglichen Produktionen pro Stunde sind in folgender Tabelle zusammengefasst:

	Franzi	Margarete
Erdbeeren	2 kg/h	5 kg/h
Käse	6 kg/h	8 kg/h

Als ersten Schritt wollen wir ermitteln, welcher Landwirt jeweils in der Produktion für welches Gut den **absoluten** Vorteil besitzt. **Kreuzen Sie dazu bitte entsprechend an, welcher Landwirt für welches Gut den absoluten Vorteil besitzt!!**

	Franzi	Margarete
Erdbeeren	☐	☑
Käse	☐	☑

Feedback:
Richtig. Gut gemacht. Sie haben alles richtig angekreuzt.

Punkte: 100/100

Systemnachricht: Gut! Sie haben die 1. von 6 Fragen absolviert.

Frage 2

Nun interessieren wir uns dafür, welcher Landwirt für welches Gut einen **komparativen Vorteil** besitzt.
Dazu berechnen wir uns zunächst, welche Opportunitätskosten jeweils bei der Produktion der beiden Güter anfallen.

Tragen Sie in die Tabelle die bei der Produktion jeweils anfallenden Opportunitätskosten ein!

	Franzi	Margarete
Opportunitätskosten für 1kg Erdbeeren	___ kg Käse	___ kg Käse
Opportunitätskosten für 1kg Käse	___ kg Erdbeeren	___ kg Erdbeeren

Fig. 8. First two steps of a larger sample exercise on economics. Several elements of the exercise including numbers, names and terms are generated randomly. The second step of the exercise ("Frage 2") is only revealed after a student made a submission to the first one.

currently offers no features for exporting or importing items in standardized formats that are compatible with other tools. Existing item pools from other tools can thus only imported manually by building each item again.

Items with several stages allow to develop large, complex scenarios and thus to create more challenging exercises than exercises with a single stage. At the same time, they allow to ask for intermediate results instead of just asking for final results and offer options to handle subsequent faults and alternative ways of problem solving. Again, this comes to the cost of higher effort for designing a single item.

Particularly in the case of mathematical content, teachers can also rely on the capabilities of computer-algebra-systems for evaluating the correctness of answers instead of figuring out corner-cases by hand. Thus, exercises may also ask students to enter complex terms instead of single numbers and computer-algebra-systems can automatically handle transformations on those terms and determine their properties. In turn, these capabilities can also be used to get fine-grained control over the generation of exercise contents.

3.4   Benefits for Students

Students can profit by the benefits for teachers in several ways. First, they get more opportunities to practice in formative assessments, as they can work on dynamically generated items repeatedly. In summer term 2018, the introductory course to botanics mentioned above used a total amount of 151 exercises. On average, students who made at least 20 submissions at all (and thus showed at least some serious interest in the exercises), made 2.04 submissions per exercise. 15 out of 133 students made more than 3 submissions per exercise. Similar figures can be found at the institute of economics with an average of 2.76 submissions per exercise in a course on statistics in winter term 2017/18 and an average of 2.09 submission per exercise in a course on microeconomics in summer term 2016.

As a second benefit, student get more opportunities to show their individual competencies, if items with several stages are used. In these cases, it is not necessary to solve the problem completely, but grades and feedback can also be assigned to smaller steps of the solution. Students appreciate that as fair grading particularly in summative assessments.

As a third benefit, students can work on more practically relevant and realistic cases, if items with several stages and vivid content are used. This helps them to not only learn the mechanics of problem solving or calculating, but also to learn how to identify and extract the relevant pieces of information from the question texts.

4   The Use of the Complementary Packages AlephQ and JACK

4.1   The Use of AlephQ and JACK to Activate Large Groups of Students

In the first term of the coming academic year 2018–2019, we intend to roll out JACK to supplement the software package AlephQ in the freshman's year Accountancy course at the faculty of Applied Business Economics at Antwerp University.

4.2   The Accountancy Course

About 700 students are enrolled in the Accountancy course. As the pass rate is relatively low, the course has a reputation for being "a difficult class". Analysis of exam results and correlating these to intake characteristics have shown that strong differences in students' prior knowledge and/or adaptation problems some students face in their freshman's year contribute to this.

Accountancy students need to digest accounting principles and regulation and be able to apply these to practical cases. That is why practicing regularly after classes is beneficial if not essential to obtain a pass grade on the exam.

Accountancy is taught over two terms in a single academic year. At the end of each term, a partial exam is set. Each term consists of six teaching units, consisting of a classroom lecture followed by a practice tutorial in smaller groups. To enhance student engagement, the lecturers set three homework assignments in the first term (at the end of each of the first two units), and just one in the second (at the end of the fourth unit).

We use the classroom lectures to explain both law and accounting principles. In the tutorial sessions, we start with some basic exercises in order to lift all students above the same minimum threshold. We then expect that the students use the compulsory homework assignments to upgrade their knowledge and skill to the required final level, which corresponds to the difficulty level of the exam.

We support our students by giving them access to a study resource of 50 short knowledge video-clips covering all the topics. Each clip is linked to the unit to which the topic belongs. Students also get access to a set of additional solved problems. Finally, we offer them and monitor a Blackboard forum to ask questions about the course material.

4.3   Use of AlephQ

Thanks to AlephQ, we are able to have students solve numerically extensive cases (as shown in Fig. 9) and give them personalized feedback on their answers in less than 24 h after the submission deadline.

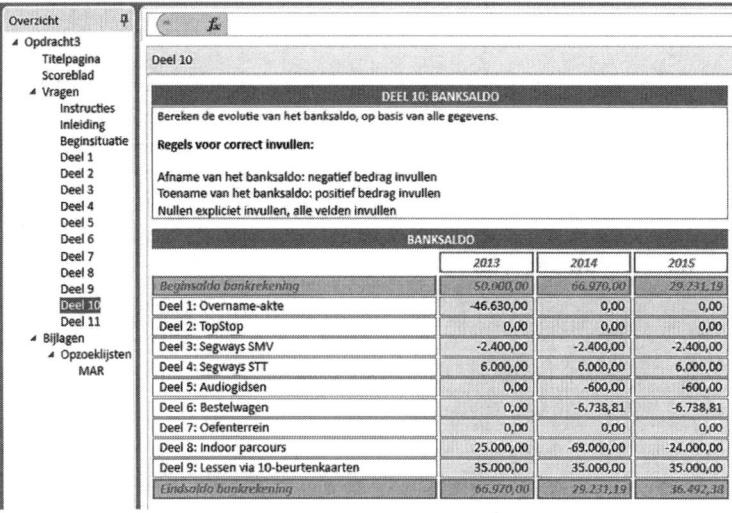

Fig. 9. Detail of the assignment

Because the difficulty level of the problems given in the assignment matches that of the problems given on the exam, and because the computerized exam is also set in the AlephQ environment, students can benefit from a familiarization effect: The assignments are an excellent preparation for both the look and feel and the difficulty level of the exam. This setup forces the students to keep up with the subject matter during the year and allows them to adjust their study approach within the semester.

Because of its user-friendliness, deploying AlephQ does not cause our teaching staff to spend more time than usual to develop new accounting cases or problem sets. Trained staff in the Accountancy department is able to develop a complete, quantitatively extensive question set in one day, which is comparable to effort they needed to produce such a question for a paper exam. The main efficiency gain is in the marking afterwards. In addition, the compilation of computerized exams allow for an easier recycling of exam questions.

The question set is not randomized, i.e. all students solve the same (complicated) case. One advantage of a unique problem case is that students can collaborate in study groups, learn from each other as well as from the lecturing and support staff.

We treat the compulsory assignments in the Accountancy class as a learning opportunity as opposed to an assessment of competence. Therefore, all questions of students are answered by the teacher on a daily basis during the period of each home assignment. The number of asked questions ranges between 40 and 70 per assignment and they cover most of the difficulties encountered by students. The forum is consulted about 1000 times per day during the brief period that the assignment is "live". The third assignment got a record 9800 student interactions (see Fig. 10).

Using a unique problem set also allows the lecturer to post a feedback video, in addition to the personalized automated feedback.

Because the assignment is administered in an uncontrolled environment (it is a homework assignment with multiple group interactions), marks on the assignment do not count towards the final exam score. By contrast, students that do not participate or that get very low scores (less than 25%) are penalized by having their final score reduced by 2 points. They can avoid this penalty by submitting additional remedial homework (which is manually set by the teaching staff and which thus inevitably means additional work for them).

	Assignment 1	Assignment 2	Assignment 3	Assignment 4
Day 1	443	575	1743	221
Day 2	1030	1251	2749	748
Day 3	986	1663	2541	1039
Day 4	1122	1066	2079	483
Day 5	1977	1449	746	534
Day 6	582	1480		673
Day 7		800		731
Day 8				782
Day 9				1383
Total	6140	8284	9858	6594
Average	1023	1183	1972	733

Fig. 10. Forum assignments: amount of views

4.4   Deploying JACK

We have recently invested the time and effort to create a set of drill-questions for Accountancy in the JACK environment. JACK is an excellent tool to generate a pool of randomized analogous problem sets. These drill-questions will help students to reach the basic skill threshold more quickly through this digitization.

JACK is also capable of handling larger quantitative concepts through its parametrization features. This requires the staff to make a one-time effort to create it, but then JACK can deliver a theoretically limitless amount of practice materials.

JACK also includes the possibility to decompose the inherent logic of a question into a programmable set of variables and instructions. To develop such flexibility within the AlephQ set-up would have required a significant rewrite of the environment. It was therefore much more time-efficient to combine JACK with AlephQ.

4.5   Advantages to the Students

For each unit, JACK exercises are offered in a module of the learning environment as materials for self-study. A big plus is that JACK offers the student instantaneous automated feedback. In addition, the offering of training materials is large due to the parametrization.

As such, these quantitatively more extensive JACK exercises form a bridge between the basic skills from the tutorial sessions and the more elaborate problem sets given in the AlephQ environment.

4.6   Advantages to the Teaching Staff

Although the initial time investment in the JACK set up is non-negligible, the effort is a one-off and the problem sets then become reusable year after year. They can also automate the remedial homeworks that teaching staff now administers to those students that have failed an AlephQ assignment.

In summary, JACK complements our existing study materials and provides an opportunity to automate the remedial work.

5   Conclusion

In this paper, we presented the case of the Accountancy course at Antwerp University, improved by rolling out both e-assessment packages AlephQ and JACK. These software packages offer complementary functionalities and complementary benefits that results in a richer learning experience for students than the standard question types from learning management systems such as Blackboard or Moodle could offer.

The combination of JACK and AlephQ allows the teaching staff to support students to master essential principals, skills and knowledge, necessary to master a discipline and to properly prepare for the exam. By offering quick and detailed feedback on a regular base, students have the opportunity to review and to optimize their study strategy. AlephQ and JACK make this feasible for large groups of students.

Annex: Longitudinal Statistical Analysis of Results Taking the Qualitative Evolution of the Accountancy Course into Consideration

A Brief Description of the Qualitative Evolution of the Accountancy Course

The authors have a well-documented record of results, course content & delivery and evaluation methods from 2005 to the present day. Up until the academic year 2007–2008 examination took place in one final exam, where students were asked to record approximately 40 journal entries from one or more case studies. A journal entry is a basic representation of a business transaction in the general journal of accounts as part of a company's accounting system. However, it doesn't show the impact of the transaction on the annual accounts, which requires an additional understanding.

The lecturing team therefore decided from 2010 onward to test this additional competence on the exam, by including questions that required the completion of (partial) annual accounts. At the same time, the number of basic journal entries was reduced. In support, home assignments were introduced to practice the skill of completing annual accounts. Inspired by the Khanacademy and other online learning tools, the team started in 2015 with a video clip library to explain some of the more technical entries and annual account updates which the students could watch a their own pace. The table below shows the complete chronology.

Academic year	Format exam	Partition exam	Journal entries per exam	Annual accounts in exam	Home assignments	Video clips
2005–2006	Paper	1 final exam	42	No	No	No
2006–2007	Paper	1 final exam	33	No	No	No
2007–2008	Paper	1 final exam	38	No	No	No
2008–2009	Paper	2 partial exams	26	No	No	No
2009–2010	Electronic	2 partial exams	22	No	No	No
2010–2011	Electronic	2 partial exams	25	Yes	Yes	No
2011–2012	Electronic	2 partial exams	?	Yes	Yes	No
2012–2013	Electronic	2 partial exams	21	Yes	Yes	No
2013–2014	Electronic	2 partial exams	27	Yes	Yes	No
2014–2015	Electronic	2 partial exams	20	Yes	Yes	No
2015–2016	Electronic	2 partial exams	13	Yes	Yes	Yes
2016–2017	Electronic	2 partial exams	19	Yes	Yes	Yes
2017–2018	Electronic	2 partial exams	20	Yes	Yes	Yes

Statistical Analysis of the Results: What Is the Impact of Electronic Assessment and the Use of Home Assignments

For each academic year, the authors had access to all exam results. The June results were taken for comparison, ignoring the retake exam in September. As of the year 2008, the result in June is computed as the sum of two exams: an exam in January (40% of the mark) and an exam in June (60% of the mark). Zero scores are ignored, because of a number of students merely present themselves on the exam for administrative reasons, and those reasons vary throughout the period. In view of the large number of exam question entries, it is highly unlikely that a real exam attempt would result in a score of zero.

The exam results are split in two groups:

Group **Situation 1** has the following features

- Exams were on paper. Each exam was only corrected once.
- There were no home assignments.
- No use was made of wiki or discussion board.
- No use was made of video (knowledge clips).

Group **Situation 2** has the following features:

- Exams were electronic. The correction of the exams happens in several iterations. In each iteration, the corrector actively searches for alternative correct answer options in the given answers.
- There were four home assignments.
- Wiki and discussion board are used to support the home assignments.
- Video (knowledge clips) are used to support the home assignments or seminars (started in 2015).

Situation 1 contains the exam results of the following academic years: 2004, 2005, 2007 and 2008. The 2006 data had to be excluded due to incompleteness of the data set. In addition to the results of the freshman students (1st bachelor year), the 2008 data also includes the results of students of the bridging program from the Master's degree Organization and Management.

Situation 2 contains the exam results over the period 2010–2017. The 2009 data was excluded because although it was the first year that the exams where electronic in that year there were no home assignments yet, making it difficult to assess to which category it would belong.

If we work under the assumption that all exams have a similar degree of difficulty, the hypothesis that education is improved can be validated by the fact that the average increases *and* the variance decreases. The data shows (see: F-test Two-Sample of Variances and t-Test: Two-Sample Assuming Unequal Variances) that Situation 2 is an educational improvement compared to Situation 1. The educational context of Situation 2 could therefore be explained by the introduction of new educational tools like a learning environment and assessment tools like AlephQ and JACK.

Supporting Data

F-Test Two-Sample for Variances

	Situation 1	Situation 2
Mean	8,02004008	9,53185145
Variance	18,71137754	13,76857577
Observations	1996	3689
df	1995	3688
F	1,358991514	
P(F ≤ f) one-tail	1,25094E−15	
F Critical one-tail	1,066413374	

Based on the *F-Test Two-Sample for Variances* we may reject the assumption of equal variance.

t-Test: Two-Sample   Assuming   Unequal Variances

	Situation 1	Situation 2
Mean	8,02004008	9,53185145
Variance	18,71137764	13,76857577
Observations	1996	3689
Hypothesized mean difference	0	
df	3592	
t Stat	−13,20534523	
P(T ≤ t) one-tail	3,25111E−39	
t Critical one-tail	1,645277949	
P(T ≤ t) two-tail	6,50222E−39	
t Critical two-tail	1,960624635	

Based on the *t-Test: Two-Sample Assuming Unequal Variances* we may reject the assumption of equal mean.

Situation 1 – Data description

	2004	2005	2006	2007	2008
Mean	8,47301	6,78667	5,55769	8,36900	8,18346
Standard error	0,18333	0,20439	0,59053	0,20417	0,16830
Median	9	7	4,5	8	10
Mode	1	10	1	8	10
Standard deviation	3,61589	3,95798	4,25839	4,36934	4,68213
Sample variance	13,07466	15,66560	18,13386	19,09112	21,92231
Kurtosis	−0,67673	−0,70065	−0,30048	−0,85753	−1,23072
Skewness	−0,10685	0,30545	0,78501	0,14507	−0,18974
Range	15	17	16	17	17
Minimum	1	1	1	1	1
Maximum	16	18	17	18	18
Sum	3296	2545	289	3833	6334
Count	389	375	52	458	774

Situation 2 – Data description

	2009	2010	2011	2012	2013	2014	2015	2016	2017
Mean	10,11472	9,96038	9,61943	9,24473	9,69196	8,87333	9,26549	9,70153	9,87958
Standard error	0,17019	0,16750	0,16330	0,16397	0,15819	0,16716	0,17914	0,18342	0,19756
Median	10	10	10	10	10	9	9	10	10
Mode	13	11	10	10	9	11	9	12	12

(continued)

(continued)

	2009	2010	2011	2012	2013	2014	2015	2016	2017
Standard deviation	3,89201	3,85615	3,62951	3,56979	3,34834	3,546D0	3,80866	3,92954	3,86126
Sample variance	15,14773	14,86988	13,17333	12,74337	11,21139	12,57412	14,50586	15,44129	14,90935
Kurtosis	−0,40575	−0,49654	−0,52408	−0,61191	−0,44519	−0,51226	−0,51574	−0,65130	−0,63667
Skewness	−0,22462	−0,16950	−0,01994	−0,16840	−0,19825	−0,17153	−0,14121	−0,30497	−0,31694
Range	IB	18	18	17	18	17	17	17	17
Minimum	1	1	1	1	1	1	1	1	1
Maximum	19	19	19	18	19	18	18	18	18
Sum	5290	5279	4752	4382	4342	3993	4188	4453	3774
Count	523	530	494	474	448	450	452	459	382

References

1. Ridgway, J., Mccusker, S., Pead, D.: Literature review of e-assessment. A NESTA Futurelab Research report - report 10 (2004)
2. Malmi, L., Korhonen, A.: Automatic feedback and resubmissions as learning aid. In: IEEE International Conference on Advanced Learning Technologies, pp. 186–190 (2004)
3. Venables, A.; Haywood, L.: Programming students NEED instant feedback! In: Proceedings of the Fifth Australasian Conference on Computing Education, vol. 20, pp. 267–272. Australian Computer Society, Inc. (2003)
4. Schwinning, N., Striewe, M., Savija, M., Goedicke, M.: On flexible multiple choice questions with parameters. In: Proceedings of the 14th European Conference on e-Learning (ECEL) (2015)
5. IMS Global Learning Consortium: IMS Question & Test Interoperability Specification, Revision 2.2.1 (2016). http://www.imsglobal.org/question/
6. Schwinning, N., Schypula, M., Striewe, M., Goedicke, M.: Concepts and realisations of flexible exercise design and feedback generation in an e-assessment system for mathematics. In: Joint Proceedings of the MathUI, OpenMath and ThEdu Workshops and Work in Progress track at CICM, co-located with Conferences on Intelligent Computer Mathematics (2014)
7. Saul, C., Wuttke, H.-D.: E-assessment meets personalization. In: IEEE Global Engineering Education Conference (EDUCON), Berlin, Germany, pp. 200–206 (2013)

Digital Exams in Engineering Education

Meta Keijzer-de Ruijter[1](✉) and Silvester Draaijer[2](✉) (iD)

[1] Delft University of Technology,
Landbergstraat 15, 2628 CE Delft, The Netherlands
M.A.Keijzer-deRuijter@tudelft.nl
[2] Faculty of Behavioural and Movement Sciences,
Department of Research and Theory in Education, Vrije Universiteit Amsterdam,
De Boelelaan 1105, 1081 HV Amsterdam, The Netherlands
s.draaijer@vu.nl

Abstract. Digital exams are rather uncommon in engineering education because general e-assessment platforms lack the ability to use advanced item types that mimic general engineering problem-solving processes and award partial scores. However, it is possible to develop such advanced items with Maple T.A.. We describe how such items are structured in scenarios and developed for a second-year bachelor's-level material science course that ran three times at the Delft University of Technology. We evaluate how these items function in practice, are scored and perform from an educational measurement perspective. The paper discusses the results of the study and future directions for development of digital exams in engineering courses.

Keywords: Digital exam · e-Assessment · Question partitioning · Partial credit · Scenario · Engineering education · Maple T.A.

1 Problem Description

In higher education, the demand for enhancement of educational quality, the rising number of students and stricter grading deadlines require teachers to rethink their exam practices, particularly their current paper-based examination processes. Digital exams could be a solution to those problems, especially since increasingly more higher education institutions have large-scale exam facilities [1, 2] and general computer-based testing systems (often available in Learning Management Systems such as Blackboard or Canvas).

However, exams for engineering courses require students to perform a complex problem-solving process, which generally requires various algebraic and numerical calculations. Figure 1 shows an example of a typical engineering exam problem and solution. It is often argued that digital exams cannot be developed for engineering courses because items are restricted to a single response field in a multiple-choice or numerical format, and students cannot provide intermediate answers that lead up to the provided answer. Both teachers and students point out that students are unable to show their problem-solving process and thus miss out on possible partial scores [3–5]. This threatens the validity and reliability of these exams, as most test information is lost with

© Springer Nature Switzerland AG 2019
S. Draaijer et al. (Eds.): TEA 2018, CCIS 1014, pp. 140–164, 2019.
https://doi.org/10.1007/978-3-030-25264-9_10

single-step questioning. Another hindrance of single-step questioning is that, in principle, each question must be independent of the others [6], but this cannot be avoided for many exam problems, including engineering problems, which require multiple interdependent questions and answers. Thus, how schools can overcome the loss of information inherent in digital exams and design test items that measure the actual problem-solving processes of students as validly and reliably as possible remains to be determined.

Engineering exam questions are typically presented as cases; the context of the engineering problem is described, the physical parameters are provided and then the student is asked to solve a main problem (for example, identify the end-state values of a process). Typically, solving the main problem requires the student to identify the right concept, choose the correct step(s) to solve the problem and execute the numerical and/or algebraic calculations correctly. Often, there are various different ways to solve a problem.

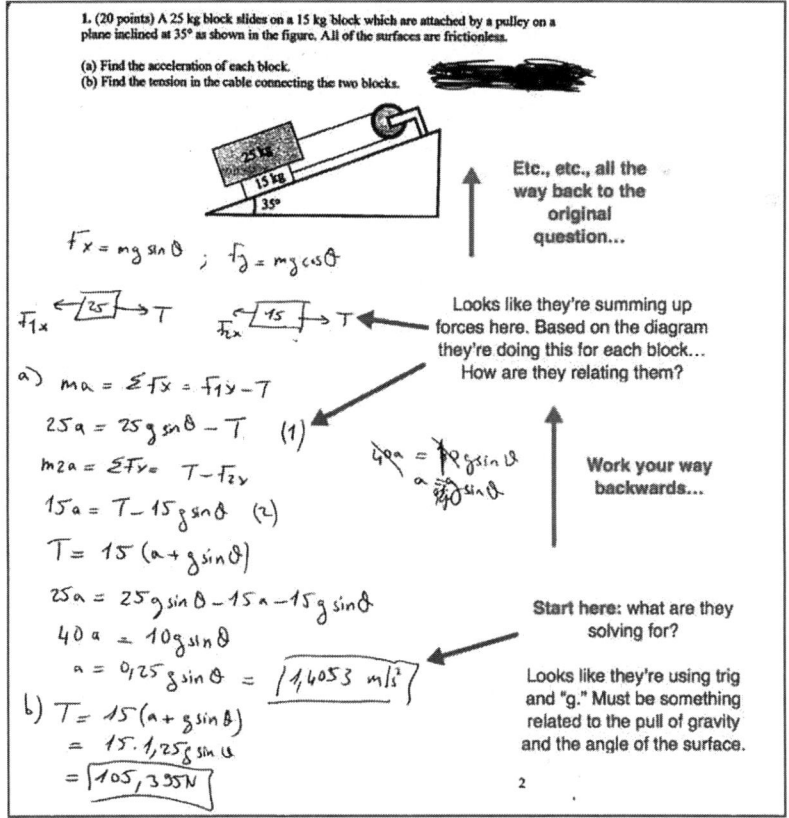

Fig. 1. A typical engineering paper-based exam question with a written solution (Source: https://collegeinfogeek.com/engineering-school-survival-guide/).

When manually grading a paper-based exam, the grader can see the student's process of solving the problem and establish where an incorrect step was taken. For example, a student might have worked based on a misconception, chosen the wrong procedure or made a calculation error. The grader deducts points based on the seriousness of the error and continues grading, correcting for the student's conceptual and/or calculation error in the previous step(s).

Converting a paper-based engineering problem into a computer-based problem that can be automatically scored is challenging. It requires careful consideration of the user interface, and decisions about how to sensibly partition of the problem-solving steps to produce test items that perform as desired from a validity perspective [7]. The question design should ensure that students are not guided too much or too little to the correct problem-solving procedure, deliver the optimal level of granularity in terms of partitioning (i.e. not too fine-grained, nor too coarse, not giving too much away about the procedure to follow) and anticipate the possible errors that students may make. It is also necessary to empirically assess whether the developed digital items meet certain requirements: Does the partitioning developed by the designer make sense to the students? Does the partitioning induce construct-irrelevant variance [8], which would unintentionally make questions too easy, too difficult or undiscriminating? Further, if students make conceptual or calculation errors, does this negatively impact the scoring process?

Of a more practical nature, but nonetheless quite important, is the issue of return on investment. Typically, in higher education, between 100–300 students are taking an engineering course at a given time. Therefore, the investment costs must be kept to a minimum. So, when developing working methods and guidelines that minimise development costs, one should incorporate methods for working with re-usable parts or design patterns [9], working sensibly with specific experts [10], automatic scoring and deploying automatic item generation techniques [11] (e.g. parametrised questions, which also hinder cheating).

Studies performed by Draaijer and Hartog [9, 10] have already addressed some of these issues in an engineering context. However, the general literature on question partitioning, partial grading and countering error propagation focuses on mathematics education, problem-solving and assessment [3, 12–14]. Thus, there is a gap in the literature regarding digital examination for engineering problem-solving. This paper seeks to fill that gap.

2   A Study of Digital Exams for Engineering at the Delft University of Technology

The current paper reports a study undertaken from 2016 to 2018 at the Delft University of Technology to investigate the processes of designing and evaluating digital engineering exams. This study is, to the authors' knowledge, the first to focus on this topic in the context of engineering material sciences. The study seeks to develop guidelines and examples through three cycles of a design-based research approach.

The project revolved around conversion of a paper-based exam to a digital version and creation of three series of digital exams and re-sit exams for a second year bachelor's-level material sciences course taught by one teacher. The project involved a cycle of analysis, conversion/design, test administration, grading and evaluation of both the grader's experience and the students' experience. The approach is in line with the design process described by, for example, Parshall and Harnes [15], which involves cyclical processes of development and evaluation of prototypes. Table 1 provides an overview of the cycles.

3   Research Questions

The goal of the project is to develop a working method and guidelines for designing engineering exams that address the challenges and scenarios described in the previous sections. The main research question is as follows: To what extent is it possible to create high-quality engineering problems using scenario-type questions? Three more specific research questions were also put forward:

1. To what extent is it feasible to construct acceptable digital engineering exams, and which guidelines are necessary to develop acceptable items?
2. How does the design of digital exams impact test-taking strategies?
3. To what extent are digital engineering exams more efficient than paper-based exams?

4   Method

The study used a design-based approach employing three cycles of construction and evaluation of a set of three series of exams. Data were collected in multiple ways: teacher input, think-aloud protocols and subsequent student interviews, manual review

Table 1. Design-based research cycles of the project.

Cycle	Exam	Main goal of cycle	Main research and data collection methods
First (2016)	1st 2nd 3rd (re-sit)	Viability of the construction of scenario-type questions	Collaborative creation, think-aloud protocol, course evaluation questionnaires, teacher comments, observations during exams
Second (2017)	1st 2nd (re-sit)	Improvement in questions' construction, improvement in students' preparation (input training), first steps toward partially automatic grading	Collaborative creation, course evaluation questionnaires, observations during exams
Third (2018)	1st 2nd (re-sit)	Improvement in the efficiency of response programming, reduction in question entry time and grading effort	Collaborative creation, course evaluation questionnaires, observations during exams

of the students' responses, reliability analysis of the exams, observation of exams by the teacher and authors and student's remarks on course evaluations. An overview of the research cycles is provided in Tables 1 and 2.

Table 2. Characteristics of the developed exams in the design cycles.

Cycle	Exam	Scenario-type questions	Single-step questions	Total score points
First (2016)	1st (for think-aloud protocol)	5	3	8
	2nd (first attempts)	6	2	14
	3rd (re-sit)	4	3	14
Second (2017)	1st	5	1	14
	2nd (re-sit)	2	2	14
Third (2018)	1st	4	2	14
	2nd (re-sit)	3	2	14

The main goal of the first cycle was to study the viability of converting paper-based material sciences exams into digital exams that would work technically, have enough face validity, were sufficiently clear for use by students and incorporated only coarse grading options. In this phase, the assessment expert, assessment system expert and teacher closely collaborated. The main goal of the second cycle was to improve questions' construction and develop the first steps toward partially automatic grading. The main goal of the third cycle was to improve the efficiency of response programming, reduce the question entry time for the teacher and reduce the effort required to grade exams. In Table 2, an overview is given of the exams that were developed including the number of more complex scenario-type questions (that will be explained in detail in Sect. 4.2) and simpler single-step questions and total score points that could be awarded to a student.

4.1   Cycle 1

Design Process. Three digital exams were developed in the first cycle. The design cycle started with conversion of all eight problems on a paper-based exam into computer-based versions. This was done in a series of sessions attended by the assessment specialist, the teacher and a specialist in the Maple T.A. test system. Prior examples, literature and systems for developing and administering digital engineering exams [3, 12–14, 16] were used. Two actual exams were designed: an exam and a re-sit.

To gain insight into the domain construct of an exam problem, the teacher began by writing down the equations that could be used to solve the problem. For instance, in a question that required shear strength to be calculated, the teacher wrote down equations including only the terms that influence shear strength in the specified situation, which must be correctly identified by students. In a scaffolding scenario, asking for the correct equation to be used would provide the grader with relevant information regarding the students' command of the domain knowledge.

From a validity perspective, the following supplementary questions turned out to be relevant for the teacher to consider how a problem can be converted into a digital form:

- What is the learning objective of the problem?
- What level of knowledge/skills do you want to assess?
- What do you want to focus on: correct use of the procedure or the correct response to the main question?
- Are there different ways to solve the problem? If so, do you want to see one specific method?
- What are the common mistakes that students make?
- Is there a chance of error propagation in the problem?
- Which scenario (scaffolding or underpinning) best suits your situation?

Based on the steps required to solve a problem, including the equations to be used and the procedures required to solve them, and the aforementioned questions and studied examples, working iteratively turned out to be the best way to approach the design process in general. A number of guidelines regarding layout, look and feel and navigation were established to ensure sufficient readability, clear access and instructions and so on.

Think-Aloud Study. Ten second-year bachelor's students taking the course in 2016 volunteered to participate in a think-aloud study [17] to test the first developed exam, which was a practice exam. The students already had some experience in using the Maple T.A. system, so basic navigation through the system was not an issue. The students were divided into two groups. One group could attempt each section four times (except for the multiple-choice questions) and used the symbol mode (i.e. an equation editor) to input equations. The other group got two attempts and used the text-entry mode.

Procedure. During a one-hour session, each student spoke aloud about whatever he or she was reading, thinking, feeling and doing while solving the exam questions. An assessment expert and the exam system expert (the first author of this paper) took notes, describing the student's strategy to solving the problem and the time they took to complete each step. The student's answers and notes during the problem-solving process were collected, and audio was recorded and transcribed for further analysis. After the session, the students had to fill out a small questionnaire regarding the difficulty of the questions and reflect on the test and think-aloud session.

4.2   Cycle 1 Results

Design Process. The first cycle revealed two main scenarios for structuring engineering exam questions in Maple T.A.: *underpinning* and *scaffolding* [18]. These two scenarios are described in detail below.

Scenario-Type Questions. Although, in general, engineering courses revolve around the notion of learning outcomes, these outcomes are primarily manifested in the ability to solve certain categories of engineering problems. Engineering exams typically consist of sets of different problems regarding specific concepts or problem-solving situations (e.g. problem categories A, B, C, D and E). For example, problems may involve systems of pulleys (A), friction (B), conservation of energy (C), equilibrium of forces (D and E). In general, similar concepts and problem-solving situations are needed across each exam as courses tend to have set rather fixed learning outcomes, so a teacher needs to design multiple variants of exam questions about categories A, B, C, D and E. For this reason, working with design patterns is very beneficial [9].

Also, engineering exam problems are designed to lead to a single correct answer. These problems are what Newell and Simon call well-defined problems [19]. To solve a group of comparable problems, a student needs to follow a fixed scenario in which students have to demonstrate their ability to follow one single problem-solving procedure. However, often, engineering problems can be solved using different combinations of routes or calculations. This is important for the scenario that we call the *scaffolding* scenario.

In this paper, a scenario is defined as a template for a series of multi-step actions and events that the author of a question can use as a point of departure and fit with an actual problem. It enables partial problem-solving and, hence, partial grading. The idea of partitioning problems into scenarios to mimic a natural problem-solving process and enable partial credit in digital testing is not new. For instance, Ashton [12] studied computer assessment with multi-step math problems and compared three types of assessment scenarios:

- S = Students have the option to solve a main problem in steps, knowing that they will not be able to receive full marks by choosing the stepwise option.
- T = Students receive instant feedback in the form of ticks and crosses to indicate whether their answer was right or wrong and can adjust their response as often as desired.
- R = Reverse translation in which a paper version of the digital assessment is a screen dump of the T type.

Ashton [12] concluded that both S- and T-type assessments may be used to replace paper-based exams, provided that the issue of error propagation is addressed and the number of attempts students can make is limited.

According to analysis of engineering problem-solving processes obtained from existing exams and evaluation of digital exams developed in the 90 s at the Delft University of Technology [16], the developed scenarios would likely best fit between the S- and T- type scenario. First, the system should present a main problem to solve (i.e. the main question). Then, when the student provides a response to the main question, the system verifies the correctness of that response. This should result in one of three possible follow-up steps:

1. *Underpinning* (U): Regardless of whether the response to the main question was correct, the student receives sub-questions to underpin the measure by which the students' process of answering the main question was valid.
2. *Scaffolding* (S1): If the response to the main question was incorrect, the system presents sub-questions that provide the correct steps to solve the problem and allow

the student to receive a partial grade. The student responds to all the questions and receives credit based on the correctness of each question.

3. *Scaffolding* (S2): If the response to the main question was correct, the system grants the full grade and continues to the next main problem in the exam. The student is thus not presented sub-questions.

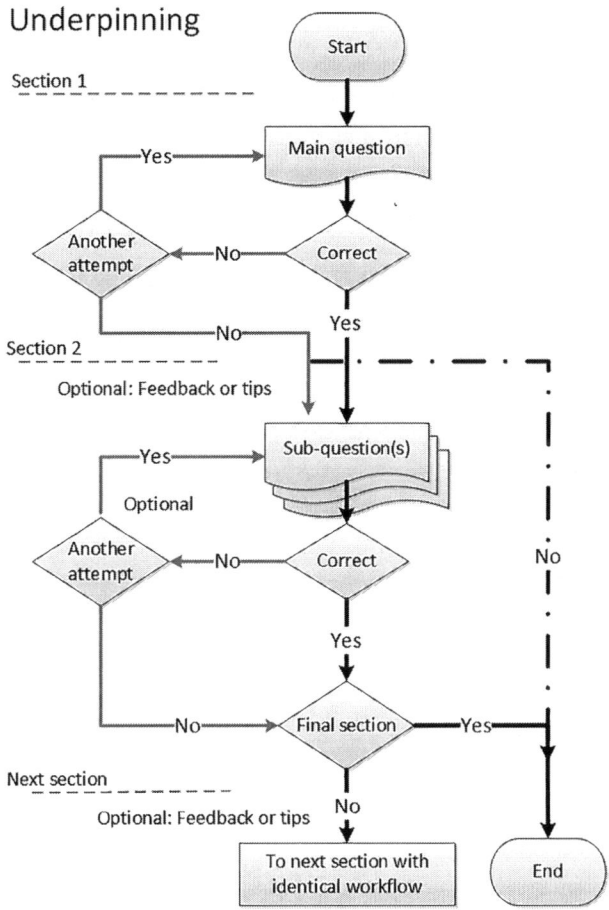

Fig. 2. Schematic of the underpinning scenario.

Underpinning Scenario. The flow diagram in Fig. 2. illustrates the underpinning scenario. In the first section, the student responds to the main problem. The number of attempts each student can make to answer the main question is set by the teacher. Then, the following steps can be performed:

– When the main question is answered correctly, the student is guided to the next section containing one or more questions that underpin the extent to which the student's response to the main question was validly reached with the correct knowledge or skill. Again, the teacher can set the number of attempts allowed per sub-question.

– When, after using the specified number of attempts, the student's answer to the main question is still incorrect, the system presents the sub-questions.

The system can handle multiple sections built into the same structure as above. The number of attempts allowed per student can vary per section. To avoid error propagation, the correct answer can be presented after the student has used up all the attempts for that section.

Appendices 1 and 2 contain examples of the underpinning scenario-type questions.

Scaffolding Scenario. The flow diagram in Fig. 3 illustrates the scaffolding scenario. This scenario allows a student to correctly solve the main question, regardless of the problem-solving procedure used.

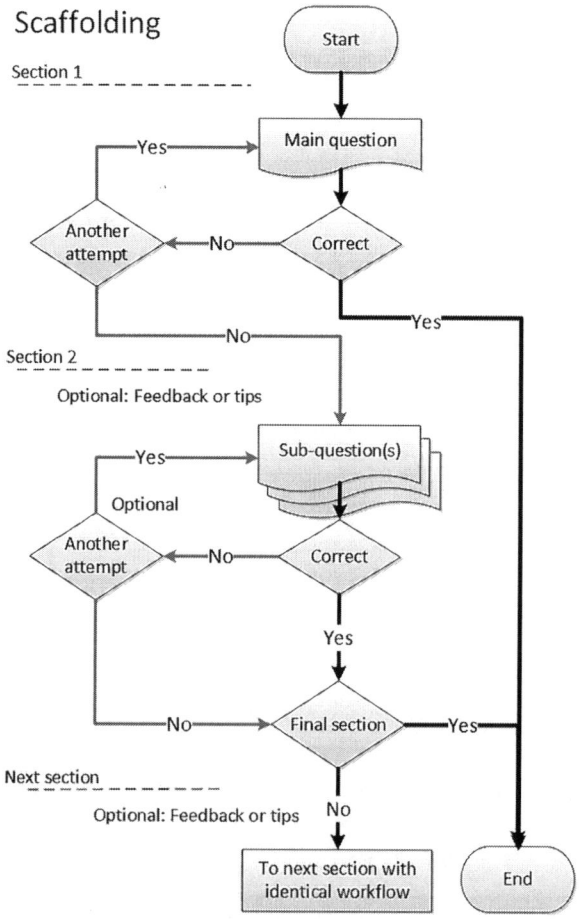

Fig. 3. Schematic of the scaffolding scenario.

In the first section of the problem, the student responds to the main question and verifies the response. When the main question is answered correctly, the student receives the full score for the problem and no sub-questions are presented. When, after using the defined number of attempts, the answer to the main question is still incorrect, the system presents the sub-questions. By answering the sub-questions correctly, the student can achieve a partial score for solving the problem.

Appendix 3 contains an example of a scaffolding scenario-type question.

Given the descriptions of the scenarios, scenario-type questions have the following advantages:

- By first posing the main question, students' ability to answer the question on their own can be evaluated.
- In case of a multiple-choice question, a correct answer due to an 'educated guess' or blind guessing is not sufficient, since the grading can be programmed to provide full marks only when the main question and all the sub-questions are answered correctly.
- In the scaffolding scenario, students are free to use their own strategies to solve the problem.
- Students can show their proficiency in smaller steps.

Of course, for these advantages to work in practice, the construction of the exam questions, the scoring algorithm and so on must be flawless. This is illustrated in the following observations regarding parametrisation and the results of the think-aloud study and other data collection methods.

Parametrisation. With respect to parametrisation, it was revealed that the parameter sets of a main question need to be selected carefully as certain combinations of parameters can make a problem harder or easier to solve or lead to unsolvable situations.

Think-Aloud Study, Observation of Test Administration and Post-course Questionnaires. The think-aloud study and post-course questionnaires produced detailed uttered and written feedback by students, which provided insights into the quality of the developed exam questions. These insights, which concern general text anxiety, readability problems, intermediate feedback effects, test-taking time, passing rates and score point distribution, are described in detail below.

General Test Anxiety. The think-aloud study confirmed the findings of previous work, such as that of Beevers [13], which found that students' anxiety increases as their confidence that the system correctly evaluates input decreases. First, students mentioned that they lacked the ability to browse all the exam questions from the start to gain a conceptual understanding of the breadth and length of the exam. This problem is inherent to scenario-type questions, as students can only be provided the main questions and not the hidden sub-questions. However, an indication can be given regarding the number of hidden sub-questions. Second, students wondered whether the computer would correctly evaluate different—but algebraically correct—syntax. Third, they were unsure of the margin within which their answer was deemed correct or whether the number of decimals would influence their grade. Finally, students mentioned that entering formulas in an equation editor was too time-consuming, leading to fear over the loss of precious exam time. Even when the text entry mode was used, the time issue was not fully alleviated, as the anxiety of using the wrong syntax increased. Students were unfamiliar with the system's notation of sub- and superscript numbers and Greek characters (for example, they may write 'ro' instead of 'rho'). During the observations of the test, several students did not use or were not aware of the preview button to check their actual input (Fig. 4) or did not use the help text (Fig. 5). This was especially true for students that missed the lectures explaining how to enter their responses into the system and those that did not engage with the practice exam that was provided.

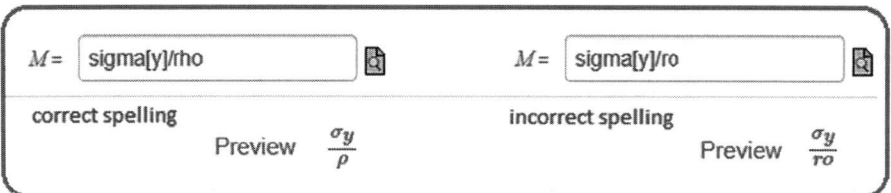

Fig. 4. Pressing the 'Preview' button shows the student their actual input. A misspelled entry is shown on the right, and the actual intended symbol, ρ, is shown on the left.

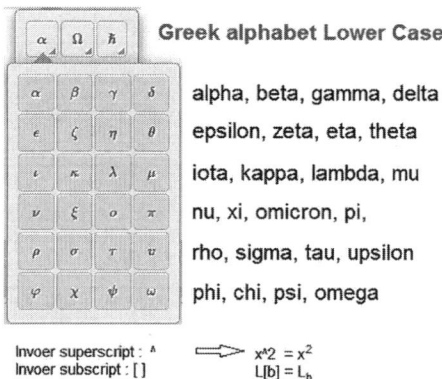

Fig. 5. Help text including the correct spellings of the Greek alphabet and the symbols to input super- and subscript characters.

Readability Problems. A rather small image was presented for one exam question because of layout constraints. Also, no zoom option was available for the image. One student noted that image was probably irrelevant because it was rather small and hard to read. This was not intended by the teacher, inducing error into the measurement. Further, many students overlooked text that was written right underneath the response field.

Intermediate Feedback Effects. Students mentioned the effect of intermediate feedback when providing correct or incorrect responses. Depending on whether they answered correctly or incorrectly, students became either more confident or more stressed and unconfident. This aligns with education research on the effects of positive or negative feedback [20–24]. Unfortunately, the extent of the effect of positive or negative feedback could not be assessed with the think-aloud approach or other means.

In the set-up of the Maple T.A., the digital exams did not show students' running score to mitigate the effect of seeing the maximum score they could obtain during the exam. For example, without such a mitigation, students may stop answering exam questions if they knew they would not achieve a passing grade on the exam. During exams conducted with Tempo+ Presto+ software in the 1990s, the second author of this paper observed that students indeed exhibited that behaviour when a running score was provided.

Grading. Although most questions in the exams in the first cycle were graded automatically with a straightforward scoring algorithm, all the questions were manually reviewed. Students' responses provided the grader with more information about the typical errors that students tend to make, allowing these to be integrated during the design phase. It turned out that a number of relatively small mistakes often led students to be awarded no credit, even though the grader thought that partial credit was more appropriate and fair.

The ability to better anticipate students' mistakes and program partial grading when these mistakes were made was needed to more fully rely on automatic grading and hence avoid time-consuming manual grading in the next cycles.

Distribution of Points Between Main and Sub-questions. During the first cycle, we investigated both underpinning and scaffolding scenarios in which students skipped the main question if they knew that the section constituted a small part of the total score. The think-aloud study revealed that students barely noticed the score point distribution. Reflecting on this after the think-aloud session, the students said that their score was not of interest because, regardless of score, they wanted to make a serious effort on the main question. Furthermore, they stated that it was a waste of time to read the text on point distribution at the top of the page. Thus, we concluded that the students did not develop a test-taking strategy based on score point distribution in the first cycle. However, we noted that they might develop such a strategy over time as they become more accustomed to this type of examination. Also, although students may not pay particular attention to the score distribution, it must remain a design element since it provides students with an overview of the exam and allows them to choose the order in which they work through the problems. Therefore, in the exams conducted in the second and third cycles, the score point distribution of the complete exam, split into main and sub-questions, was given on the first page of the exam.

4.3 Recommendations Based on First Cycle

Given the findings of the first cycle, we provide the following recommendations.

Layout and On-Screen Presentation. Presenting a question on a screen requires a different layout than when presenting a paper-based question. We propose the following rules of thumb for laying out questions:

- Use a sans-serif font.
- Apply blank lines between paragraphs.
- List parameters in a table.
- Make the maximum width of a line of text 600 px.
- Place images on the right side of the text.
- Try to avoid the need to scroll, if possible; the Verify button for the first section of the problem should be visible when students open the question page.

Design and Construction Guidelines

- Scenario-type questions are necessary in multiple conversion situations, but not for all questions.
- Carefully consider and test the range of parametrisation values and specific values.
- In line with recommendations for digital math exams [3, 12, 25], it is necessary to at least reword paper-based questions for use in a digital exam.
- Specify the accuracy that is expected from students in their responses.
- Specify the allowed margin of error and the units in which the answer must be expressed.
- Provide a fixed list of variables that students should use in their response; for example, make sure to not confuse T (temperature) and t (time).
- Place crucial remarks about the expected answer, such as response accuracy, *above* the response field.
- Make sure that images are readable and of sufficient size. Possibly, allow for a zoom function.

Feedback Guidelines

- Clearly describe the maximum score that can be attained.
- Clearly provide the total number of main questions and the number of possible sub-questions in the exam.
- Do not display the running score.
- Clearly describe in the text what happens after clicking the Verify button.
- Clearly state the number of possible attempts when clicking the Verify button.
- When students submit an incorrect response, design the feedback to be as positive as possible. Restate the number of possible attempts.

Pedagogic Embedding

- Ensure ample opportunity for students to practice with an actual, but dummy, exam.

4.4   Cycles 2 and 3

In the subsequent courses, students could practice with the exams developed in the first cycle. Students were encouraged to practice, and for that reason, preparation for the computer-based exam was integrated into weekly examples and homework. Further, students were trained to use the Preview button to help them discover syntax mistakes, and help text was added to the question texts.

Design Process. Speeding up the design process was emphasised in cycles 2 and 3 by limiting development of completely new questions and rely on adapting the already-developed exams and fine-tuning the grading with adaptive grading to better cater to minor errors.

Adaptive Grading Scheme. While scenario-type problems allow for partial grading of a problem, the system should also allow for partial grading of a minor mistake in a response. This would allow score deduction for error propagation to be restricted to a specific part of the scenario.

As an example, let us consider the case of deduction of the material index (Appendix 2). In the sub-questions, the target function and constraint need to be combined so the free geometrical parameter can be found. The target function can be written as follows:

$$m = AL\rho = \pi\left(R_0^2 - R_1^2\right)L\rho = 2\pi R_i tL\rho \tag{1}$$

The equation for the constraint is as follows:

$$S = \frac{C_1 EI}{L^3}$$

$$\text{with } I = \frac{\pi}{4}\left(R_0^4 - R_1^4\right) = \pi R_i^3 t \tag{2}$$

Rewriting Eq. (2) gives the free geometrical parameter:

$$t = \frac{SL^3}{\pi C_1 E R_i^3} \tag{3}$$

Small mistakes in Eqs. (1), (2) and (3), such as in the surface area, A, or in I, are deducted only in the final step, when Eqs. (1) and (3) are combined:

$$m = \frac{2SL^4}{C_1 R_i^2} * \frac{\rho}{E} \tag{4}$$

With an adaptive grading scheme, error propagation could be regulated and point deduction for a minor mistake could be restricted to a specific part of the scenario. For students, this leads to less anxiety; instead of showing three red Xs since all rows contain mistakes, only the final row has a red X (Fig. 6).

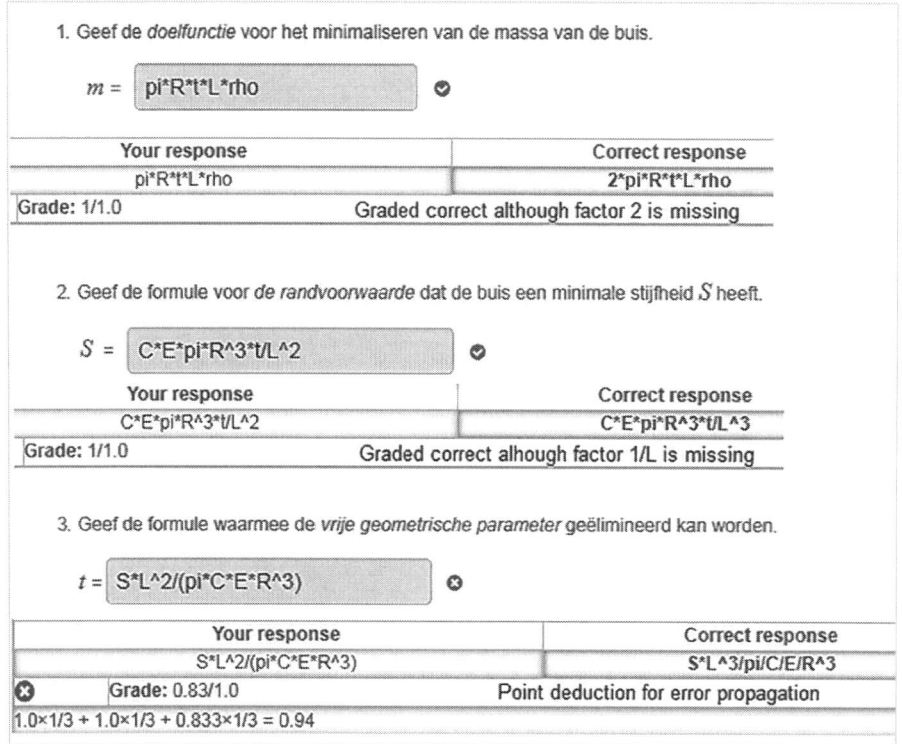

Fig. 6. Example of an adaptive grading scheme in which minor errors are not propagated. Without adaptive grading, students would see three red Xs. With adaptive grading, they see two green checkmarks and only one red X with the same score reduction. The figure also shows how feedback is provided to the students when all attempts have been used. Students see their answer, the correct answer and the grade for each question. (Color figure online)

Syntax Errors. Multiple aspects need to be taken into account when grading open response fields, like numeric values or equations. For example, value, precision and syntax play a role in correct grading; the margins of error of these factors in the answer model define the range in which the student's response is still graded as correct. Syntax can be of importance when scientific notation is needed or, in this case, notation of symbols, super- and subscript numbers and character captions.

Over time, the grading scheme was optimised to allow for additional mistakes to be scored correctly. Differences in the case sensitivity of answers and inclusion of multiple correct scoring syntax formulas resulted in more robust exams. These typical score-error-countering measures were put in a database so they could be quickly applied to future exams, significantly reducing the time required to enter problems into the system for exams.

Test-Taking Time and Passing Rate. Observation of test administration revealed that students took more time to complete a computer-based exam using scenario-type questions compared to the paper-based version. This seemed to be mainly caused by the fact that students receive immediate feedback during the digital exam and start to correct their responses based on this feedback. This process is not present in paper-based exams.

Further, there were doubts about the extent to which students were able to easily submit answers from a user interface design perspective and the extent to which the number of allowed attempts to answer a question lead the student to apply an unin-tended answering strategy. Table 3 shows an overview of the typical values for the average difficulty of the exams and reliability expressed in Cronbach's alpha and passing rate. For comparison, data regarding the last paper-based exam is included in the table. The table shows that the average difficulty seemed to decrease when turning to digital exams, but in the third cycle, the average difficulty seemed to return to the previous level. Expressed in terms of passing rate, there does not seem to be any effects, but this could be due to score-to-grade considerations. The reliability of the first attempt at exams is, on average, not very high, though given the rather low number of score points that could be awarded, the reliability is not that poor. Further, the relia-bility of the exams does not seem to change dramatically.

Table 3. Characteristics of the developed and administered exams in the design cycles.

Cycle	Exam	Total score points	Number of students	Average difficulty (P-value)	Cronbach's alpha	Passing rate
Pre-Pilot Paper-Based	1st	17	320	0.63	0.63	56%
	2nd (re-sit)	17	181	0.54	0.38	42%
First Digital (2016)	1st (think-aloud protocol)	3	10	–	–	–
	2nd (first attempts)	14	454	0.46	0.61	nnb
	3rd (re-sit)	14	280	0.43	0.57	52%
Second Digital (2017)	1st	14	523	0.45	0.68	47%
	2nd (re-sit)	14	295	0.45	0.68	72%
Third Digital (2018)	1st	14	414	0.54	0.73	61%
	2nd (re-sit)	14	221	0.66	0.59	78%

Test-Taking Strategies. The test-taking strategy of a student can be defined as the tactic used by the student to determine how seriously he or she will attempt to answer the main question.

Maple T.A. can allow students to make multiple attempts at answering a question correctly. During the think-aloud study, the students used the attempts as many times as possible, saying, 'I still have plenty of attempts'. This resulted in loss of precious exam time. One student noted, 'The fewer attempts given, the more valuable they are.

It forces you to give it your best effort'. This aligns with a statement by Ashton [12]: 'in the T-type scenario it was unclear whether students were guessing or doing serious attempts'. During the think-aloud study, we also observed that the students spent too much time attempting to get one problem right and ran out of time to completely finish the assignment.

During the exams, we analysed which changes students made to the answers they submitted for their first attempt. In most cases, the follow-up attempts were only used to make small changes to the first answer (for example, rounding off) or checking their calculations. Seldom did they choose a different problem-solving process or correct their syntax.

We concluded that providing too many attempts, in general, only led to a loss of time for the students. Allowing for two attempts in a time-constrained test would be optimal to provide students with a fair opportunity to correct a possible mistake but also restrict them from losing too much time and running into time problems.

Design Effort Reduction. As was expected, the first conversion from paper-based to computer-based problems took a lot of time. However, with experience, more efficiency was achieved. After three cycles of developing digital material science exams, the teacher claimed that it did not take more time to design a digital exam with the same quality as a paper-based exam.

Entering Questions in the System. Due to improvements in the grading code by collecting grading and response checking procedures, creating fixed structures for some problems (e.g. questions about material selection and material index derivation) and applying score-error-countering algorithms from a database, the time required to enter questions is, in general, about eight hours.

Grading the Exam. For the first two exams of the first cycle, a lot of time was spent reviewing the automatic grading and adjusting grades in the system. Writing an answer model for the computer-based exam forced the teacher to document students' decisions quite intensively. However, because of this elaborate, strict answer model and automatic partial grading, the teacher could have colleagues help review the grades in cycles two and three.

It became apparent that the gradebook of Maple T.A. is not well suited for making manual adjustments to grades. It takes a lot of time to navigate the system and access each student's answer and score for each question. In particular, essay-type questions, which cannot be scored automatically, required a labour-intensive process. For these questions, a smart combination of question types was introduced that combines a numerical or multiple-choice response field - which is automatically graded - with an essay comment field (not worth any points). If the student's response is correct, and the comment corroborates the response, no adjustments need to be made. Only if the comments give a reason for the student to receive partial credit does the grade need to be adjusted.

Because of the measures described above, the lead time to get grades out to students was reduced to one week for the digital exam, compared to at least three weeks for the paper-based exam.

5   Conclusion and Discussion

Based on the three cycles of design and evaluation of a series of material sciences digital exams, we can answer our main research questions, summarise some limitations of the study and describe its implications for practice.

With respect to the first research question, the project showed that it is feasible to construct acceptable digital engineering exams that are comparable to paper-based versions in terms of eliciting student responses and the ability to partially score relevant steps in the problem-solving process. In that sense, the exams have sufficient face validity. The developed scenarios fit well with the intended measurement of students' skill in solving engineering-type problems. The project provides a number of example items and guidelines to aid assessment experts and teachers in engineering education in developing exams.

Regarding the average difficulty of the digital exams, they seem to be somewhat more difficult than the paper-based exams. The reasons for this are not fully clear, but the results of the study suggest that intermediate feedback could have an effect. On the one hand, providing feedback helps to keep students on track to eventually solve a problem. On the other hand, this causes students to spend more time answering questions, which can cause timing problems. Also, receiving positive or negative feedback during execution of an exam, which is not provided in a paper-based exam, may have effects. However, the reliability of the exams does not seem to have changed. That in itself is encouraging, as it does not dismiss digital exams as a suitable assessment method. In general, however, digital exams need extra questions to reach acceptable reliability levels (i.e. more than 0.8).

With regards to the second research question, we found that students indeed display different test-taking strategies for digital exams compared to paper-based exams. This seems to be due to the possibility of making multiple attempts to answer a question. Limiting the number of attempts to two seems to be acceptable, as this allows the student to correct small errors.

With regards to the final research question, we found that digital engineering exams are not more expensive to develop or score than paper-based exams. However, doing so does require an investment in experience and fluency in constructing exams and building fixed design patterns for scenario-type questions, problem categories and scoring algorithms to achieve improved efficiency. The finding that it is not more expensive is welcome given the sophistication that is achieved in the construction of these exam questions.

In terms of limitations, we tried to cover the general methods to construct engineering type of exams. However, the generalisability of the results of this design study may be limited as we focussed mainly on material sciences. So, the study would need replication in the other fields that constitute engineering.

Further, the study took into consideration the possibilities and limitations of the Maple T.A. platform. It is very likely that higher education institutions using other assessment platforms face some limitations, as the developed methods of incorporating intermediate steps into questions and possibilities for algebraic input and automatic scoring are very specific to Maple T.A.

In view of the many engineering courses that are conducted worldwide each year at higher education institutions, the development process and example digital exam questions described in this study can have a great impact on practice. The results show that, within comparable bounds of investment time and development time, digital exams of comparable difficulty and reliability to paper-based exams can be achieved. Further, the time to provide students with grades is shorter for digital exams than for paper-based exams. In short, the method to develop digital exams for engineering education developed in this study is general and robust enough to be applied on a large scale for multiple engineering courses.

Appendix 1: Example 1—Underpinning Scenario

Learning Objective
The student is able to choose the most suitable material following prescribed steps.

In this example, the student is first presented with a multiple-choice question (the original paper-based question). After correctly answering this question, the student underpins the choice by answering the sub-questions that represent the prescribed steps.

After correctly answering the main question you will get 3 additional questions, to corroborate your choice. All questions must be correct to get a score on this question.

A supercapacitor can be used to store electrical energy. This requires a material with dielectrical properties. In the graph below the dielectrical constant ε_r is presented versus the dielectric strength E_b (MV/m) for four different materials.

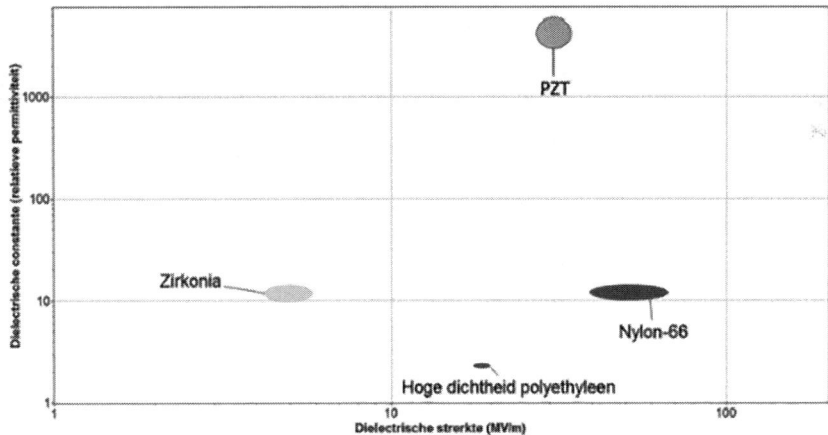

Which dielectrical material has the highest energy density E (kJ/m³) for the storage of dielektrical?

(Click for List) ▼

Section Attempt 1 of 1

Verify

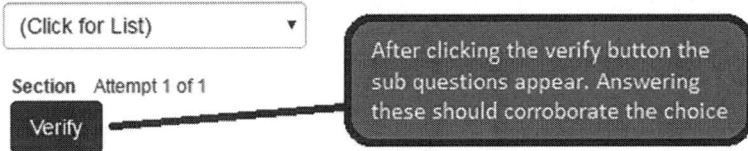

After clicking the verify button the sub questions appear. Answering these should corroborate the choice

a. Give the materials index that is maximised to find the material with the highest energy density.

$M =$ [   ] 🔍 📄

Click here for an overview of the Greek Symbols and how to write them

b. What is the slope of the line of constant material index ?

[Number]

c. In what direction should this line be shifted to determine the maximal material index?

(Click for List) ▼

Section Attempt 1 of 1

Verify   **Image 2: Example of a multiple choice underpinnning scenario**

Appendix 2: Example 2—Underpinning Scenario

Learning Objective

The student is able to produce a material index for a given situation following a prescribed method.

After answering the main question you get 3 additional questions to corroborate your response.

A long, thin-walled, cylindrical tube with a given length L (m) and inner en outer radius R_i (m) and R_u (m), respectively, is exposed to a force F (N). Both ends of the tube are supported as shown in the figure below.

We aim to minimize the material cost under the constraint that the tube's outer fiber is not allowed to deform plastically due to the bend momentum M_{brig} (Nm).

The tube's wall thickness t (m) is, to a certain extend, the free parameter of this system. The only restriction is that the wall thickness is far less than the inner radius of the tube: $t \ll R_i$. The following simplification can be used:

$$R_i + t \approx R_i \text{ and}$$
$$R_u^2 - R_i^2 \approx 2 \cdot R_i \cdot t$$

The material the tube is made of has the following properties: density ρ (kg/m³), yield stress σ_y (Pa) and cost per kilograms C_m (€/kg).

Main question

Derive the material index that has to be maximized to select the right material for minimal material cost C for the forementioned situation and constraint.

Material index = [_____] 🗔 📄

Click here for an overview of Greek symbols and their spelling

Section   Attempt 1 of 2

[Verify] ─────────────────   After clicking the verify button the sub questions appear. Answering these should corroborate the choice

a. Give the formula for the target function:

$C =$ [_____] 🗔 📄

b. Give the formula for the constraint:

$M_{brig} =$ [_____] 🗔 📄

c. Derive the equation for the free parameter:

Give yhe symbol for the free parameter in the first cel and the formula for the free parameter in the second cel

[_____] 🗔 📄 = [_____] 🗔 📄

Section   Attempt 2 of 2

[Verify]   Image 3: Example of a numerical question underpinning scenario

In the paper-based exam, the steps were given leading up to the main question, which concerned the material index (MI). The computer-based version shows the main question first, requiring students to try and solve the problem by themselves. Since it was an open-book exam, students could have derived the MI by comparing the situation with example MIs from the book and not performing the proper derivation. This is why they needed to show they understand the separate steps.

Appendix 3: Example 3—Scaffolding Scenario

Learning Objective
The student can correctly calculate the process conditions that influence the properties of certain materials by selecting the proper equations from the book, filling in the parameters and correctly performing the calculations.

In the paper-based exam, the main question is posed. Since students hand in their complete calculation, the grader can see where the student went wrong and grant a partial score if appropriate. In a digital numerical version, the student is able to give only the final response, which can be scored either 0 or 1. The scenario version shows intermediate calculations, allowing for a partial score.

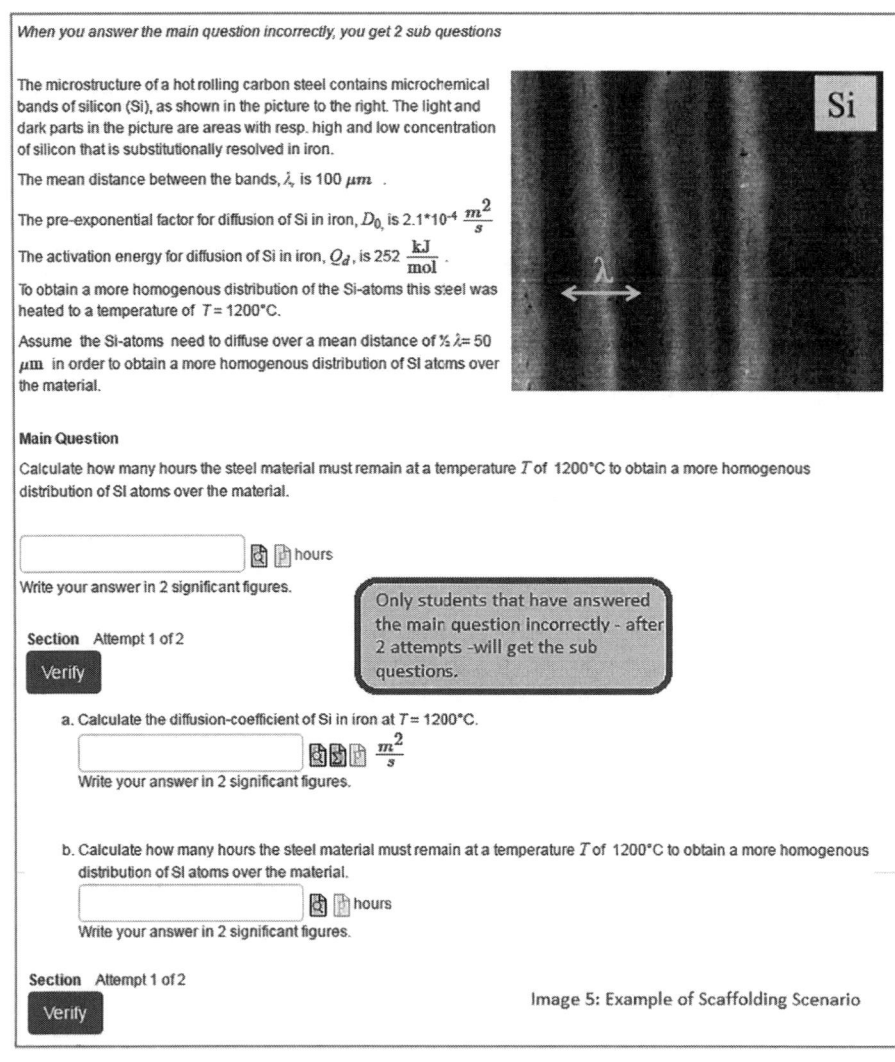

When you answer the main question incorrectly, you get 2 sub questions

The microstructure of a hot rolling carbon steel contains microchemical bands of silicon (Si), as shown in the picture to the right. The light and dark parts in the picture are areas with resp. high and low concentration of silicon that is substitutionally resolved in iron.

The mean distance between the bands, λ, is 100 μm .

The pre-exponential factor for diffusion of Si in iron, D_0, is $2.1*10^{-4}$ $\frac{m^2}{s}$

The activation energy for diffusion of Si in iron, Q_d, is 252 $\frac{kJ}{mol}$.

To obtain a more homogenous distribution of the Si-atoms this steel was heated to a temperature of $T = 1200°C$.

Assume the Si-atoms need to diffuse over a mean distance of $½ \lambda = 50$ μm in order to obtain a more homogenous distribution of Si atoms over the material.

Main Question

Calculate how many hours the steel material must remain at a temperature T of 1200°C to obtain a more homogenous distribution of Si atoms over the material.

[   ] 🔲🔲 hours

Write your answer in 2 significant figures.

Section   Attempt 1 of 2

[Verify]

> Only students that have answered the main question incorrectly - after 2 attempts -will get the sub questions.

    a. Calculate the diffusion-coefficient of Si in iron at $T = 1200°C$.

    [   ] 🔲🔲🔲 $\frac{m^2}{s}$

    Write your answer in 2 significant figures.

    b. Calculate how many hours the steel material must remain at a temperature T of 1200°C to obtain a more homogenous distribution of Si atoms over the material.

    [   ] 🔲🔲 hours

    Write your answer in 2 significant figures.

Section   Attempt 1 of 2

[Verify]

Image 5: Example of Scaffolding Scenario

In this example, the parameters are randomised so each student has his or her own set. This discourages cheating. If the student answers the main question correctly, no sub-questions are presented. If it is incorrectly answered, the student is asked the same question but in a two-step process.

References

1. Draaijer, S., Warburton, B.: The emergence of large-scale computer assisted summative examination facilities in higher education. In: Kalz, M., Ras, E. (eds.) CAA 2014. CCIS, vol. 439, pp. 28–39. Springer, Cham (2014). https://doi.org/10.1007/978-3-319-08657-6_3
2. Draaijer, S., Jefferies, A., Somers, G.: Online proctoring for remote examination: a state of play in higher education in the EU. In: Ras, E., Guerrero Roldán, A.E. (eds.) TEA 2017. CCIS, vol. 829, pp. 96–108. Springer, Cham (2018). https://doi.org/10.1007/978-3-319-97807-9_8
3. Bacon, D.R.: Assessing learning outcomes: a comparison of multiple-choice and short-answer questions in a marketing context. J. Mark. Educ. **25**, 31–36 (2003). https://doi.org/10.1177/0273475302250570
4. Scott, M., Stelzer, T., Gladding, G.: Evaluating multiple-choice exams in large introductory physics courses. Phys. Rev. Spec. Top. - Phys. Educ. Res. **2**, 020102 (2006). https://doi.org/10.1103/PhysRevSTPER.2.020102
5. Lawson, W.D.: Reliability and validity of FE exam scores for assessment of individual competence, program accreditation, and college performance. J. Prof. Issues Eng. Educ. Pract. **133**, 320–326 (2007). https://doi.org/10.1061/(ASCE)1052-3928(2007)133:4(320)
6. Hambleton, R.K., Jones, R.W.: An NCME instructional module on: comparison of classical test theory and item response theory and their applications to test development. Educ. Meas. Issues Pract. **12**, 38–47 (1993). https://doi.org/10.1111/j.1745-3992.1993.tb00543.x
7. Ashton, H.S., Youngson, M.A.: Creating questions for automatic assessment in mathematics. LTSN MSOR Maths CAA Series, pp. 1–11 (2004)
8. Downing, S.M.: Construct-irrelevant variance and flawed test questions: do multiple-choice item-writing principles make any difference? Acad. Med. **77**, 103–104 (2002)
9. Draaijer, S., Hartog, R.: Design patterns for digital item types in higher education. E-J. Instr. Sci. Technol. **10**, 1–31 (2007)
10. Hartog, R., Draaijer, S., Rietveld, L.C.: Practical aspects of task allocation in design and development of digital closed questions in higher education. Pract. Assess. Res. Eval. **13**, 2–15 (2008)
11. Gierl, M.J., Haladyna, T.M.: Automatic Item Generation: Theory and Practice. Routledge, New York (2012)
12. Ashton, H.S., Beevers, C.E., Korabinski, A.A., Youngson, M.A.: Incorporating partial credit in computer-aided assessment of mathematics in secondary education. Br. J. Educ. Technol. **37**, 93–119 (2006)
13. Beevers, C.E., Wild, D.G., McGuine, G.R., Fiddes, D.J., Youngson, M.A.: Issues of partial credit in mathematical assessment by computer. ALT-J. **7**, 26–32 (1999)
14. Clariana, R., Wallace, P.: Paper-based versus computer-based assessment: key factors associated with the test mode effect. Br. J. Educ. Technol. **33**, 593–602 (2002)
15. Parshall, C.G., Harmes, J.C.: The design of innovative item types: targeting constructs, selecting innovations, and refining prototypes (2008)
16. Draaijer, S., Van Gastel, L., Peeters, V., Frinking, P., Reumer, C.: Flexibilisering van Toetsing [Flexibility in Testing and Assessment]. Digitale Universiteit, Utrecht (2004)
17. van Someren, M.W., Barnard, Y.F., Sandberg, J.A.C.: The Think Aloud Method: A Practical Guide to Modelling Cognitive Processes. Academic Press, London (1994)
18. Goedee, C., Keijzer-de Ruijter, M., Offerman, E.: Digitaal toetsen van Engineering Lesstof [Digital testing of Engineering Instructional Materials]. Examens. Tijdschr. voor Toetspraktijk., 16–24 (2017)

19. Newell, A., Simon, H.A.: Human Problem Solving. Prentice-Hall, Upper Saddle River (1972)
20. Spilt, J.L., Leflot, G., Onghena, P., Colpin, H.: Use of praise and reprimands as critical ingredients of teacher behavior management: effects on children's development in the context of a teacher-mediated classroom intervention. Prev. Sci. **17**, 732–742 (2016). https://doi.org/10.1007/s11121-016-0667-y
21. Pintrich, P.R., Blumenfeld, P.C.: Classroom experience and children's self-perceptions of ability, effort, and conduct. J. Educ. Psychol. **77**, 646 (1985)
22. Worrall, C., Worrall, N., Meldrum, C.: The consequences of teacher praise and criticism. Educ. Psychol. **3**, 127–136 (1983). https://doi.org/10.1080/0144341830030204
23. Gable, R.A., Hester, P.H., Rock, M.L., Hughes, K.G.: Back to basics: rules, praise, ignoring, and reprimands revisited. Interv. Sch. Clin. **44**, 195–205 (2009). https://doi.org/10.1177/1053451208328831
24. Deci, E.L., Ryan, R.M.: Intrinsic Motivation and Self-Determination in Human Behavior. Springer, New York (1985). https://doi.org/10.1007/978-1-4899-2271-7
25. McGuire, G.R., Youngson, M.A., Korabinski, A.A., McMillan, D.: Partial credit in mathematics exams - a comparison of traditional and CAA exams. Presented at the 6th International Computer Assisted Assessment Conference, Loughborough, Loughborough University, UK (2002)

A Cost–Benefit Analysis for Developing Item Banks in Higher Education

Silvester Draaijer[(⊠)] [iD]

Faculty of Behavioural and Movement Sciences,
Department of Research and Theory in Education, Vrije Universiteit Amsterdam,
De Boelelaan 1105, 1081 HV Amsterdam, The Netherlands
s.draaijer@vu.nl

Abstract. Item banks in higher education can be regarded as important assets
to increasing the quality of education and assessment. An item bank allows for
the flexible administration of computer-based achievement tests for summative
purposes, as well as quizzes for formative purposes. Developing item banks,
however, can require quite an investment. A well-worked-out business case can
help with convincing stakeholders to start an item bank development project. An
important part of such a business case should be the increase in item quality and
the estimated reduction in costs, particularly for the collaborative development
of an item bank. However, a theoretical underpinning of a business case,
incorporating considerations based on classical test theory is lacking in the
literature. Therefore, a model is described to make estimations of reductions in
misclassifications and per-unit costs. Examples are presented of the likelihood of
reducing misclassifications and cost per unit based on findings in the literature.
Implications for research and practice are discussed.

Keywords: Item banking · Question development · Test development ·
Educational measurement · Economics · Multiple-choice questions · MCQs ·
Higher education

1 Background

In many higher education institutions (HEIs), computer-based assessment systems
nowadays are seen as integral parts of the e-learning landscape. Benefits of
e-assessment are generally acknowledged, such as the ability for anytime anyplace
testing, increasing the quality of assessment, support for and improvements to formative assessment, support for more authentic testing and testing using multimedia. It
has become more evident however that simply leaving the use of these systems to the
disposal of individual teachers results most often in an underused and less productive
educational tool [1–3]; hence, the benefits are not realised. More and more, HEIs are
looking for ways to optimise the use and deployment of e-assessment in a more
systematic manner, such as by developing and using *item banks* of selected response
test items.

Multiple advantages and opportunities of item banks for higher education can be
identified. Advantages of both item banking systems on the one hand, as well as item

© Springer Nature Switzerland AG 2019
S. Draaijer et al. (Eds.): TEA 2018, CCIS 1014, pp. 165–179, 2019.
https://doi.org/10.1007/978-3-030-25264-9_11

bank content on the other are seen as opportunities to increase the quality of education and assessment [4, 5]. Specifically for higher education, Draaijer and De Werk [6] sum up some of these advantages of item banking such as increasing the quality of assessment by improving item quality, increasing accountability and the transparency of the development process [7], increasing the durability of investments, improving test security, improving efficiency and increasing utility. This list of advantages is often used as part of a business case for item banking. Further, Draaijer and De Werk argue that *collaboration* between teachers is important because of the need for explicit development procedures and quality assurance, hence raising item quality. Conversely, collaboration could lower the cost per collaborator involved, despite the initially high investment.

However, when it comes down to actual numbers in terms of (1) decreases in cost (for example per test item used by students) or (2) reductions in the number of false negative and false positive pass-fail decisions (misclassifications), data and arguments run mostly thin. In addition, the literature provides no clear guidance on this issue in the context of classical test theory, which is the theory most relied upon in higher education[1]. This is an important omission, as convincing arguments from these two perspective can make business cases for starting an item bank development project stronger.

This paper therefore seeks to fill this gap by providing a theoretical and practical underpinning for the balance between cost and benefits using classical test theory and concepts of economies of scale. Based on anecdotal and research findings, an assessment is made of the practical applicability of this model. Finally, implications of the presented approach are discussed.

2   Cost and Benefits

The balance between cost and benefits is central to this paper. First, the concepts of cost and benefits will be described in the context of item banking using a selected response test item in higher education. Cost will be expressed in development cost. Benefits will be expressed in increasing validity, increasing reliability and hence reduction in misclassifications. Finally, benefits are expressed in the possibilities for re-use and hence cost reduction per teacher, test, student and test item.

---

[1] This is unsurprising because in the case of adaptive testing programmes using item response theory, the main argument for using this complex assessment technique relates largely to being able to develop up to 25% shorter tests for test takers and better controllable reliability. It also relates to preventing item exposure [8]. However, it does not aim to calculate the percentage of misclassifications [5, 8, 9]. It also must be noted that developing multi-stage tests (MSTs) and computer-adaptive tests using IRT methods should be regarded as only feasible for the professional testing industry [10] or in some selected cases for the domain of medicine [11].

2.1   Cost: Development

It can safely be assumed that the cost of developing test items for an item bank is the greatest factor in the total cost of a testing programme [5]. Quite some research is for example devoted to methods and systems for automatic item generation (AIG) to minimise the cost of the development of test items, whilst remaining in control of the content and psychometric characteristics of test items [see for example 12–15]. However, in the context of higher education, AIG has limited applications apart from maybe the domain of medicine [16]. Therefore, developing test items in general requires manual labour [17]. How much time it takes to design test items manually and the associated cost are therefore important variables in a model of the cost–benefit analysis for developing an item bank.

With respect to more fully supported item banking projects, as described by Hartog et al. [18], investment costs increase compared to personal test item banks (PTIBs). This is of course due to the fact that it requires multiple specialties to make an item banking project successful [5, 6, 18]. That is, more specialised expertise is needed per test item, more handling and control are needed; per test, the number of discarded items will most likely increase to meet the higher shared standards (for example more higher-order thinking questions); per test item, more time for design, review and editing is needed, etc. In various handbooks, elaborate methods and procedures are described [5, 6, 18, 19]. However, these will not be described here in further detail. Of course, the total cost of developing test items will increase when more complexity is added to the process of designing test items. How expansive such a project is, is a matter of balancing the cost against the benefits, which we will touch upon later.

2.2   Benefits: Increasing Validity and Reliability

The quality of test items can be related to a number of criteria. Below are five criteria for item banking deemed important for higher education applications, namely, (1) face validity, (2) the absence of item flaws, (3) validity with respect to the balance of factual questions versus higher-order thinking questions, (4) the level of difficulty and (5) the discrimination value of the tests items.

First, the face validity of tests will increase if test items in a bank adhere to a coherent set of editorial and style guidelines [20]. The impact of poor adherence to style and lay-out results most likely in low perceived quality by students. In particular, it can reinforce the opinion that selected response test items are not deemed appropriate for educational assessment purposes in higher education [21].

Second, with respect to *flawed* test items [22], the quality of items can increase if flaws can be avoided. Flawed test items can be considered test items that do not adhere to generally acknowledged test item construction guidelines, for example, the 31 guidelines of Haladyna and Rodriguez [22].

Additionally, concerning the quality of face validity and flawed test items, both cannot be regarded item characteristics that sit on a linear scale from low to high quality. Students can become quite upset when they feel test items are not 'fair' [21, 23], but are not necessarily very happy when flaws are absent. Test item quality falls in that respect into the category of 'must-be' quality, according to an easy to make interpretation using the Kano model [23, 24]: a single flawed test item in an achievement test can result quickly in the perception of a loss of quality. In contrast, must-be quality implies that users do not perceive the higher quality of test items when style problems or flaws are absent. A good test item without style problems or flaws is simply a precondition resulting in what could be called 'baseline quality'.

Third, with respect to validity, in general, at least two cognitive categories [25] of items are supposed to be part of achievement tests in higher education, namely, on the one hand, facts and knowledge-based questions and on the other hand knowledge application questions or problem-solving questions [26, 27]. What is regarded as low quality in higher education is the overuse of facts and knowledge-based questions. This is regarded as lower validity [21] and adds to the conception that selected response test items are 'intrinsically bad' and 'factual'. Therefore, with a limited number of higher-order thinking items, the test specification criteria are harder to meet. Hence, to raise test quality, an item banking project could be started to focus on designing relatively more higher-order thinking questions than factual recall questions.

Fourth, with respect to the *difficulty* of test items, benefits can also be sought in an item bank project. For achievement tests (based on classical test theory) in particular, the difficulty of test items must be on average neither too high nor too low, as average difficulty items allow for better discrimination of the level of attaining students for a specific domain [28, 29]. Given the random guess score of selected response test items, the optimal level of difficulty could differ, but it should preferably lie between 0.5–0.8 for selected response test items. The level of difficulty can, with sufficient effort and expertise, be influenced by good item design and a good understanding of the material and characteristics of the student population [30].

Finally, with respect to ability to identify justly more and less competent students, one aim of an item bank project could be to increase test reliability. First, the most straightforward option to increase reliability is to increase *the number of items* in a test [31, 32]. In higher education, this should not be overly problematic, as achievement tests in general already consist of between roughly 30 and 80 items [33]. Item banking in itself could lead to additional test items being available so longer tests can more easily be assembled. A second aim could be to increase the *discriminating power* of items (and hence to increase test reliability) in an item bank project. When test items have higher discriminating power, tests that are more reliable would be obtained with the same number of items. Conversely, with fewer items on a test, the same level of reliability could be achieved.

2.3   Benefits: Decreasing Misclassification in Achievement Tests

When an item bank project succeeds in designing test items with more favourable item difficulty and discrimination values, the reliability of the assembled tests—given the average number of items in these tests—will result in a lower percentage of misclassifications. The latter must be seen as an important pursued benefit of an item banking project, as it helps the students and the HEIs to minimise costs.

It is possible to estimate the percentage of misclassifications of a test based on a few basic variables derived from classical test theory. For this estimation, based on dichotomously scored selected response test items, the standard deviation of a test,

SD_{test}, based on Gibson and Weiner [34] can be used. Gibson and Weiner use the item-test point-biserial correlation values r_{it}, the level of difficulty p and the number n of items in a test to calculate a test's standard deviation. When using the average of all the items $\bar{r}_{it}$, $\bar{p}$, and the average number of items $\bar{n}$ in a test or an item bank, the average standard deviation $\overline{SD}_{test}$ of all tests based on the items can be calculated according to formula (1). Using the $\overline{SD}_{test}$, the average reliability $\overline{KR20}$ (which is equal to Cronbach's α for dichotomous items) can be calculated according to formula (2).

$$\overline{SD}_{test} = \bar{n} * \bar{r}_{it}[\bar{p}(1-\bar{p})]^{\frac{1}{2}} \tag{1}$$

$$\overline{KR20} = \frac{\bar{n}}{\bar{n}-1}\left[1 - \frac{\bar{n} * \bar{p}(1-\bar{p})}{\overline{SD}_{test}^2}\right] \tag{2}$$

Formula (2) can be simplified to formula (3).

$$\overline{KR20} = \frac{\bar{n}}{\bar{n}-1}\left[1 - \frac{1}{\bar{n} * \bar{r}_{it}^2}\right] \tag{3}$$

The values for r_{it} can easily be retracted from current computer based assessment systems and hence averages can be calculated. It follows from formula (3) that with an increasing number of items per test and increasing r_{it} values, $\overline{KR20}$ will also increase. Interestingly, the average level of difficulty $\bar{p}$ of the test items is not relevant to the value of $\overline{KR20}$, as becomes clear from formula (3).

Following this procedure and given an average percentual fail rate for the students of $\bar{c}$ on these tests, the average percentage of misclassifications for an achievement test can be calculated based on Douglas [35]. Specific percentages of misclassifications can be looked up in a table provided for example by Eggen and Sanders [36], as shown in Table 1.

Table 1. Percentage of two-sided misclassifications on a test as a function of the percentage of failed test-takers and the test–retest reliability.

Percentage fails	Test-retest reliability						
	0.0	0.50	0.60	0.70	0.80	0.90	1.00
5	10	8	7	6	5	4	0
10	18	14	12	11	9	6	0
15	26	18	17	14	12	8	0
20	32	23	20	17	14	10	0
25	38	26	23	20	16	11	0
30	42	29	25	22	18	12	0
35	46	31	27	23	19	13	0
40	48	32	29	24	20	14	0
45	50	33	29	25	20	14	0
50	50	33	30	25	20	14	0

For example, if $\bar{r}_{it} = 0.25$ and $\bar{n} = 40$, then it follows that $\overline{KR20} = 0.61$. If further it is given that $\bar{c} = 30\%$, then the percentage of misclassifications (false positive and false negatives combined) would be about 25% of the student population. When increasing for example $\bar{r}_{it}$ to $\bar{r}_{it} = 0.30$ and adding 10 items on average to the tests, it would increase $\overline{KR20}$ up to 0.79, and the number of misclassifications would decrease to about 18% of the student population.

The decrease in misclassifications could be considered cost savings *as a result* from an item bank project and as such a benefit. For example, HEIs need to accommodate fewer unnecessary re-sits that are a cause of study hold-up, and society can be surer that fewer students acquire unjustified course credit. These benefits could be monetised for a business case.

2.4   Benefit: Re-use

For balancing the cost against the benefits, as well as to decrease misclassifications, this paper proposes using the number of uses of test items in a bank. For example, when a test item is used by two teachers instead of one, the cost *per teacher* will be halved. When a test item can be used in two tests instead of one, the cost *per item per test* will be halved. When a test item can be used by twice as many students, the cost *per student* will be halved. In business terms, the fundamental laws of 'economies of scale', in which investments in production methods are recovered through a decrease in cost per unit produced, are applicable. The amount of re-use of items must therefore be used in a business case for an item bank development project to uncover the financial benefits in terms of reduction in the cost per unit: cost per teacher, cost per test and cost per student.

2.5   Example

Given the concepts and variables described in Sects. 2.1, 2.2, 2.3, 2.4 and 2.5, a model and example calculations are worked out below. They illustrate the possibilities by drawing up two scenarios. The first scenario (A) is the bottom-line scenario, where a teacher works alone to develop test items for a series of tests. The second scenario (B) is the situation in which multiple teachers who teach the same subject would engage in an item banking project for the same number of tests and use the items in their tests.

First, the model takes as the input the number of tests and test-takers for which items are developed, as well as the number of items per test. Second, assumptions are made concerning the average effort to develop a test item. The first and second numbers result in a particular cost per test item and test. Third, assumptions must also be made concerning the quality of test item in terms of average discrimination value. It is to be assumed that a collaborative development effort increases the total effort per item and, based on Rush [37], will increase the discrimination value of those test items. Fourth, using the average discrimination value, achieved reliabilities can be calculated. Additionally, assuming a certain pass–fail ratio and the number of test-takers, we can then look up the percentage and number of misclassifications. This number of mis-classifications can be evaluated in terms of benefits, even in financial terms. Finally, the calculated values can be used to compute the cost per unit, such as per teacher, per test, per student and per item.

Table 2 provides an overview of a specific comparison of scenarios. In scenario A the teacher teaches 200 students and needs to make three tests. The teacher uses 40 items for the test [33]. The teacher needs therefore to develop an item bank containing 120 items. In scenario B, the situation of three collaborating teachers is worked out. It is assumed that each teacher teaches also 200 students, so the test will be used for 600 students in total instead of 200 students. The teachers will develop three tests that they will all use. To increase quality, first, the teachers increase the number of items per test from 40 to 50. The teachers develop therefore an item bank of 150 items. Second, by having a more systematic and intensified item development process, in which it is estimated that two times as much time per test item will be invested, the average discrimination value is expected to increase from 0.25 to 0.3. The resulting total development cost per test, based on these assumptions increases considerably from EUR 2,000 to EUR 5,000. Additionally, given these assumptions, it can be calculated that the number of misclassifications per test decreases from 25% to 18%. This percentage can be translated to numbers of students and, assuming a certain monetisation (say EUR 50 per misclassified student), can be used in consecutive calculations for the cost per teacher, per test and per student.

Table 2. Overview of model results for two item bank development scenarios and their differences expressed as delta and percentage change.

Variables	Scenario A	Scenario B	delta (B-A)	delta percentage
Assumptions				
Number of teachers	1	3	2	200%
Number of students	200	600	400	200%
Number of items in test	40	50	10	25%
Number of tests to develop	3	3	0	0%
Total resulting number of items to develop	120	150	30	25%
Assumption of average work load per test item in hours	0,5	1	0,5	100%
Assumption investment cost per test item for item development (1 hour for EUR 100,-)	€ 50	€ 100	€ 50	100%
Resulting development cost per test	€ 2.000	€ 5.000	€ 3.000	150%
Total resulting development cost	€ 6.000	€ 15.000	€ 9.000	150%
Assumption of quality of test items in terms of rbis	0,25	0,3	0,05	20%
Resulting average reliability KR20	0,62	0,79	0,18	29%
Resulting average percentage of misclassifications	0,25	0,18	−0,07	−28%
Resulting number of misclassified students per test	50	36	−14	−28%
Resulting cost effects per test				
Resulting cost of misclassified students (assume for example EUR 50,- per student) per test	€ 2.500	€ 1.800	€−700	−28%
Resulting cost per teacher per test (incl. misclassifications)	€ 4.500	€ 2.267	€−2.233	−50%
Resulting cost per student per test (incl. misclassifications)	€ 22,50	€ 11,33	€−11,17	−50%
Resulting cost per item per student per test (incl. misclassifications)	€ 0,56	€ 0,23	€−0,34	−60%

Table 2 shows that initial investment cost increases considerably. However, the costs per student per test and per item per student per test decrease dramatically. The example shows that an additional 150% increase in development costs can result in a 50% lower cost per student. Further, given that in general teachers receive payment based on the number of students that take a particular course, this decrease in cost per student must be regarded as having the highest practical impact.

The described approach also allows for identifying combinations of assumptions and numbers in which break-even points are reached. For example, what is the minimum number of collaborators or students needed to achieve benefits? What is the maximum extra effort needed to achieve benefits? What is the minimum increase in item discrimination needed to achieve benefits? Or what is the minimum number of extra items in our test to achieve benefits?

3   Practical Value

Given the concepts and variables described above, a reality check of the values of the model with empirical data should be made to underpin the realistic nature of the approach. Are the numbers and assumptions provided in the example in Table 2 to be expected or achievable? For that purpose, in this paper, the findings from the literature will be listed with respect to a typical workload for developing test items and psychometric values and the possibilities of influencing the value of these variables intentionally.

3.1   Cost and Workload

First, with respect to *financial* data, we can only rely on a few anecdotal sources for some tangibles numbers. These sources report costs ranging from $1,000 [38] up to $2,500 for the development of IRT-calibrated items for large-scale licensure programmes [5]. The numbers indicate indeed that developing high-quality items comes with considerable costs. The financial number can be attributed largely to the working hours of experts, including the training and organisation of item writers, item reviewers and item editors. Therefore, by using an hourly payment rate, one could find the average workload (for example, with an hourly payment rate of € 100) that would require between 10 and 25 h per final calibrated and approved item. As has been stated, however, the higher education context does not lend itself easily for full-fledged IRT-based item banks. Therefore, these numbers should be regarded as a significantly high upper limit.

Second, with respect to *workload*, handbooks for computer-based testing acknowledge that the manual process is labour-intensive, but the handbooks do not elaborate on this load in practical detail [8, 22, 39, 40] or concrete numbers. However, it is in general acknowledged that it requires specialised domain knowledge and knowledge about testing to be able to produce higher-order thinking items [17, 30]. Therefore, it costs more effort to design higher-order thinking questions than facts and knowledge-based questions. Mayenga [41] further identified in his study that teachers in particular found developing a third distractor for a multiple-choice question most difficult and time consuming. As research suggests, 3-option multiple-choice questions in practice perform equally well as 4-option versions [42], and cost benefits can be achieved if an item banking project chooses a 3-option database. One study focused on the development workload for three item writing models [43]. The study estimated an average number of hours worked by support staff to reach acceptable levels of quality of test items ranging from an average of 1.5 up to 2.4 h, depending on the development method. The presented effort was excluding the effort of the item authors.

Third, within the context of more fully developed and supported item banking projects in higher education, Hartog et al. [18] collected evidence in which development times for test items ranged from an average of 1.9 to 2.1 h.

Fourth, within the context of higher education, personal test item banks [3] are developed and used by individual teachers. The development of items for personal item banks mostly takes place in an informal setting with little quality control processes [20]. Development times between 15 min up to one hour were once observed by the author in a local item banking project [44].

In all, little is actually known about the financial numbers and workload for developing test items, but assuming a lower limit of 15 min (for a teacher left to his or her own devices and quickly designing some items) and an upper limit of 2.5 h (for a collaborative item development project) seems reasonable for further practical use when using a calculation model.

3.2 Flawed Test Items and Their Impact on Item Quality

Currently, the quality of teacher-developed item banks is most likely rather low [2, 3, 45–47], mainly because of the presence of many flaws. Tarrant and Wade [46] found for example between 28–75% flawed test items in teacher-made tests. Downing [48] found between 36 and 65% flawed test items in teacher-made tests. Rush et al. [37] identified about 29% flaw-free questions in teacher made tests. When items were more elaborately scrutinised and were developed in more systematic item development projects, it was possible to decrease the number of flaws significantly [49, 50] with relatively limited effort.

However, research shows some mixed results as to whether flaws influence item difficulty or discrimination. For example, Downing [48] studied the effects of flaws as described above and found that passing rates declined as flawed items were 0–15% points more difficult than standard items measuring the same construct. Passing rates would decline for example from 53% to 47% for a particular exam. The study of Tarrant and Wade [47] however showed mixed effects in which sometimes flawed items were more difficult and sometimes less difficult than flawless items. They attributed this to the type of flaws that were in the sample test as some flaws provide information regarding the correct answer while other flaws obscure the correct answer. The latter is also described by Rush et al. [37]. Wadi et al. [49] also found no effect on mean exam scores of a vetting procedure that focused on detecting and repairing flawed test items. In their study, 10–30% of test items were changed during the development stage, yet no effect was found on passing rates. Therefore, for practical purposes, it is a defensible position that the level of difficulty is in practice *not* dependent on item flaws.

Additionally, it is also too simple a thought that avoiding item flaws raises discriminating power. However, Downing [48] found small effects on test score reliability or other psychometric quality indices for a 22-item test with flawed and unflawed test items. The reliability of such a test was about 0.61 and the average r_{bis} was 0.34 for the unflawed items and 0.30 for the flawed items. Further, Rush et al. [37] studied the impact of item-writing flaws and item complexity on item difficulty and discrimination value for a set of 1,925 examination items. They found that about 38% of questions in a third-year veterinary study programme contained item flaws, the average difficulty was 83% and the average discrimination index was about 0.18. However, they did *not* find that item-writing flaws impacted the indices of difficulty or discrimination, apart from a limited set of flaws (implausible distractors, use of "all of the above" and series of true/false response options). Rush et al. however did find that higher cognitive skill items were associated with higher item difficulty and increased discrimination values.

The reported two average discrimination values presented by Downing and Rush are also of practical interest. They describe typical values of average test item characteristics as found in the realm of the author. With respect to acceptable or good item discrimination values, the literature however is inconclusive, and debate is ongoing [51, 52]. For use in a business case, as described in this study, the actual values however are of less interest. Of much more importance is the change in value (delta) of the item discrimination that can be accomplished when executing an item bank development project.

In conclusion, research suggests that improving the psychometric properties of test items is not an easy task accomplished simply by avoiding flaws. Hence, the specific content and item design knowledge of the teachers who design test items remains paramount to achieving benefits concerning the discriminating power of test items [30].

3.3   Discussion of the Presented Model

Given the findings presented in Subsects. 3.1 and 3.2 regarding the outlook of the practically attainable values of the variables in the model, two lines of improving item quality can be identified.

First, in relation to face validity and avoiding flaws, it is possible with relatively limited effort to realise relatively large improvements. Imposing a limited vetting procedure can result in a significant decrease in item flaws. Hence, for example, it could be a realistic assumption that when raising item development time by say 50%, this form of quality could be improved considerably. However, test-takers will regard this factual lack of flaws as a baseline and not necessarily perceive it as a large quality improvement.

Second, in relation to difficulty and discriminating power, item banking projects could result in more stable and favourable levels of difficulty or discrimination power of test items if ample effort is put in to selecting item writers, training, design and reviewing processes. It would be a defensible stance that it requires at least a 100–200% increase in item development effort to achieve such an improvement in item quality.

The studies suggest in a way with respect to difficulty and discriminating power that the infamous 80/20 rule applies, where 80% of quality is reached with 20% of effort [53]. This implies that one should not overestimate the possibilities of increasing those quality characteristics with an item banking project, unless rigor is applied through an elaborate approach. Economies of scale and the weight of an achievement test in a programme of study should justify such a rigorous and elaborate approach.

Also, the current study has some resemblance to concept put forward in an article of Winer and Thissen [54]. They put forward empirical data that compared the cost for scoring a test and resulting reliabilities of constructed-response test items versus multiple-choice test items. They coined this the concept of ReliaBuck that represents the ratio between the money needed and the attainment of a particular reliability. Though the model in this paper is not directly focussing on achieving a particular reliability for tests but seeks relative improvements, I believe that the developed model of this study could be an interesting addition to the ReliaBuck concept.

Finally, with respect to the example analysis in Subsect. 2.5, it could be concluded that the assumptions and provided numbers could indeed represent a realistic situation. The chosen workload for developing test items and achievable item discrimination values, as shown in Table 2, can be encountered in practice.

4 Conclusion and Limitations

In this study, a relative simple model for a cost–benefit analysis of developing item banks in higher education is described. An example calculation was developed in which the balance of cost and benefits is worked out using the model. The model is based on classical test theory and some additional variables. In the calculations, the increase in discriminating power of the test items is used to determine the decrease in the numbers of misclassified students. This decrease represents a concrete benefit as a result of an item banking project. Additionally, by assuming a certain level of re-use of developed items, the cost per student can decrease considerably. The approach allows for calculating the effects of various variants and assumptions underlying the item bank development project. Additionally, the findings in the literature of the presented values and assumptions of the example support the realistic value of the worked-out example using the model.

The limitations of this study lie in the fact that the approach is typical for higher education and that use in other contexts might differ. There is for example hardly a need to say that approaches in which item response theory is used with adaptive testing procedures would shed a completely different light on the given cost-benefit question. Even further, the used concept of calculating average test reliabilities using average item test correlations has limitations and cuts quite a number of corners. It requires for example minimum values for the number of test items in a test and item test correlations to yield sensible outcomes. This requires further theoretical and mathematical underpinning. Further, when using classical test theory, the relations between the characteristics of the student population, the quality of education, reliabilities, levels of difficulty and item discrimination values are all dependent on one another. Further research is needed to establish guidelines for minimum values for the number of test items, item discrimination values that would yield practical useful outcomes.

Another limitation is that the effects of providing formative quizzes to support the learning process [55] are not part of the model with respect to re-use or increased passing rates when such quizzes are embedded in the course design [see for example 56, 57]. Such a model could be developed. However, when combining summative and formative goals, consideration should also be given to the problem of item exposure [58]. With item exposure, items become known amongst the student population and, because of that, impact the items classification performance. This would limit the items use for successive summative purposes. For item banking development projects, the suggestion would be to develop separate item banks for summative and formative purposes [6] and fill formative banks with test items from summative banks who show declining performance because of item exposure. Adding interacting variable would increase the complexity of the model, but would be an interesting line of further development.

Further, in the description of the model and its variables, the development and provision of feedback to students has been omitted. Yet, feedback is regarded an important learning tool for students [59, 60] and hence could increase benefits. Developing feedback for test items comes at a cost that might be comparable to the cost of developing the test item itself [18]. Considering the cost and benefits of developing feedback would be an important avenue for further development of the model also.

With respect to the work load of developing test items, the study shows that more research is needed in that area to inform the practice of test item design. In addition, the effects of training and experience of item writers and the effect on development efforts is a domain that is hardly touched upon [17]. Therefore, setting up an empirical study in which the model is used in an actual item banking project is needed to inform the realism of the model and approach. In particular, the question should be studied to what extent different interventions and intensities of test item design effort result in an increase on average item discrimination values.

The implications for practice of this study are important. The study shows that the business case for project plans for developing item banks in higher education can and should incorporate the approach to a cost–benefit analysis as presented in this paper. The approach allows practitioners to improve their business cases and set clearer goals regarding the number and quality of test items a project needs to deliver. In addition, when projects are underway and need evaluation, clearer criteria are present to allow targeted project adjustment (e.g. extra training or stricter development).

In all, further validation of the proposed model in practice is clearly needed, however I believe that this work provides an important first step. A step that can lead to an improved practice for developing item banks in higher education.

References

1. Anderson, S.B.: The role of the teacher-made test in higher education. New Dir. Community Coll. **1987**, 39–44 (1987). https://doi.org/10.1002/cc.36819875907
2. Jozefowicz, R.F., Koeppen, B.M., Case, S.M., Galbraith, R., Swanson, D., Glew, R.H.: The quality of in-house medical school examinations. Acad. Med. **77**, 156–161 (2002)

3. Jugar, R.R.: An inquiry on the roles of personal test item banking (PTIB) and table of specifications (TOS) in the construction and utilization of classroom tests. Int. J. Educ. Res. **1**, 1–8 (2013)
4. Vale, C.D.: Computerized item banking. In: Downing, S.M., Haladyna, T.M. (eds.) Handbook of Test Development. Lawrence Earlbaum Associates, Mahwah (2006)
5. Lane, S., Raymond, M.R., Haladyna, T.M.: Handbook of Test Development. Routledge, New York (2015)
6. Draaijer, S., De Werk, J.: Handboek In 5 stappen naar een itembank [Handbook In 5 steps to an item bank]. SURF (2018)
7. Downing, S.M., Haladyna, T.M.: Test item development: validity evidence from quality assurance procedures. Appl. Meas. Educ. **10**, 61–82 (1997). https://doi.org/10.1207/s15324818ame1001_4
8. Davey, T.: Practical Considerations in Computer-Based Testing. ETS Research and Development Division (2011)
9. Van der Linden, W.J., Glas, C.A.W.: Computerized Adaptive Testing: Theory and Practice. Springer, Dordrecht (2000). https://doi.org/10.1007/0-306-47531-6
10. Rudner, L.M., Guo, F.: Computer adaptive testing for small scale programs and instructional systems. J. Appl. Test. Technol. **12**, 1–12 (2011)
11. Baumeister, H., Abberger, B., Haschke, A., Boecker, M., Bengel, J., Wirtz, M.: Development and calibration of an item bank for the assessment of activities of daily living in cardiovascular patients using Rasch analysis. Health Qual. Life Outcomes **11**, 133 (2013). https://doi.org/10.1186/1477-7525-11-133
12. Attali, Y.: Automatic item generation unleashed: an evaluation of a large-scale deployment of item models. In: Penstein Rosé, C., et al. (eds.) AIED 2018. LNCS (LNAI), vol. 10947, pp. 17–29. Springer, Cham (2018). https://doi.org/10.1007/978-3-319-93843-1_2
13. Gierl, M.J., Haladyna, T.M.: Automatic Item Generation: Theory and Practice. Routledge, New York (2012)
14. Gierl, M.J., Lai, H.: Instructional topics in educational measurement (ITEMS) module: using automated processes to generate test items. Educ. Meas. Issues Pract. **32**, 36–50 (2013)
15. Glas, C.A.W., Van der Linden, W.J.: Computerized adaptive testing with item cloning. Appl. Psychol. Meas. **27**, 247–261 (2003). https://doi.org/10.1177/0146621603027004001
16. Gierl, M.J., Lai, H.: Evaluating the quality of medical multiple-choice items created with automated processes. Med. Educ. **47**, 726–733 (2013). https://doi.org/10.1111/medu.12202
17. Draaijer, S.: Supporting teachers in higher education in designing test items (2016). http://dare.ubvu.vu.nl/handle/1871/54397
18. Hartog, R., Draaijer, S., Rietveld, L.C.: Practical aspects of task allocation in design and development of digital closed questions in higher education. Pract. Assess. Res. Eval. **13**, 2–15 (2008)
19. ETS: How ETS creates test questions. http://www.ets.org/s/understanding_testing/flash/how_ets_creates_test_questions.html
20. Osterlind, S.J.: Constructing Test Items: Multiple-Choice, Constructed-Response, Performance, and Other Formats. Kluwer Academic Publisher, Norwell (1998)
21. Cizek, G.J.: More unintended consequences of high-stakes testing. Educ. Meas. Issues Pract. **20**, 19–27 (2001). https://doi.org/10.1111/j.1745-3992.2001.tb00072.x
22. Haladyna, T.M., Downing, S.M., Rodriguez, M.C.: A review of multiple-choice item-writing guidelines for classroom assessment. Appl. Meas. Educ. **15**, 309–333 (2002). https://doi.org/10.1207/S15324818AME1503_5

23. Gerritsen-van Leeuwenkamp, K.: Het relatieve belang van vijftig kwaliteitskenmerken van toetsing voor studententevredenheid in het hoger beroepsonderwijs [The relative importance of fifty quality indicators for measurement of student satisfaction in higher education] (2012). http://hdl.handle.net/1820/4295

24. Kano, N., Seraku, N., Takahashi, F., Tsuji, S.: Attractive quality and must-be quality. J. Jpn. Soc. Qual. Control **14**, 39–48 (1984)

25. Bloom, B.S.: Taxonomy of Educational Objectives, the Classification of Educational Goals – Handbook I: Cognitive Domain. McKay, New York (1956)

26. Haladyna, T.M.: Writing Test Items to Evaluate Higher Order Thinking. Allyn & Bacon, Needham Heights (1997)

27. Haladyna, T.M.: Developing and Validating Multiple-Choice Test Items. Lawrence Erlbaum Associates, London (2004)

28. Ebel, R.L.: Essentials of Educational Measurement. Prentice-Hall, Englewood Cliffs (1979)

29. De Gruijter, D.N.M.: Toetsing en toetsanalyse [Testing and test analysis]. ICLON, Sectie Onderwijsontwikkeling Universiteit Leiden, Leiden (2008)

30. Olsen, J.B., Bunderson, B.: How to write good test questions [powerpoint presentation] (2004)

31. Spearman, C.: Correlation calculated from faulty data. Br. J. Psychol. **3**(271–295), 1904–1920 (1910). https://doi.org/10.1111/j.2044-8295.1910.tb00206.x

32. Brown, W.: Some experimental results in the correlation of mental abilities. Br. J. Psychol. **1904–1920**(3), 296–322 (1910)

33. Draaijer, S.: Rule of thumb: 40 questions in a 4-choice multiple-choice test. Why? – Draaijer on Assessment and Testing. https://draaijeronassessmentandtesting.wordpress.com/2014/10/23/rule-of-thumb-40-questions-in-a-4-choice-multiple-choice-test-why/

34. Gibson, W.M., Weiner, J.A.: Generating random parallel test forms using CTT in a computer-based environment. J. Educ. Meas. **35**, 297–310 (1998). https://doi.org/10.1111/j.1745-3984.1998.tb00540.x

35. Douglas, K.M.: A general method for estimating the classification reliability of complex decisions based on configural combinations of multiple assessment scores (2007)

36. Eggen, T., Sanders, P.: Psychometrie in de praktijk [Psychometrics in Practice]. Cito Instituut voor Toetsontwikkeling, Arnhem (1993)

37. Rush, B.R., Rankin, D.C., White, B.J.: The impact of item-writing flaws and item complexity on examination item difficulty and discrimination value. BMC Med. Educ. **16**, 250 (2016)

38. Fitzgerald, C.: Risk management: calculating the bottom line of developing a certification or licensure exam (2005). https://www2.caveon.com/2005/02/08/risk-management-calculating-the-bottom-line-of-developing-a-certification-or-licensure-exam/

39. Parshall, C.G., Spray, J.A., Kalohn, J.C., Davey, T.: Practical Considerations in Computer-Based Testing. Springer, New York (2002). https://doi.org/10.1007/978-1-4613-0083-0

40. Downing, S.M.: Construct-irrelevant variance and flawed test questions: do multiple-choice item-writing principles make any difference? Acad. Med. **77**, S103–S104 (2002)

41. Mayenga, C.: Mapping item writing tasks on the item writing ability scale. In: XXXVIIth Annual Conference on Canadian Society of Safety Engineering, Carleton University, Ottawa, Canada (2009)

42. Rodriguez, M.C.: Three options are optimal for multiple-choice items: a meta-analysis of 80 years of research. Educ. Meas. Issues Pract. **24**, 3–13 (2005). https://doi.org/10.1111/j.1745-3992.2005.00006.x

43. Case, S.M., Holtzman, K., Ripkey, D.R.: Developing an item pool for CBT: a practical comparison of three models of item writing. Acad. Med. **76**, S111–S113 (2001)

44. Draaijer, S., Van Gastel, L., Peeters, V., Frinking, P., Reumer, C.: Flexibilisering van Toetsing. [Flexibility in Testing and Assessment]. Digitale Universiteit, Utrecht (2004)
45. Downing, S.M.: Threats to the validity of locally developed multiple-choice tests in medical education: construct-irrelevant variance and construct underrepresentation. Adv. Health Sci. Educ. Theory Pract. **7**, 235–241 (2002). https://doi.org/10.1023/A:1021112514626
46. Tarrant, M., Knierim, A., Hayes, S.K., Ware, J.: The frequency of item writing flaws in multiple-choice questions used in high stakes nursing assessments. Nurse Educ. Pract. **6**, 354–363 (2006). https://doi.org/10.1016/j.nepr.2006.07.002
47. Tarrant, M., Ware, J.: Impact of item-writing flaws in multiple-choice questions on student achievement in high-stakes nursing assessments. Med. Educ. **42**, 198–206 (2008)
48. Downing, S.M.: The effects of violating standard item writing principles on tests and students: the consequences of using flawed test items on achievement examinations in medical education. Adv. Health Sci. Educ. **10**, 133–143 (2005). https://doi.org/10.1007/s10459-004-4019-5
49. Wadi, M.M., Abdul Rahim, A.F., Yusoff, M.S.B., Baharuddin, K.A.: The effect of MCQ vetting on students' examination performance. Educ. Med. J. **6** (2014) https://doi.org/10.5959/eimj.v6i2.216
50. Hassan, S., Simbak, N., Yussof, H.: Structured vetting procedure of examination questions in medical education in faculty of medicine at universiti sultan zainal abidin. Malays. J. Public Health Med. **16**, 29–37 (2016)
51. Nabil Demaidi, M.: Why is the threshold of Point Biserial correlation (item discrimination) in item analysis 0.2? https://www.researchgate.net/post/Why_is_the_threshold_of_Point_biserial_correlation_item_discrimination_in_item_analysis_02
52. Crocker, L., Algina, J.: Introduction to Classical and Modern Test Theory. Holt, Rinehart and Winston, Orlando (1986)
53. Leahy, J.M., Smith, A.: Economics of item development: key cost factors impacting program profitability. Asia ATP (2014)
54. Wainer, H., Thissen, D.: Combining multiple-choice and constructed-response test scores: toward a marxist theory of test construction. Appl. Meas. Educ. **6**, 103 (1993)
55. Karpicke, J.D., Roediger, H.L.: The critical importance of retrieval for learning. Science **319**, 966–968 (2008). https://doi.org/10.1126/science.1152408
56. Roediger, H.L.I., Agarwal, P.K., McDaniel, M.A., McDermott, K.B.: Test-enhanced learning in the classroom: long-term improvements from quizzing. J. Exp. Psychol. Appl. **17**, 382–395 (2011). https://doi.org/10.1037/a0026252
57. Slusser, S.R., Erickson, R.J.: Group quizzes: an extension of the collaborative learning process. Teach. Sociol. **34**, 249–262 (2006). https://doi.org/10.1177/0092055X0603400304
58. Davey, T., Nering, M.: Controlling item exposure and maintaining item security. In: Mills, C.N., Potenza, M.T., Fremer, J.J., Ward, W.C. (eds.) Computer-Based Testing, Building the Foundation for Future Assessments. Lawrence Erlbaum Associates, Mahwah (2002)
59. Hattie, J., Timperley, H.: The power of feedback. Rev. Educ. Res. **77**, 81–112 (2007). https://doi.org/10.3102/003465430298487
60. Butler, M., Pyzdrowski, L., Goodykoontz, A., Walker, V.: The effects of feedback on online quizzes. Int. J. Technol. Math. Educ. **15**, 131–136 (2008)

Advantages of Using Automatic Formative Assessment for Learning Mathematics

Alice Barana[1]($\boxtimes$) ⓘ, Marina Marchisio[2] ⓘ, and Matteo Sacchet[1] ⓘ

[1] Department of Mathematics, Università di Torino, Turin, TO, Italy
{alice.barana,matteo.sacchet}@unito.it
[2] Department of Molecular Biotechnology and Health Sciences,
Università di Torino, Turin, TO, Italy
marina.marchisio@unito.it

Abstract. Automatic Assessment Systems empowered by mathematical engines allow the development of online assignments for Mathematics, which goes beyond multiple-choice modality. Automatically assessed assignments, used with formative purposes, can support teaching and learning from several perspectives, such as conceptual and procedural understanding, metacognition, enactment of adaptive strategies, and teachers' management of the class. This paper reports on an experimentation where automatic assessment has been used in a blended modality according to a model of formative assessment and interactive feedback to enhance learning. The experiment involved a total number of 546 students of 8th grade in the town of Turin (Italy). The use of the automatic assessment is shown and exemplified. Data from learning tests, questionnaire and platform usage are analyzed and used to show the effectiveness of the interactive materials for enhancing mathematical understanding and self-assessment skills. Moreover, a profile of the students who did not use the online opportunities, defined as "reluctant users", is drawn and discussed.

Keywords: Automatic assessment · Formative assessment ·
Mathematics education · Reluctant users · Self-assessment

1 Introduction

In the last decades, national and international directives have largely encouraged the adoption of learning technologies at the school level, prompted by the idea that a stronger technological education will help the future citizens to cope with a digitalized society, to find employment opportunities in a revolutionized industry and to understand the continuous developments that affect our world [1]. Moreover, there are several findings in the research which show that technologies can generate positive effects on students, both from a cognitive and from a metacognitive point of view [2].

One of the features of technology identified as a key promoter of learning, especially in the research in Mathematics Education, is its interactive nature: stimulated by the student's action, a digital tool reacts and returns some information [3]. This kind of feedback, when processed by the learner, can be relevant for several issues, such as fostering deep reflection, putting the learner at the center of the learning process and

© Springer Nature Switzerland AG 2019
S. Draaijer et al. (Eds.): TEA 2018, CCIS 1014, pp. 180–198, 2019.
https://doi.org/10.1007/978-3-030-25264-9_12

helping students become responsible for their learning [4]. Under this perspective, the automatization of feedback can represent a considerable advantage and digital learning materials with automatic assessment can be valuable resources, since they are easily sharable by teachers, accessible by students and they offer interesting learning experiences to improve understanding.

On the students' access to technologies, some issues can be raised that potentially hinder the widespread adoption of digital tools in education. First of all, the equity issue must be taken into account: digital tools should support every student's opportunity to learn fundamental Mathematics, as well as other subjects. Equity mainly involves socio-economic circumstances, but also differences in physical capabilities, gender or teachers' development should not prevent students from getting quality instruction [5]. Secondly, the complexity of the technological tools should be suitable to the students' digital skills: some findings suggest that "digital native" students do not easily transfer their skills in browsing social networks to a fluent use of technologies in a learning context [6]. Lastly, while the use of technology at school is commonly appreciated by the students, there is still a small percentage of pupils that prefer a paper-and-pen approach to learning. The little appreciation of computer-aided instruction seems to be correlated to the dislike of computers in general [7] or to the little perceived usefulness of the learning activities with that particular instrument [8].

This paper deals with the use of automatic assessment to design digital materials for learning Mathematics at lower secondary school. After an overview of the state of the art in the field of digital and automatic assessment in Mathematics, an experimentation on the use of automatic formative assessment in a blended Mathematics course for students of grade 8 is presented. The use of digital assessment by students is analyzed in light of the results of learning tests and of appreciation questionnaires, to the purpose of comparing the results of the students who did use the technologies with those of the students who made little use of the online activities. An analysis of the group of the "reluctant users" of the technology is made in order to understand the reasons for their behavior.

2 Theoretical Framework

2.1 Automatic Formative Assessment

Automatic formative assessment (AFA) in Mathematics is widely used in online courses, with the aim of keeping the learner involved and increasing motivation. Research centers and universities have developed systems that are able to process open-ended answers from a mathematical point of view and to establish if they are equivalent to the correct solutions, in order to widen the possibilities of student interaction with the digital tools. Example of similar Automatic Assessment Systems (AAS) are CALM, developed by the Heriot-Watt University in the programming language of Pascal [9]; STACK, developed by the University of Edinburgh and relying on the Computer Algebra System (CAS) Maxima for its Mathematics capabilities [10]; Moebius Assessment, developed by the University of Waterloo and running on the engine of the Advanced Computing Environment (ACE) Maple [11]. By Exploiting programming languages or mathematical packages, these AASs allow instructors to build interactive worksheets based on algorithms where answers, feedbacks and values are computed over random parameters and can be shown in different representational registers. The use of similar AASs becomes powerful when combined with the principles of formative assessment. According to Black and Wiliam [12], "a practice is formative to the extent that evidence about student achievement is elicited, interpreted, and used by teachers, learners, or their peers, to make decisions about the next steps in instruction that are likely to be better, or better founded, than the decisions they would have taken in the absence of the evidence that was elicited". Among the strategies for enhancing formative assessment, the provision of feedback that moves learners forward is one of the most acknowledged. Hattie and Timperley's [13] definition of feedback conceptualizes it as "information provided by an agent regarding aspects of one's performance or understanding"; they draw a model for designing effective feedback, which should provide relevant information about learning achievements, learning goals and current performance.

Research and experimentations have shown that digital materials which provide a feedback through an AAS empowered by a mathematical engine can be useful under different perspectives, such as learning, problem solving, metacognition, adaptive teaching and teacher's practice.

First of all, they are effective to *enhance learning*. Taking advantage of all the potential of the technology, questions can now be created that could not be replicated with paper and pen, but that stimulate students' cognitive processes. Stacey and Wiliam [5] suggest new solutions for computer-based items where situations or solutions can be explored dynamically; Sangwin [14] shows examples of implicit feedback provided to the student instead of explicit solutions and in relation to their answer, in order to enhance reflection and promote understanding. Questions can be enriched with dynamic images, animations, geometrical visualizations, symbolic manipulations, tables and other features that can be created through the computing environments running behind the ACE, thus offering students experiences of mathematical construction and conceptual understanding [15].

Secondly, they help *master problem solving procedures and strategies*. Beevers and Paterson discuss the use of step-by-step automatically graded resolutions of complex tasks that students are not able to solve on their own [16]. They state that the stepped approach guides learners towards breaking problems into smaller and manageable parts and helps them acquire control over the solving process. Students can thus develop procedural knowledge that, in Mathematics, is strictly connected to conceptual understanding [17]. Adaptive stepping capabilities are supported by several AASs and this area of research flows into studies on adaptive tutoring systems, which are at the most cutting-edge solutions in terms of e-assessment [18].

Third, automatic assessment proves to be useful at a *metacognitive level*. Nicol and Milligan [19] have analyzed e-assessment in the light of seven principles of good feedback practices to promote self-regulation, suggesting several question formats or uses of the online assessment in order to help students become aware of their knowledge, draw abstract concepts out of the examples, reflect on their own mistakes, and set goals for their learning.

Another relevant opportunity offered by interactive materials with AFA is that of *facilitating adaptive teaching strategies*. In fact, formative automatic feedback can work as an online tutor while students attempt the assignments at their own pace; the absence of restriction on the number of attempts allows weaker students to repeat the questions, while their most skillful classmates can put themselves to test with new ones [20]. Data collected by the platform can help teachers monitor learning and adjust instructional strategies accordingly. Moreover, digital interactive materials are particularly helpful for students with learning disabilities: in fact, the organization and presentation of the worksheets, the multimodality and the computing environments enhanced by technology can make up for their cognitive difficulties and motivate them to study.

Lastly, *teachers' work* can benefit from AFA, and not only for the time saved from manual correction. As mentioned above, data collected from the platform inform them about students' understanding and they can be useful to shape teaching and to have a complete picture of the students' gains. Many systems also allow teachers to author their own materials, or to adjust existing ones, and to share their work with colleagues. This permits to overcome dissatisfaction with textbooks and contributes to the development of professional communities and the growth of teachers' competences. Moreover, assignments prepared for one class can be easily reused and transferred to new courses the following years, thus the effort for producing online tests yields advantages and time saved in the future [21].

Using Maple TA AAS, the Department of Mathematics of the University of Turin has designed a model for the automatic formative assessment for STEM (Science, Technology, Engineering and Mathematics) disciplines, based on the following principles [22]:

1. availability of the assignments to the students, who can work at their own pace;
2. algorithm-based questions and answers, so that at every attempt the students are expected to repeat solving processes on different values;
3. open-ended answers, going beyond the multiple-choice modality;
4. immediate feedback, returned to the students at a moment that is useful to identify and correct mistakes;
5. contextualization of problems in the real world, to make tasks relevant to students;
6. interactive feedback, which appears when students give the wrong answer to a problem. It has the form of a step-by step guided resolution, which interactively shows a possible process for solving the task.

The last point recalls Beevers and Paterson's step-by-step approach to problem solving with automatic assessment, but here it is conceptualized in terms of feedback, highlighting the formative function that the sub-questions fulfill for a student who failed the main task. The interactive nature of this feedback and its immediacy prevent students from not processing it, a risk well-known in literature, which causes formative feedback to lose all of its powerful effects [23]. Moreover, students are rewarded with partial grading, which improves motivation [24].

2.2   Reluctant Learners and Reluctant Users

Every teacher, especially at secondary level, have met at least one "reluctant learner" in his or her career. Reluctant learners are those students who achieve low academic results as a consequence of their scarce motivation, self-esteem and low efficacy. They are usually disengaged with school and they do not easily get involved in learning activities; they often end up leaving school without any formal qualification. Since Mathematics is considered one of the hardest disciplines, developing negative aptitudes towards it is rather more common than other subjects [25]. The use of digital learning environments, in particular for formative assessment, is generally considered successful to engage reluctant learners in Mathematics. In fact, the presence of digital and dynamic elements can offer them new ways of engaging with mathematical thinking and of facilitating understanding [26].

In this framework, we propose a distinction between the reluctant *learners*, who are dissatisfied with school, or with Mathematics, in general, and reluctant *users*, who cannot be engaged in the use of learning technologies. In particular, we define "reluctant learners" as those students who make too few attempts to the AFA activities in a course to benefit of their effects on learning, metacognition and self-regulation. They are counterposed to the "active users", who can be actively involved in the online activities. Activity and reluctance here concern only the use of the automatically graded assignments; an a priori relation with learning is not assumed, however, it will be discussed through the following analysis.

3   Research Questions

The Department of Mathematics of the University of Turin (Italy) has been active for years in the research on automatic formative assessment. In light of the theoretical framework illustrated above, the Department has started a research project aimed to study the effectiveness of the learning approach based on the model of AFA and interactive feedback previously developed [22] in Mathematics education at lower secondary level. Our first goal was the study of the effectiveness of the AFA model on the point of view of learning, in order to understand the advantages of using these kinds of online activities for improving learning results. Interesting insights can be drawn from the comparison of an experimental group of classes which uses the AFA with a control group of classes which received traditional instruction, but also from the comparison between active users' and reluctant users' results. Secondly, we were interested in understanding to what extent the reluctant users of the online activities are reluctant learners, and what the reasons are that motivate their scarce use of the AFA.

These purposes led us to the formulation of the following research questions:

1. Are mathematical knowledge, procedural understanding and self-assessment skills influenced by the regular adoption of the formative automatic assessment for learning Mathematics at secondary school level?
2. Who are the reluctant users of the AFA and are there any differences between active and reluctant users in the learning achievements?

In the next paragraphs these research questions will be addressed and discussed through the results of a didactic experimentation.

4 Experimentation and Research Method

4.1 The Experimentation "Educating City"

The didactic experimentation on which this paper focuses is part of a bigger project, called "Educating City" ("Città Educante" in Italian), funded by the National Research Council, with the aim of rethinking the learning processes through the application of the newest advances in educational technologies [27]. Within the project the University of Turin undertook an experiment during the school year 2017/2018, involving 24 classes of 8th grade of 6 different lower secondary schools, with a total amount of 546 students, with their teachers of Mathematics. 13 of these classes (299 students), randomly chosen, formed the test group and they carried on several didactic activities proposed by experts from the Department; the remaining 11 classes (247 students) constituted the control group for the comparison of results. The six schools were located in different areas of Turin; about half of the classes belonged to a low socioeconomic status with a high presence of immigrants' children, while the other half of the sample belonged to a middle-high social class and wealthier families. Of each school, a similar number of classes was inserted in the control group and in the test group, so that the two groups were homogeneous under this point of view.

The classes in the test group had access to an online course with automatically assessed digital materials for revising and learning mathematical contents relevant for the competences to be acquired by the end of 8th grade. The materials were prepared by experts from the University of Turin, after agreeing on the topics with their Mathematics teachers; the online course was then shared with teachers, who were trained on the use of the platform. Teachers could use the interactive materials in class during their lessons and assign the automatically assessed questions as homework. Moreover, a particular relevant topic in Mathematics education for grade 8, that is formulas, symbolic manipulation and modeling, was chosen as didactic goal for the experimentation, and a series of lessons around it were held in collaboration with a PhD student of the Department.

4.2 Instruments

All the students of both test and control classes took a test at the beginning of the school year, an intermediate test halfway through and a final one in June. The initial test was aimed to gain a picture of students' abilities and competence in Mathematics; it was composed of 19 items with different levels of difficulty and varied topics. The test was of an acceptable level of reliability (Cronbach's alpha: 0.773). The intermediate test was mainly focused on symbolic manipulation and modeling, and it was administered before starting that particular module, so that it measured students' prior modeling skills. It was composed of 25 items with different levels of difficulty, all on the same topic; its Cronbach's alpha is 0.800, revealing a high level of internal reliability. The final test aimed to assess high-level mathematical competences that students should develop during the lower secondary school; it was composed of 11 items, all of them rather difficult; its level of reliability is acceptable, considering that the number of items was lower (Cronbach's alpha: 0.652). During the final test students were also asked to fill a self-assessment form after solving the exercises: for each question, they were asked to indicate if they thought that their answer was correct, incorrect or whether they did not know it. All the tests were paper-and-pen based so that students in the test group would not be favored by their experience with the use of the AAS.

At the beginning of the experimentation all the students filled in a questionnaire about their motivation and approach to school in general and to Mathematics in particular; one more questionnaire was distributed only to the test classes at the end of the school year to investigate the appreciation of experimental methodologies. Questionnaires were delivered online that were mainly composed of Likert-scale questions, with a few open questions for comments and explanations.

4.3   The Automatically Assessed Learning Materials

The online course prepared for the experimentation was created in a Moodle platform dedicated to the project (https://cittaeducante.i-learn.unito.it/). The course was organized in 10 modules, corresponding to 10 mathematical topics; an additional initial section included introductory materials and interactive tutorials on how to use the platform and how to insert answers in the online tests. The course was replicated in 13 separated courses so that each class could constitute a virtual community, easily monitored by its teacher. In each section there were two kinds of materials: problems with interactive solutions that teachers could use in class with the IWB (Interactive White Board) and online assignments conceived for students' homework. The latter are the main focus of this paper, while classroom problem solving activities will not be discussed here. Teachers were free to use all the sections that they needed; materials about "formulas and functions", the most considerable section for the topic involved and for the quantity of materials, were compulsory for all the classes in the test group. Working with formulas and functions is one of the most important part of 8th grade Mathematics and it was deeply dealt in the control classes as well. Teachers of the control group were not provided with didactic materials; they were asked to teach their lessons in a traditional way covering all the topics as they usually do with 8th grade classes. Figure 1 shows the homepage of the online course with 10 topic sections and an initial one; Fig. 2 shows the content of one section, with problems and the related automatically graded assignments.

The online assignments were created through Moebius Assessment. The choice of this system is motivated by its powerful assessing capabilities for STEM, long known by the main scientific universities [17] and recently developed with new interactive functionalities and a simple interface that makes it usable even at school level; moreover, it has been successfully adopted by the University of Turin for online courses and in several projects involving secondary schools [28, 29], so that the research group involved in this experimentation has gained deep experience in the technical and methodological use of this AAS.

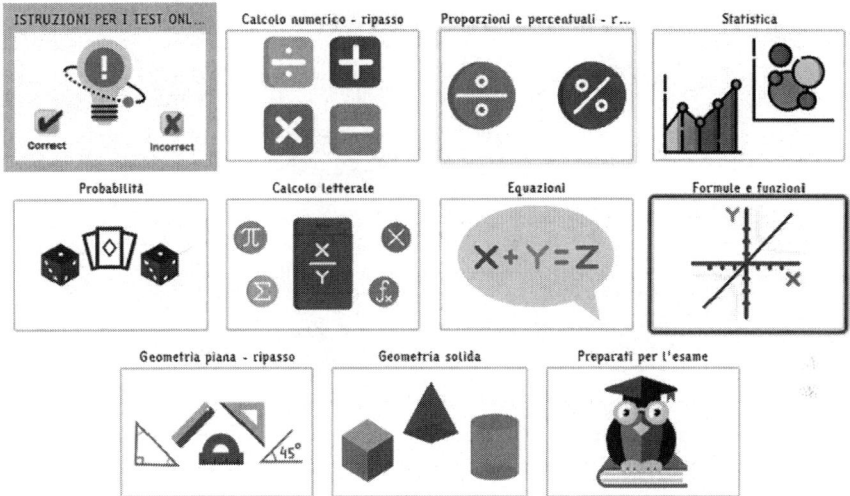

Fig. 1. Online course available to teachers and students of the test group.

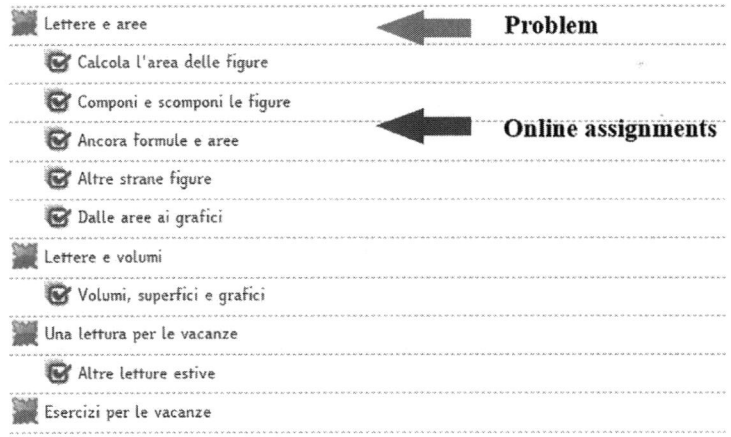

Fig. 2. One section's content

The assignments were created according to the above-mentioned model of formative assessment. Questions involved a mathematical task, which was often contextualized in reality or in another discipline; verbal and symbolic registers were associated with graphical visualizations in two or three dimensions, tabular representations to be completed by students and other interactions that fostered understanding. The feedback was given interactively either after giving the incorrect answer to the main task, or through a series of subtasks that were necessary parts of the procedure that helped students check if their computations were correct before inserting the final answer. As an example, Fig. 3 shows a question where students were guided into drawing a line in the cartesian plane. As a first step they were asked to fill in a table with the coordinates of

We are going to represent the line of equation $y = -2x + 1$ on the Cartesian plane.

Let's start from finding **two** points belonging to the graphic of the line. Two points are sufficient to identify one line.

x	y	
0	1	✓
1	-1	✓

Click on the **Verify** button to check your answer and draw the line.

Attempt 1 of 1   Verify

Now draw the line in the following Cartesian plane. To sketch the line, click on two points of the Cartesian plane.

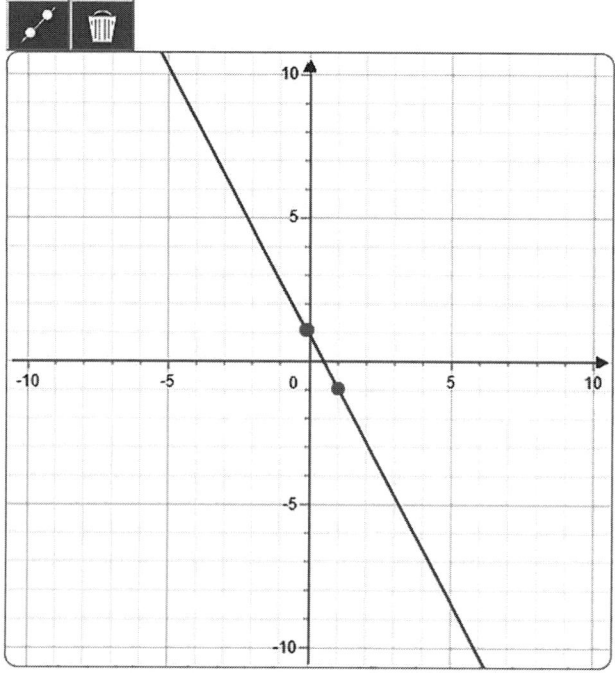

Click on the **Verify** button to check your answer.

Attempt 1 of 1   Verify

Fig. 3. An example of question made through the AAS Maple TA. The Italian text has been translated into English for the paper's comprehension.

two points belonging to the graphic of the line; once they checked that the values were correct, they were asked to interactively draw the line in the cartesian plane. A feedback showing the correct line was then provided to all students after their sketch was graded. At the following attempt, another line with a different equation would be displayed. Each assignment was made up of no more than three questions of this kind, or even only one question if it involved a more complex problem.

4.4 Data Collection

In order to discuss the answers to the research questions, five main sources of data were collected and cross-checked:

1. the percentage of correct answers of the initial, intermediate and final tests returns the information about the learning achievements made by the two groups of students (test and control group);
2. answers from the self-assessment form expressing students' self-assessment skills. For each item, one point was assigned if the student's impression of giving the correct or incorrect answer matched the item's evaluation, while no points were assigned in case it did not match or in case students were unsure of their answers. The sum of the points earned in the whole test was then scaled from 0 to 10;
3. students' answers to the initial questionnaire indicate their motivations to study Mathematics – and to schoolwork in general – before the experimentation;
4. the answers of the test group to the final questionnaire – and in particular to the set of questions about the online assignments – shows students' satisfaction with the online interactive materials;
5. data about the platform usage have been extracted, in particular the number of attempts made and the grades obtained, to analyze the relationship between learning achievements and frequency of usage.

The last point deserves some additional clarifications. For each student, the number of attempts to all the available tests – included repeated attempts to the same tests – was drawn from the platform. Only the fully completed attempts were considered as "attempt", meaning that students requested and obtained feedback and grade. This choice is in line with the value of the formative feedback proposed in this discussion, as we maintain that without automatic grading and interactive feedback, students would not appreciate all the potentialities offered by the system, and this is what makes this assessment different from a traditional one. Thus, all the times students opened a test just to have a look without completing it were not taken into account.

The number of attempts was used to define the two sub-groups of students in the test group: we defined "active users" as those who made at least 5 graded attempts for the assignments in the course, while the students who made less than 5 attempts were defined "reluctant users". The latter represent about 25% of the students in the test group. As active and reluctant users were defined on the basis of the number of accesses to online materials, a parallel definition is not provided for students belonging to the control group, who did not have access to online activities. Data have been analyzed using SPSS 25; the main results and conclusions will be reported in the following paragraphs.

5   Results

The main results of the experimentation are positive, as the students in the test group performed significantly better in the final test than their school-mates in the control group. The mean of the final test results, corrected with the initial test results through covariance analysis, are shown in Table 1. Values are statistically significant ($p = 0.002$). The sample has been restricted to the only students who took both the initial and the final test, being present at school on the days the tests were administered.

Table 1. Corrected means of the final test's results.

	N	Mean	Standard error
Control group	197	43.99	1.185
Test group	255	49.01	1.040

In order to better understand the relationship between active users and reluctant users in the test group with regard to learning gains, the analysis of variance (ANOVA) has been performed on their results in the initial, intermediate and final tests and in the self-assessment of the final test. Results are summarized in Table 2; they include 62 reluctant users and 193 active ones. It emerges that active users performed a little, but not significantly better in the initial and intermediate tests than reluctant users. However, active users performed significantly better in the final test and in the self-assessment of the final test. Given the similarity in the initial results, it is not possible to reach the conclusion that reluctant users were initially weaker than their active class-mates; the regular use of the automatic formative assessment, however, led to higher learning achievements and to more effective self-assessment skills.

Table 2. Comparison between learning results of reluctant and active users.

		Reluctant users	Active users	p-value
Initial test	Average	36.94	42.51	0.060
	St. dev.	19.26	19.12	
Intermediate test	Average	55.41	59.85	0.091
	St. dev.	17.07	16.37	
Final test	Average	43.16	49.13	0.049
	St. dev.	18.20	20.21	
Self-assessment	Average	3.64	4.47	0.011
	St. dev.	2.09	2.13	

An analysis on the platform usage leads to affirm that the questions implemented with automatic assessment according to the above-mentioned educational models were effective under several points of view. The number of attempts that students made to any test is, on average, 15.81; this value obviously grows when considering only active users (average: 20.76). Active students attempted the same assignments an average rate of 1.75 times, which means that they have generally made more than one attempt to the online quizzes. The feedback gained with the automatic assessment has been used to improve the performance in subsequent attempts, where tasks were repeated with different numerical values, functions, and geometrical figures which varied algorithmically. This can be statistically shown using the assignments results from the platform, comparing the average score of students' first assignment attempts with the average score of their last attempt. Active students' results grew from an average value of 51.97 at their first attempts to 60.25 at their last attempts (values are expressed in percentage of correct answer); a pairwise t-test shows that the difference is statistically significant ($p < 0.001$). It is interesting to notice that the average grade of the first attempts made by reluctant users (49.76), is similar to that of active students: the ANOVA test shows that there is no statistically significant difference between the two means ($p = 0.524$). This fact confirms what emerged from the initial and intermediate tests, namely that reluctant users were not initially weaker than active users in terms of learning. However, in the platform, like in the learning tests, reluctant users did not improve their results: the average of their last attempts increased only of 2.15 points out of 100, rising up to 51.91, while the average active users' grade increased by 8.28 points out of 100, rising up to 60.25. The difference in the improvements between the two groups can be seen as a consequence of the time spent in the use of the online assignments: reluctant users' average rate of attempts per assignment is 1.22. Table 3 summarizes the statistics on the platform usage for active and reluctant users.

Table 3. Comparison of data from platform usage between active and reluctant users.

		Reluctant users	Active users	p-value
Number of attempts	Average	1.48	20.76	<0.001
	St. dev.	1.52	15.63	
Rate of attempts per test	Average	1.22	1.75	0.001
	St. dev.	0.43	0.90	
Average of the first attempts	Average	49.76	51.97	0.524
	St. dev.	24.90	18.49	
Average of the last attempts	Average	51.91	60.25	0.016
	St. dev.	22.82	18.80	

The improvements registered through the platform suggest that the automatic assessment format helped students develop problem solving strategies, acquire procedural understanding, identify and correct their mistakes. The answers of active users to the final questionnaire support this hypothesis: they affirmed that it was useful to visualize the feedback immediately after giving the answer, and in particular it helped them understand how to solve a task; step-by-step guided resolutions were useful to understand the solving process. Their answers are compared with the reluctant users' ones, which are lower, as expected. Interestingly, ANOVA results show that, between the two groups, there is no statistically significative difference neither in the appreciation of AFA as a support to study, nor in the effectiveness of AFA to raise the awareness of one's capabilities, while the main differences in appreciation are due to the ability of the system to help learn a method to solve problems. It means that reluctant users acknowledged the potential of the automatic assessment; anyway, the effectiveness of the system to learn problem solving strategies could actually be appreciated only after multiple attempts and after an adequate time spent on online homework. The data are summarized in Table 4.

Table 4. Active users' answers to questions about automatic assessment in the final questionnaire. Answers are in a Likert scale from 1 (lowest value) to 5 (highest value).

		Active users	Reluctant users	p-value
It is useful to visualize the correct answer immediately after giving a response	Av.	4.29	3.93	0.047
	S.D.	0.89	0.91	
The immediate assessment helped me understand how to answer the questions	Av.	4.16	3.77	0.042
	S.D.	0.95	0.97	
Problems with step-by-step guided resolution helped me understand how to solve the exercises	Av.	3.91	3.47	0.025
	S.D.	0.96	1.01	
Online assignments helped me learn to solve problems autonomously	Av.	3.34	2.83	0.015
	S.D.	1.00	1.08	
Online tests are a valid support for studying	Av.	3.62	3.43	0.362
	S.D.	0.99	1.07	
Online assignments helped me acquire awareness of my preparation	Av.	3.69	3.43	0.20
	S.D.	0.99	1.00	

Students' appreciation of the automatic assessment is confirmed by their answers to the open question "Why do you think that online tests are useful for learning Mathematics?". Examples of comments repeated in the answers collected are the following:

- "I appreciated the fact that the exercises were on the computer, which made them more interesting. In my opinion, giving an evaluation to each exercise pushed me to put more effort in my homework and to improve my results."
- "They are useful because if you give an incorrect answer you can try it again, while you cannot do the same on the book".
- "The online exercises are useful because you can access them whenever you need. Also, the problems that gave the correct solution immediately after your answer were excellent, since you could understand the solving process and try them again with different data."
- "In my opinion, they are useful because they help you understand the topic, and the presence of figures and graphs helped you better understand the task."

As using the automatic assessment provides such good effects on learning, it seems a pity that there were students who missed this opportunity and barely opened the online assignments. Data collected during the experimentation help understand who the reluctant users are. As emerged above, reluctant users do not coincide with reluctant learners, in fact their initial learning achievements were not significantly far from the active users' ones. We supposed that students who made little use of the online platform had a preference for a paper-and-pen learning approach, so we analyzed their answers to the question inserted in the final questionnaire: "do you prefer doing computer-based or paper-based homework?", to which students could chose one of the two options. It turned out that the 60% of active users opted for "computer-based homework", while 45% of reluctant users made the same choice (Cramer's V: 0.117, p-value: 0.11). This means that, among reluctant users, there is a slight preference for a paper-and-pen learning style, but it does not explain the difference in the platform's usage. At least, the 45% of reluctant users who stated that they preferred using the computer for doing their homework, actually did not do it.

We investigated reluctant users' general approach to learning through their answers to the initial questionnaire, provided in a Likert scale from 1 (strongly disagree) to 4 (strongly agree) and displayed in Table 5. It emerges that they are as aware as active users of the importance of studying Mathematics for their educational and professional future; however, they do not appreciate the subject per se as much as their classmates (Cramer's V: 0.22, p = 0.006). Some differences emerge in the extent to which they appreciate the way Mathematics is taught at school: reluctant users are slightly less willing to attend Mathematics lessons. They are aware that good results depend on their dedication to the same extent of their classmates, they arrive at school with their homework done, however they work less hard on their homework and they usually do not help their friends with homework as much as active students (Cramer's V: 0.24, p = 0.002). There are no statistically significant differences in questions asking about their attitude towards problem solving, even though reluctant users seem to be a little less persistent in problem solving.

Table 5. Answers of reluctant and active users to questions of the initial questionnaire, given in a Likert scale from 1 (strongly disagree) to 4 (strongly agree).

		Reluctant users	Active users	Cramer's V (p-value)
Mathematics is an important subject as it will be useful for my future studies	Av.	3.43	3.46	0.15 (0.093)
	S.D.	0.61	0.75	
It is worth working hard in Mathematics because it will be useful for my professional future	Av.	3.46	3.51	0.14 (0.167)
	S.D.	0.53	0.66	
I'm looking forward to having Mathematics lessons	Av.	2.20	2.45	0.151 (0.116)
	S.D.	0.73	0.81	
I study Mathematics because I like it	Av.	2.58	2.74	0.22 (0.006)
	S.D.	0.83	0.88	
If I work hard, I can be successful in Mathematics	Av.	3.42	3.42	0.086 (0.595)
	S.D.	0.68	0.66	
I finish all my Mathematics homework before the lessons	Av.	2.94	2.94	0.073 (0.716)
	S.D.	0.97	1.03	

(*continued*)

Table 5. (*continued*)

		Reluctant users	Active users	Cramer's V (p-value)
I work hard on my Mathematics homework	Av.	2.69	2.94	0.148 (0.129)
	S.D.	0.79	0.69	
I help my friends in Mathematics	Av.	1.89	2.29	0.244 (0.002)
	S.D.	0.89	0.86	
I get easily discourage when I try to solve a problem	Av.	2.52	2.32	0.107 (0.565)
	S.D.	1.17	1.14	
I put aside difficult problems	Av.	2.45	2.20	0.145 (0.246)
	S.D.	1.25	1.04	

Sociocultural factors did not affect students' usage of the automatic assessment: the percentage of reluctant users is similar and even lower in schools located in areas with low socioeconomic conditions (24%) than in wealthy areas (27.1%).

Summing it up, the picture of the reluctant users emerging from data is that of students who are not lacking talents or economic conditions for accessing the platform or performing well; they are conscious that school is important even though they do not like Mathematics. This lack of inner motivation could be linked to the scarce effort they put in studying. An important element of distinction of reluctant users from the general reluctant learners is their acknowledgement that school success depends on their effort in studying. It is interesting that they hardly help their friends with Mathematics: associated to the fact that they complete their homework without working hard on it, it suggests that they are mainly the students who are usually helped by others or even copy their homework, a thing that becomes nearly impossible with an online system. This insight was also confirmed by teachers' opinions collected through a focus group at the end of the experimentation: they affirmed that the online work was really appreciated by the weakest students with learning disorders or little self-awareness; it was useful for skilled students to improve even more, however the most undisciplined and lazy students did not seize the opportunities given by digital tools, they worked very little on the platform, just like they did with paper-and-pen homework.

6 Main Conclusions and Implications for Research and Practice

This study has several limitations that hinder the generalization of the results: numbers are significative, but not that high; moreover, all the participants come from the same city in Italy: regional differences are not taken into account in this study. However, it offers some interesting insights that deserve to be deepened in future research.

The data collected in the experimentation help answer the research questions: (1) Are mathematical knowledge, procedural understanding and self-assessment skills influenced by the regular adoption of the formative automatic assessment for learning Mathematics at secondary school level? and (2) Who are the reluctant users of the AFA and are there any differences between active and reluctant users in the learning achievements?

Regarding the first research question, it resulted that the immediate feedback, given at the right time and in an interactive way, helps students master a process for solving mathematical tasks and find problem solving strategies. In fact, when students repeated the exercises with similar tasks but different data, they improved their grades, as shown in the analysis before (Table 3). This finding is rather in disagreement with many findings in literature, which show that students pay little attention to feedback information and consequently do not use it to improve [30]; in this study, the key strength was the interactivity of the feedback, which managed to engage students in processing the information. Enhancements in understanding also emerged from the comparison of initial and final tests, compared with other students in similar conditions who did not use the platform. The gains involve not only mathematical knowledge, but also metacognitive factors, self-assessment skills above all. This fact emerged clearly from the performance in the self-evaluation of the final test of students that regularly used the automatic assessment, when compared with that of students who rarely worked on the platform. Hence, we have positively answered the first research question: mathematical knowledge, procedural understanding and self-assessment skills are positively influenced by the regular adoption of the formative automatic assessment for learning Mathematics at secondary school level.

Regarding the second research question, through an analysis of the data usage, we have selected a group of students who made few or no attempts with the online assignments and we defined them "reluctant users", opposed to the "active users". Data show that students that did not take advantage of this chance did not improve in learning as much as their classmates. Their profile can be inferred from their answers to the initial questionnaire, thus answering the second research questions. Reluctant users are basically students who put little effort in school in general, and who dislike Mathematics in particular. Economic disadvantages or learning disorders did not prevent students from working in the online courses, as reluctant users' social distribution and their initial results show. Some of them prefer a paper-based approach to learning, but it is not the main reason why they did not use the technologies.

The results of this experimentation lead to consider other aspects of the integration of the automatic assessment in Mathematics courses at school level. First of all, teachers need to be prepared to carry out this step. The materials included in the online course presented in this paper were all designed and developed by university researchers, who are expert both in the technical use of the platform and in didactic methodologies for teaching and learning Mathematics. The teachers who participated to the experimentation, satisfied with the impact of this kind of technology in their classes, started a training aimed at making them autonomous in authoring digital materials of this kind. For a similar training to be effective, teachers should have constant support by expert tutors, and inner motivation to change their teaching method. All the online activities, which resulted to be successful in delivering learning, have been made available to all the Italian teachers through the national project "Problem Posing and Solving", supported by the Italian Ministry of Education, where didactic methodologies and technologies as the automatic formative assessment are proposed and used by teachers supported by tutors [21]. Moreover, the results of this experimentation gave prompts to the research on adaptive assessment about which the department of

Mathematics of the University of Turin is very active [31, 32]. The main output of this research is the design of an automatic system that provides students with questions according to their level of competence, choosing them among a database of shared items appositely clustered. Our hope is to broaden the set of good experiences and examples of learning through technologies by means of the cooperation of research, training and practice, in order to offer more and more students effective opportunities of education.

References

1. World Economic Forum: Eight Futures of Work. Scenarios and their Implications (2018)
2. Drijvers, P., Ball, L., Barzel, B., Heid, M.K., Cao, Y., Maschietto, M.: Uses of Digital Technology in Lower Secondary Mathematics Education: A Concise Topical Survey. Springer, New York (2016). https://doi.org/10.1007/978-3-319-33666-4
3. Olive, J., Makar, K.: Mathematical Knowledge and Practices Resulting from Access to Digital Technologies. In: Hoyles, C., Lagrange, J.-B. (eds.) Mathematics Education and Technology-Rethinking the Terrain. NISS, vol. 13, pp. 133–178. Springer, New York (2010). https://doi.org/10.1007/978-1-4419-0146-0_8
4. Heid, M.K.: The technological revolution and the reform of school mathematics. Am. J. Educ. **106**(1), 5–61 (1997). https://doi.org/10.1086/444175
5. Stacey, K., Wiliam, D.: Technology and assessment in mathematics. In: Clements, M., Bishop, A., Keitel, C., Kilpatrick, J., Leung, F. (eds.) Third International Handbook of Mathematics Education. SIHE, vol. 27, pp. 721–751. Springer, New York (2013). https://doi.org/10.1007/978-1-4614-4684-2_23
6. ECDL Foundation: The Fallacy of the 'Digital Native': Why Young People Need to Develop their Digital Skills (2014)
7. Mitra, A., Steffensmeier, T.: Changes in student attitudes and student computer use in a computer-enriched environment. J. Res. Comput. Educ. **32**(3), 417–433 (2000)
8. Armstrong, D.A.: Students' perceptions of online learning and instructional tools: a qualitative study of undergraduate students use of online tools. Turk. Online J. Educ. Technol. **10**(3), 222–226 (2011)
9. Beevers, C.E., Cherry, B.S.G., Clark, D.E.R., Foster, M.G., McGuire, G.R., Renshaw, J.H.: Software tools for computer-aided learning in mathematics. Int. J. Math. Educ. Sci. Technol. **20**(4), 561–569 (1989)
10. Sangwin, C.: Computer aided assessment of mathematics using STACK. In: Cho, S.J. (ed.) Selected Regular Lectures from the 12th International Congress on Mathematical Education, pp. 695–713. Springer, Cham (2015). https://doi.org/10.1007/978-3-319-17187-6_39
11. Barana, A., Marchisio, M., Rabellino, S.: Automated assessment in mathematics. In: Proceedings of 2015 IEEE 39th Annual Computer Software and Applications Conference, pp. 670–671. IEEE, Taichung (2015). https://doi.org/10.1109/COMPSAC.2015.105
12. Black, P., Wiliam, D.: Developing the theory of formative assessment. Educ. Assess. Eval. Account. **21**(1), 5–31 (2009)
13. Hattie, J., Timperley, H.: The power of feedback. Rev. Educ. Res. **77**(1), 81–112 (2007)
14. Sangwin, C., Makar, K., Cazes, C., Lee, A., Wong, K.L.: Micro-level automatic assessment sup-ported by digital technologies. In: Hoyles, C., Lagrange, J.-B. (eds.) Mathematics Education and Technology-Rethinking the Terrain. NISS, vol. 13, pp. 227–250. Springer, New York (2010). https://doi.org/10.1007/978-1-4419-0146-0_10

15. Paiva, R.C., Ferreira, M.S., Mendes, A.G., Eusébio, A.M.J.: Interactive and multimedia contents associated with a system for computer-aided assessment. J. Educ. Comput. Res. **52**(2), 224–256 (2015)
16. Beevers, C.E., Paterson, J.S.: Automatic assessment of problem solving skills in mathematics. Act. Learn. High Educ. **4**(2), 1–14 (2003)
17. Bokhove, C., Drijvers, P.: Digital tools for algebra education: criteria and evaluation. Int. J. Comput. Math. Learn. **15**(1), 45–62 (2010)
18. Helder, E., Sosnovsky, S., Dimitrova, V.: Adaptive intelligent learning environments. In: Duval, E., Sharples, M., Sutherland, R. (eds.) Technology Enhanced Learning: Research Themes, pp. 109–114. Springer, New York (2017). https://doi.org/10.1007/978-3-319-02600-8_10
19. Nicol, D., Milligan, C.: Rethinking technology-supported assessment practices in relation to the seven principles of good feedback practice. In: Innovative Assessment in Higher Education, pp. 1–14. Taylor and Francis Group Ltd., London (2006)
20. Barana, A., Fioravera, M., Marchisio, M., Rabellino, S.: Adaptive teaching supported by ICTs to reduce the school failure in the project "Scuola Dei Compiti". In: Proceedings of 2017 IEEE 41st Annual Computer Software and Applications Conference (COMPSAC), pp. 432–437. IEEE (2017). https://doi.org/10.1109/COMPSAC.2017.44
21. Brancaccio, A., Marchisio, M., Palumbo, C., Pardini, C., Patrucco, A., Zich, R.: Problem posing and solving: strategic italian key action to enhance teaching and learning mathematics and informatics in the high school. In: Proceedings of 2015 IEEE 39th Annual Computer Software and Applications Conference, pp. 845–850. IEEE (2015)
22. Barana, A., Conte, A., Fioravera, M., Marchisio, M., Rabellino, S.: A model of formative automatic assessment and interactive feedback for STEM. In: Proceedings of 2018 IEEE 42nd Annual Computer Software and Applications Conference (COMPSAC), pp. 1016–1025. IEEE (2018). https://doi.org/10.1109/COMPSAC.2018.00178
23. Sadler, D.R.: Formative assessment and the design of instructional systems. Instr. Sci. **18**(2), 119–144 (1989)
24. Beevers, C.E., Wild, D.G., McGuine, G.R., Fiddes, D.J., Youngson, M.A.: Issues of partial credit in mathematical assessment by computer. Res. Learn. Technol. **7**(1), 26–32 (1999)
25. Sanacore, J.: Turning reluctant learners into inspired learners. Clear. House **82**(1), 40–44 (2008)
26. Calder, N., Campbell, A.: Using mathematical apps with reluctant learners. Digit. Exp. Math. Educ. **2**(1), 50–69 (2016)
27. Barana, A., Boffo, S., Gagliardi, F., Marchisio, M.: Problem Posing & Solving: a Digital Way to Learn Mathematics (in press)
28. Barana, A., Bogino, A., Fioravera, M., Marchisio, M., Rabellino, S.: Open platform of self-paced MOOCs for the continual improvement of academic guidance and knowledge strengthening in tertiary education. J. E-Learn. Knowl. Soc. **13**(3), 109–119 (2017). https://doi.org/10.20368/1971-8829/1383
29. Barana, A., Marchisio, M., Miori, R.: MATE-BOOSTER: design of an e-learning course to boost mathematical competence. In: Proceedings of the 11th International Conference on Computer Supported Education (CSEDU 2019), pp. 280–291 (2019)
30. Timmers, C., Veldkamp, B.: Attention paid to feedback provided by a computer-based assessment for learning on information literacy. Comput. Educ. **56**(3), 923–930 (2011)

31. Marchisio, M., Di Caro, L., Fioravera, M., Rabellino, S.: Towards adaptive systems for automatic formative assessment in virtual learning communities. In: Proceedings of 2018 IEEE 42nd Annual Computer Software and Applications Conference (COMPSAC), pp. 1000–1005. IEEE (2018). https://doi.org/10.1109/COMPSAC.2018.00176
32. Barana, A., Di Caro, L., Fioravera, M., Marchisio, M., Rabellino, S.: Ontology development for competence assessment in virtual communities of practice. In: Penstein Rosé, C., et al. (eds.) AIED 2018. LNCS (LNAI), vol. 10948, pp. 94–98. Springer, Cham (2018). https://doi.org/10.1007/978-3-319-93846-2_18

Getting to Grips with Exam Fraud: A Qualitative Study Towards Developing an Evidence Based Educational Data Forensics Protocol

Christiaan J. van Ommering[1(✉)], Sebastiaan de Klerk[1(✉)], and Bernard P. Veldkamp[2(✉)]

[1] Xquiry (eX:plain), Disketteweg 6, 3821 AR Amersfoort, The Netherlands
{c.vommering,s.dklerk}@explain.nl
[2] Department of Research Methodology, Measurement and Data Analysis, Faculty of Behavioral Sciences, University of Twente, P.O. 217, 7500 AE Enschede, The Netherlands
b.p.veldkamp@utwente.nl

Abstract. This design research was focused on developing standards covering the entire process of examination to limit the chances of security risks (e.g., the prevention of exam fraud as much as possible, and detection by means of data forensics), together these standards form the Educational Data Forensics Protocol. Two research questions guided this study. The first question was, which standards regarding preventing and detecting fraud in the process of examination need to be included into the EDF protocol? In addition, practitioners must be able to act on indications of exam fraud based on these standards. Therefore, a second research question was formulated, namely which conditions must be considered during development of the EDF protocol to support practitioners in detecting possible gaps in the security of their examination process?

The EDF protocol was developed and validated in five consecutive steps. This study analyses on the theoretical base of developing the EDF protocol (*Step 1*) and the considerations for developing a prototype (*Step 2*). The prototype was being validated (e.g., establishing correctness of the content) through seven semi-structured interviews with content experts in the field of either test security or data forensics (*Step 3*). Statements from these interviews were used to adjust the prototype into a final version of the EDF protocol (*Step 4*). Finally, to determine the practical value, the final version of the EDF protocol was used to flag gaps in the security of the exam process and determine possible security risks for one of eX:plain's exam programs (*Step 5*).

Keywords: Data forensics · Academic integrity · Test security · Exam fraud

1 Introduction

1.1 Problem Description

In education, performance is measured mainly by using grades. These grades appear to have a major impact on student lives by means of pressure to perform well, and being

© Springer Nature Switzerland AG 2019
S. Draaijer et al. (Eds.): TEA 2018, CCIS 1014, pp. 199–218, 2019.
https://doi.org/10.1007/978-3-030-25264-9_13

concerned about failing [1]. Hence, cheating reflects the need to get passing grades, especially considering high-stakes testing. Over the last two decades, interest in exploring ways of detecting and preventing cheating, fraud, or (test) misconduct in education has been growing. Literature provides separate definitions, due to this diversity it can be difficult to make a clear distinction between these terms. In all cases (i.e., cheating, fraud or misconduct) they refer to the intention of deliberately influencing (parts of) the examination process with the aim of obtaining a different result on the exam or for personal gain. Rather than try to define these terms separately, this definition applies when these terms are used alternately in this study.

McCabe [2] reported that 26% of the students admitted to cheat during test taking back in 1961, this percentage increased to 52% in 1991. In a 1999 study 75% of students admitted to cheat during tests. In similar fashion, based on a longitudinal research [3], reported an increase in cheating over the last decades, while they also found that the severity of individuals perceived dishonest behavior has decreased. Although this research is outdated, it does show a certain trend in behavior. In fact, in a more recent study, both Novotney [4] and Witherspoon, Maldonado and Lacey [5] state that students whom cheat during college are also more likely to partake in other unethical behavior, for example cheat on their spouse, and cheat at work. Although prevalence numbers on cheating differ amongst research findings, ranging from 50% to 95% [1, 2, 5, 6, 24], there seems to be consensus in the fact that cheating is a growing problem in contemporary education.

In similar fashion, Computer-Based Testing (CBT) is becoming a more popular administration mode for examination. CBT is particularly popular with standardized testing, because of its operational advantages [7]. Although CBT provides many advantages in terms of testing and analyzing the test data, it also comes with new security risks, for example the ability to obtain and share test information [7, 8]. Fortunately, next to the technological progress that brought CBT, also various methods are the topic of research in detecting cheating, for example (educational) data forensics [8, 9].

Educational Data Forensics (EDF) offers a promising opportunity to detect cheating behavior, for example by looking at aberrant response patterns, response time, and suspicious test results on individual levels as well as group level by comparing test results to prior examinations. Despite these advantages on the levels of securing the examination program, analyzing examinees' behavior and the exam results, it is important to proceed with caution when using data forensics. Mainly because few studies report on the practical use and the reliability of data forensic methods [10]. Therefore, caution is advised in terms of decision making, for example. After all, data forensic indices provide indications of potential fraud rather than detect actual fraud. Therefore, the results of data forensics analysis should lead to further investigations (e.g., discuss possible irregularities during examination), rather than sanctioning an examinee based on the results. The number of high-stakes testing programs that use data forensics is growing, due to the increasingly popular idea that it is essential to act on evidence of test misbehavior to protect the validity of test programs [11]. These aberrant patterns may not always be caused by exam fraud, which stress the demand for reliable and accurate data forensics to detect aberrant patterns.

Two questions rise from the promising prospect of using data forensics to detect potential misconduct during the process of examination; can we be sure that indications of cheating are based on flawless and validated data forensics, and can we be sure students are not innocently accused of fraud? These questions support the vital need for an evidence based protocol when it comes to detecting and indicating misconduct after analyzing exam data. Detecting fraud remains an extremely difficult endeavor [8]. While some students who get accused of cheating acknowledge it, many do not [12]. Therefore, it is the responsibility of testing agencies, such as eX:plain, to stay aware of the latest developments in terms of how test takers cheat, and can react on that with fitting responses, to preserve the integrity of examination standards [12].

To that aim, eX:plain started a data forensics project (called Xquiry) involving both fixed and randomized exams. In fixed exams, all examinees are presented with the same set of questions. For randomized CBT, the questions are randomly drawn from an item bank, and the answers are presented in randomized order. In practice this means that a group of examinees answer completely different sets of items. In collaboration with the University of Twente, eX:plain developed a data forensics monitor (DFM). The DFM is an online web application that can analyze large amounts of data using multiple data forensic indices. Van Noord [10] reported, by means of an experimental study, on the validity of the data forensics monitor. The DFM flagged 38% of potential cheaters with a reliability of 97%. As far as the usability of the DFM is concerned, these findings are promising. However, what remains unanswered is the question if we, to some extent, can prevent cheating from happening, and what the follow-up steps should be when cheating is detected by means of the DFM.

Therefore, the current study is considered a follow-up on the experimental study by Van Noord [10]. The aim of this study was to provide evidence based security standards, in the form of an EDF protocol for preventing, detecting and acting on indications of exam fraud. In practice, this protocol should be able to be implemented, both with and without the application of the data forensics monitor. The educational data forensics protocol can be regarded as an audit on the safety and fraud resistance of the exam and/or exam process. This audit shows possible security gaps and provides the user with practical guidelines to act, hence preventing misconduct in the future. To determine the practical value, the EDF protocol was validated through interviews with experts from the field and subsequently implemented at one of eX:plains exam programs.

1.2 Educational Data Forensics Protocol

The EDF protocol is a quality assurance system, validated by content experts, which is aimed at prevention (i.e., the prevention of exam fraud as much as possible) and detection of exam fraud. Although exam fraud can never be fully banned, the protocol provides security standards to limit the chance of exam fraud. These standards can be used to determine whether there is a security risk (e.g., a high, medium, or low security risk). That is why the interaction with the EDF monitor is of the utmost importance, because it can highlight fraud trends and possible security gaps. By using the EDF protocol, based on scientifically based standards, gaps in the exam security can be detected [13].

The standards in the EDF protocol that relate to the prevention of exam fraud can be divided into two categories, namely physical and technological standards. Physical standards relate to how candidates enter the examination room, what kind of materials they can bring, and what precautions are taken against (technological) aids etc. The technological standards have an ICT technical impact. This relates to test construction (test items), the way items are manufactured and exchanged between test experts, and how an item bank is secured etc. In terms of detecting exam fraud, the EDF protocol standards can also be divided into physical and technological standards. Surveillance during exams, and the detections of unwanted objects in the examination room are examples concerning physical standards. The technological standards are mainly based on the EDF monitor [13].

1.3 Research Question and Model

This research was focused on developing standards covering the entire process of examination in order to limit the chances of security risks (e.g., the prevention of exam fraud as much as possible, and detection by means of data forensics). Accordingly, the corresponding research question was:

1. Which standards regarding preventing and detecting exam fraud in the process of examination need to be included into the EDF protocol?

   In addition, practitioners should be able to act on indications of exam fraud based on these standards, this study therefore also answered a second research question:

2. Which conditions must be considered during development of the EDF protocol to support practitioners in detecting possible gaps in the security of their examination process?

1.4 Scientific and Practical Relevance

What makes writing an EDF protocol a challenging endeavor lies in the fact that this is unchartered territory. So far, data forensics had only been used in analyzing fixed examinations. Xquiry however, like mentioned before, only just determined the validity of their fraud indices by means of an experimental study on randomized exams. Exam fraud is a serious threat to the validity of the exam. Most examination organizations put a lot of time, money and effort into developing reliable exams. However, the time, money and effort invested into fraud prevention and especially detection is often very little. Even though this is a vital part of ensuring exam validity. Therefore, a practical and evidence based protocol for fraud prevention and detection is indispensable for practitioners to guarantee the quality of the exam. This study aims to provide an in-depth understanding of factors to prevent, detect, and act on indications of exam fraud and thereby add to the examination practice.

2 Method

The EDF protocol was constructed and validated in five consecutive steps: (I) a literature search relating relevant standards and criteria on security of the examination process, and also prevention and detection of exam misconduct; (II) development of the

EDF protocol prototype; (III) validation of the prototype standards and criteria through semi-structured interviews with content experts; (IV) adjustment of the prototype towards a final version of the EDF protocol; and (V) empirical testing of the protocol by putting the protocol to practice.

2.1   Step 1 - Literature Search

For the first step the PRISMA framework [14] was used for conducting the literature review. To compile an evidence base for the development of the EDF protocol, three major databases were searched: Scopus, Web of Science, and Google Scholar.

For the main topic of the study several search terms were used (see Table 1). Boolean search operators were also used during this step (e.g., AND, OR, NOT, and *). The initial search findings were thinned through excluding duplicates. Hereafter, the articles were first screened on title, and secondly the abstract. Articles were included in the study if the main topic of the paper or chapter related to security of examination, or if the paper or chapter provided a structured set of guidelines or standards on security of examination. This method not only summarized existing literature, but also aimed to generalize and transfer findings for policy making and practice [15]. Prior to the development of the EDF prototype, an overview was made of the most important findings from the literature review. These insights were used to develop an EDF prototype.

Table 1. Search terms used in the literature search

Keywords	Related/more specific/broader
Test security	Educat*, Prevention, Detection, Standards, Fraud, Cheating
Data forensics	Educat*, Fraud, Cheating

2.2   Step 2 - Developing an EDF-Protocol Prototype

Based on the literature findings, a consultation with the scientific advisor and manager of Xquiry was organized in order to ensure that development was in line with their goals and expectations. The insights gathered in the consultation were used in the development of the prototype standards, as well as a corresponding grading system. This initial prototype was again discussed during consultation with the Xquiry team. The intention was to make the standards (concerning prevention of misconduct during the process of examination) as complete as possible before starting the interviews. The insights gathered in the literature search were used in the development of the first set of standards of the prototype (Part A), as well as a corresponding grading system. The intention was to make the standards (concerning prevention of misconduct during the process of examination) as complete as possible before starting the interviews.

The development of part B (i.e. the standards and criteria for detection of misconduct by means of using data forensics) took more time and effort. Although there is a considerable amount of scientific literature on the possibilities of using data forensics, research is mostly focused on case- or compare studies, and thus often lacking proper directions for practical implementation. The intention with this part of the prototype was therefore to enter the interviews more open minded, hence gain insight on what the content experts deem to be included or excluded in terms of data forensic standards.

During this step a deliberate choice was made for a distinction between a set of standards for prevention as well as a set of standards for detection (by means of data forensics) because these actions not always coincide in practice.

2.3   Step 3 - Validating the EDF-Protocol Standards

Participants

The prototype was validated by means of seven semi-structured interviews. All approached experts have practical and theoretical experience on the subject. These interviews were held with content experts from different backgrounds, amongst them psychometricians, policy makers and practitioners in the field of test security or education. Multiple experts who focus their work on (parts of) test security have been approached with the question to partake in this design research to gain an insight on their opinions and experiences concerning standards for securing the process of examination. To keep development of the prototype and validation of the content separate steps, the participating experts were not involved during the development of the prototype.

Procedure and Materials

Systematic expert interviews offer the possibility of identifying strengths and weaknesses in the content [16, 17]. This method is a valuable source of data collection, particularly when establishing the content correctness (e.g., validating) of a product [18]. The interview format consists of four categories; category one focused on general questions concerning the protocol (n = 7), category two focused on questions concerning the protocol content (n = 4), category three related to the grading of the protocol (n = 5), and category four focused on the data forensic standards (n = 5). An example of an interview question would be: "The goal of the protocol is to provide a good check whether the process of examination is secure. Do you think this is feasible in the current form?"

All potential respondents were first contacted through e-mail or Linked-In. This e-mail contained a brief introduction of the researcher, a short explanation of the context of the design research (e.g., the duration of the interview, and method of the interview), and finally the request for an interview. Initially eight requests have been sent to potential respondents. However, due to a possible conflict of interest, one candidate preferred not to take part in an interview. A second e-mail was sent to the seven remaining respondents. Through e-mail a more thorough explanation of the protocol's goal was provided, the respondents were asked to read the prototype and the interview questions in preparations of the interview, finally an appointment was set for the interview. This was either face-to-face (n = 2), through phone (n = 2), or through Skype (n = 3). The choice for the interview method was in consultation with the respondents, and mainly based on convenience for both parties.

At the start of the interview, each respondent was asked for consent verbally. This means that they were asked whether the interview could be recorded and whether the input from the interview could be used to validate the content of the prototype. It was also agreed in advance with the participants that they would receive the transcript of the interview, to be completely transparent about the input that was collected. The semi-structured interviews were conducted between April 17th and June 1st of 2018.

After the interviews, all the recordings have been converted to verbatim transcripts to keep statements in their proper context. Cues and codes were written in the margin of the transcript to indicate a reference to a specific question or part of the prototype. Subsequently, text fragments were summarized based on the interview categories (n = 4). The selection of usable statements was done on an individual basis by the author.

2.4   Adjustment of the Prototype and Final EDF Protocol

In the fourth step, the statements from the experts were used to transform the prototype into a final version of the EDF protocol. In the result section an overview is provided on all changes made based on statements from the interviews. These statements provided several new insights, especially in terms of usability and assessment. This emphasizes the significant impact of the interviews on the validation process.

2.5   Implementation of the EDF Protocol

The first four steps mainly focused on validating the design, purpose and content of the protocol. In order to be able to determine the actual value for practice it had to be used in a real situation. In the fifth step of this design research the final EDF protocol was used to determine if there was a possible security risk within one of eX:plain's exam programs. This step has been taken to determine the actual practical value of the protocol.

3   Results

In this section the results for each consecutive research step are described.

3.1   Literature Search

The literature search was split into two main topics. Firstly, the search for literature on 'Test Security', and secondly the search for 'Data Forensics' related literature. The literature found is up to June 2018. As was described in the method section the PRISMA framework was used in this step [14] (Fig. 1).

The first major topic was 'Test Security'. The key search term was based on the research question, namely test security. To broaden or specify the search, the following search terms were also used: prevention, detection, standards, fraud and cheating. Not all search terms provided usable information. Figure 2 shows the steps of the search process.

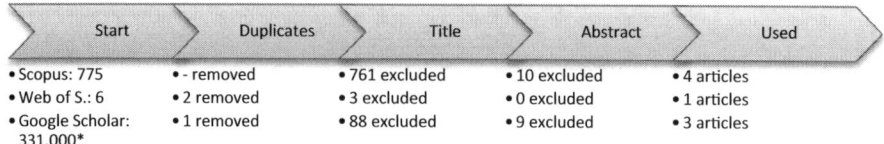

Start	Duplicates	Title	Abstract	Used
• Scopus: 775	• - removed	• 761 excluded	• 10 excluded	• 4 articles
• Web of S.: 6	• 2 removed	• 3 excluded	• 0 excluded	• 1 articles
• Google Scholar: 331.000*	• 1 removed	• 88 excluded	• 9 excluded	• 3 articles

Fig. 1. PRISMA flow chart showing the search process in the query of test security. Note: *only the first 10 pages were scanned (n = 100 hits)

Start	Duplicates	Title	Abstract	Used
• Scopus: 108	• 2 removed	• 102 excluded	• 3 excluded	• 3 articles
• Web of S.: 2	• 2 removed	• 0 excluded	• 0 excluded	• 0 articles
• Google Scholar: 24.200*	• 1 removed	• 84 excluded	• 7 excluded	• 8 articles

Fig. 2. PRISMA flow chart showing the search process in the query of data forensics. Note: *only the first 10 pages were scanned (n = 100 hits)

The second major topic of this step was focused on gathering literature on data forensics. For this topic, the main keyword, data forensics, directly relates to the main research question. Again, to broaden or specify the search at certain points, the following search terms were also used: educat* standards, fraud and cheating. Figure 3 shows the steps of the search process.

Because the literature search did not yield the desired results, a snowballing approach [19], was used to find more relevant literature on the topic of test security. As a result of this method, scanning the reference lists of the articles and handbooks that were found during the initial literature search provided new information on studies in the field of data forensics and test security (n = 20), see Table 2.

Some of these are highlighted here, because they have proved to be very valuable for this study. For example, the handbook of test security [20] provided several directions for prototype content in terms of prevention criteria as well as input for the data forensics standards. Secondly, the Handbook of Quantitative Methods for Detecting Cheating on Tests [21] provided the ground work for the data forensics standards in the EDF prototype through offering multiple methodologies for identifying cheating of tests. The third handbook, Test Fraud [22], provided a solid summary of statistical detection methods. In terms of justification, these handbooks were very valuable since they summarize lessons learned from practice and involve numerous content experts in writing these handbooks.

There is a multitude of frameworks and handbooks available in literature on security guidelines (Table 3). However, to a certain degree these guidelines lack direction for assessing a possible security risk. Most guidelines are very precise in stating what to consider, yet a distinction between a high, medium or low security risk are often absent. On this note, the COTAN rating system for test quality, and the RCEC

Table 2. Overview of additional literature findings based on the snowball method (n = 20)

Document title	Authors	Year	Source
Utilization of Response Time in Data Forensics of K-12 Computer-Based Assessment	Liu, Primoli & Plackner	2013	Google
Combating academic fraud: are students reticent about uncovering the covert	Malgwi & Rakowski	2009	Google
Educator cheating and the statistical detection of group-based test security threats	Maynes	2013	Google
Fraude onder studenten	Scholten	2013	Essay. utwente.nl
The role and responsibility of auditors in Prevention and Detection of Fraudulent Financial Reporting	Zager, Malis & Novak	2015	Google
Detecting and Preventing Cheating During Exams	Yee & MacKown	2010	Google
Fraud and plagiarism in school and career	Agud	2014	Google
Testing for Aberrant Behavior in Response Time Modeling	Marianti, Fox, Avetisyan, Veldkamp & Tijmstra	2014	Google
Comparing the Performance of Eight Item Preknowledge Detection Statistic	Belov	2015	Google
Detecting Test Tampering Using Item Response Theory	Wollack, Cohen & Eckerly	2015	Google
Detecting test tampering at the group level	Wollack & Eckerly	2017	Google
An Investigation of Answer Changing on Large-Scale Computer-Based Educational Assessment	Tiemann	2015	Google
Beat the Cheat	Novotney	2011	Google
Cheaters should never win: Eliminating the benefits of cheating	Fendler & Godbey	2015	Google
Observing and Deterring Social Cheating on College Exams	Fendler, Yates & Godbey	2018	Google
Countering Fraud for Competitive Advantage	Button & Gee	2013	Google
Detecting fraud: the role of the anonymous reporting channel	Johansson & Carey	2016	Google
Using response times to detect aberrant responses in computerized adaptive testing	van der Linden & van Krimpen-Stoop	2003	Google
Using response time to detect item pre-knowledge in computer-based licensure examinations	Qian, Staniewska, Reckase & Woo	2016	Google
A bivariate lognormal response-time model for the detection of collusion between test takers	Van der Linden	2009	Google

Table 3. Overview of openly available guidelines (n = 8)

Document title	Authors	Year	Source
Framework of Standards for Educational Assessment	AERE, APA & NCME	2014	Google
Richtlijnen voor het beschermen van de inhoud van examens	NVE & Caveon	2016	Google
Test Fraud Threats	Caveon	2016	Google
Security Planning Rubric	CoSN	2017	Google
Guidelines of the Security of Tests, Examinations, and Other Assessments	ITC	2014	Google
Richtsnoer Veilige digitale toetsafname	SURF	2014	Google
COTAN Beoordelingssysteem voor de kwaliteit van tests	COTAN	2010	Google
RCEC Beoordelingssysteem voor de kwaliteit van studietoetsen en examens	RCEC	2015	Google

rating system for quality test and exams both provide valuable input. All literature described in this section was used to support and justify the content of the prototype.

3.2   Developing an EDF Protocol Prototype

Based on the literature review and reading through similar protocols, manuals and handbooks, two main areas for development were identified. First, an area concerning standards and criteria with a focus on preventing misconduct during the process of examination (Part A). Second, an area with a set of standards concerning the detection of misconduct after examination by means of data forensics (Part B). The EDF prototype's body of content is presented in Fig. 3.

Part A: Standards for Fraud Prevention
1.   Security Plan
2.   Security Team
3.   Exam development process and maintenance
4.   Security of Examination
5.   Security of Results
6.   Internet Screening
7.   Security Incident Response
8.   Performing Security Audit

Part B: Standards for Fraud Detection through Data Forensics
1.   Detecting Preparatory Fraud Threats: Pre-knowledge and Item Compromise
2.   Detecting Test Score Similarity and Answer Copying
3.   Detecting Unusual Gain Scores and Test Tempering

Fig. 3. Overview of the EDF prototype content

The prototype standards each relate to the most commonly used and accepted guidelines on test security: The Security Guidelines by NVE (Dutch Association for Assessment) and Caveon, the guidelines by SURF (ICT cooperation for education and research in the Netherlands), and the Standards for Educational and Psychological Testing [23] as well as other literature to support the inclusion of these criteria in the prototype.

An important note for the development of the EDF protocol must be made beforehand. Namely, internally within eX:plain a protocol has been developed, for which the NVE & Caveon guidelines have been adopted. To continue this path, the same guidelines also form an important base in the development of the current prototype. If there is no additional argumentation or reference to literature considering a certain standard or criterion, then the inclusion is considered valid because it already reflects the policy of eX:plain.

3.3   Validating the EDF Protocol Standards

The content of the prototype was validated by means of seven semi-structured expert interviews. The interview is divided into four categories; category one focused on general questions (n = 7) concerning the protocol, the results are shown in Table 4. The second category focused on questions (n = 4) concerning the protocol content, see Table 5. Category three (n = 5) related to the grading of the protocol, see Table 6. Category four focused on the data forensic standards (n = 6), see Table 7.

Table 4. Overview of expert statements on the general category

	Statements:	N
First impression	The protocol looks clear and applicable	4x
	The protocol looks well-thought-out and manageable	3x
Design	The design of the protocol looks clear/intuitive	4x
	The design of the protocol is currently not very sexy	2x
Feasibility	Securing the process of examination by using this protocol is feasible	5x
	There will always be a chance of fraud, but minimalizing the chance is feasible	1x
Current content	The current standards seem to be sufficient	6x
	Currently criteria on responsibility and integrity are missing	1x
	I would have the assessor as a separate standard	2x
Comparison	Not to my knowledge. We have our own internal documents regarding security	3x
	I see duplications with what we have in our manuals	1x
Ideal protocol	Ideally, this protocol should initiate awareness	4x
	Ideally, this protocol provides users with insight into possible security gaps	2x
Usage	I would use the protocol myself or recommend it to colleagues	5x
	I would use the protocol, provided that it would be made more explicit	1x

Table 5. Overview of expert statements on the content category

		Statements:	N
Standards	1	The inclusion of this standard makes sense	4x
	1	Include more detailed information	1x
	2	The inclusion of this standard makes sense	5x
	2	Awareness should be part of this standard	1x
	3	The inclusion of this standard makes sense	4x
	3	Currently it is mainly operational, add a certain level of awareness	1x
	4	The inclusion of this standard makes sense	5x
	5	The inclusion of this standard makes sense	2x
	6	The inclusion of this standard makes sense	4x
	6	Maybe this should not be a separate standard	1x
	6	Hacking could be an addition to this standard	1x
	7	The inclusion of this standard makes sense	5x
	8	The inclusion of this standard makes sense	4x
	8	Maybe this should not be a separate standard	2x
Current criteria		They seem to be clear	5x
		Some criteria are very similar (std. 4)	2x
Criteria missing		They seem to be complete and clear	2x
		Examples could be included	2x
Equivalency		Most criteria are equality important	3x
		Impact should weight more than equality of the criteria	4x

Table 6. Overview of expert statements on the grading category

	Statements:	N
Grading system	The current grading system is relevant and good	4x
	Add the option 'not applicable'	1x
	An insufficient or sufficient score would already be sufficient	1x
Concreteness	Being more concrete may lower the usability of the protocol	5x
Rubric scores	The current scores have added value	2x
	Scoring should be interactive when 'not applicable' is included	1x
	An insufficient or sufficient score would already suffice	1x
Security labels	These terms fit, and are realistic	4x
Security assessment	Determining the security risk depends on the impact of a score	4x
	When a criterium is scored insufficient, a high risk is fine	1x

The third step of the research yielded several valuable statements made by the content experts, which have been incorporated into the final version of the EDF protocol. The way these statements are embedded in the protocol and the arguments for inclusion are described in step four.

Table 7. Overview of expert statements on the data forensics category

	Statements:	N
Feasibility	Yes. In the sense that it is aimed to provide information	1x
	Currently, this part is quite compelling	1x
Current standards	Currently, the classification is not identical	2x
Completeness	The question is whether it should be standards	1x
	The question is whether this is logical	1x
Types of fraud	No real fraud types are missing	1x
	Collusion is broad	1x
	Correcting by an assessor is not described within de fraud types	1x
Missing indices	No, obvious analyses are missing	3x

3.4   Adjustment of the Prototype and Final EDF Protocol

The interview statements were summarized into three categories. The first category describes adjustments based on statements referring to the protocol in general (e.g., "include possible evidence in the protocol"). The second category include adjustments referring to the content (e.g., "include awareness in the protocol"). The third category include grading adjustments (e.g., "add the option 'not applicable"). The EDF protocols' body of content is shown in Fig. 4. An excerpt from content is shown in Table 8.

```
EDF-Protocol Standards
    1.   Security Plan
    2.   Involved Personnel
    3.   Exam development process and maintenance
    4.   Security of Examination
    5.   Security of Results
    6.   Data Forensics I: Detecting aberrant patterns in test data
    7.   Security Incident Response
    8.   Internet Screening
    9.   Data Forensics II: Following suspicion of fraud
    10.  Performing Security Audit
```

Fig. 4. Overview of the EDF protocol content

General Protocol Adjustments

The first adjustment made, was that there no longer is a distinction between part A and part B. After statements from several content experts, the three data forensics standards have been revised into two standards, and hereafter included within part A. Thus, resulting in a set of ten standards concerning security of the examination process. The first data forensics standard (standard 6), describes several criteria around detecting aberrant patterns in test data. The second data forensics standard (standard 9) include criteria aimed for handling a suspicion of fraud or misconduct. Subsequently, these two data forensics standards now have the same grading system as the other standards.

These adjustments have been made to make the EDF protocol more fluid in general and the content more consistent.

The second adjustment, was the introduction of an evidence table for each standard. This adjustment was based on two categories of statements. First, this table offers the opportunity to gather concrete insights per standard on how each criterion is currently dealt with. Secondly, the provided evidence gives the opportunity to enter a discussion. For example, to determine potential security risks, and decision making in terms of change management. The third general adjustment, was a change in the order of the standards. They have been adjusted to make the standards more logically reflect the process of examination in a chronological way.

Table 8. Excerpt of the EDF protocol content

Criteria	Description	na	0	1	2
Data forensics	[1]Clearly described whether personnel is assigned to analyse exam results (internal or external). [2]This/these member(s) deliver periodic reports with findings and recommendations	☐	☐	☐	☐
Compromised items	Data forensics include analysing the test items' validity (analysis of: P-value, Differential Item Functioning). Strong aberrant patterns may indicate one or more compromised items	☐	☐	☐	☐
Response similarity	Data forensics include analysing the test on similarity of responses between candidates. Strong aberrant patterns may indicate answer copying or collusion	☐	☐	☐	☐
Response time	Data forensics include analysing the test on candidates' or item response time. Strong aberrant patterns may indicate collusion or harvesting	☐	☐	☐	☐

Content Adjustments

Standard two has been revised based on several expert statements. Firstly, the name 'Security team' raised questions, and was considered too big or too vague. The image created with this standard was that a separate team should be responsible for securing the exam process. However, this was not intended with this standard. This idea was also caused, because 'human actions' were already included in other standards. However, the aim for this standard was to support awareness and to offer guidance in assessing the responsibility and integrity of all involved personnel within the process of examination. Accordingly, the name of standard two was revised into 'Involved personnel: tasks and responsibilities'. Also, the description of the four criteria have been revised to support security awareness.

Another clearly voiced point of feedback in some interviews was the lack of a standard concerning the assessor of exams or tests. The significance of including this in the protocol was made very clear, however instead of devoting an entire standard to the assessor, several criteria have been revised, and new criteria were developed to meet the statements made in this area (e.g., standard 2: criteria 2, 3 and 4, standard 4: criteria 5, and standard 5: criteria 4). An argument for doing so was that the integrity of all personnel involved was already included in the revised second standard.

Finally, several adjustments have been made in terms of naming the criteria. Reason for these adjustments were not always found in the interview transcripts, but were for example based on the fact that the original naming of some criteria did not fully represent what a criterion aimed for. Therefore, adjustments were in some cases necessary to better indicate the direction of these criteria. In one case, however, two content experts rightly pointed to the fact that criteria one (Proctoring) and four (Use of materials) of standard four, of the prototype, aimed to measure the same. Namely, the use of unauthorized materials.

Grading Adjustments

In all interviews, on various topics, statements were made about the risk of drawing conclusions by means of the rubrics could be risky, especially considering the impact these conclusions might have. In the prototype the impact of the assessment was not clearly reflected in the criteria when considering assessing a diversity of exam programs. Therefore, several adjustments have been made to make the protocol even more manageable in terms of grading. First the rubrics have been revised. In the prototype all levels of grading (e.g., insufficient, sufficient and good) had a description. To focus on what is sufficient, only a clear description of the 'sufficient' level was now included in the rubric. The descriptions of the other levels have become fixed, namely: (0) Insufficient: the described criteria are not met; (2) Good: the criteria are amply met/demonstrates how this is acted upon. Because they now have a fixed character they are excluded from the rubrics and included as a note under each standard. The new grading system is shown in Table 9.

Table 9. Overview of the grading system

Determining security risk for Standard 2	
The total score on this standard is '4' or 'higher', without an 'insufficient' score (a 'not applicable' score lowers the total possible score)	→ Low security risk
Depending on the impact for the exam, one or more 'Insufficient' score(s) on one of the criteria *Advise*: Direct your resources towards the criteria with the 'Insufficient' score	→ Medium/High security risk

Secondly, a new grading option was introduced, the option 'Not applicable' has been included. This adjustment is based on comments from experts whom stated, 'I understand that you've included this criterion, but for me this would not apply'. In the prototype, there was no way of indicating applicability of certain criteria. Thirdly, a minor change was made in terms of usability. In the prototype the awarding of a score was open. This could be done, for example, by filling in an 'X' by hand. In the final version blocks have been added, when clicking a particular block an 'X' will automatically be applied. This makes the protocol slightly more user-friendly and more intuitive.

3.5   Implementation of the EDF Protocol

During the fifth step, the EDF protocol was used to evaluate and measure possible security risks within one of eX:plain' s exam programs. In the scope of the current study, this step has been taken to determine the actual practical value of the protocol. A one hour consultation with the manager of the exam program was organized to implement the EDF protocol. The application of the protocol in the exam program was the final validation strategy for the content of the protocol. In doing so, the application of the protocol has demonstrated that it is functioning as intended, and therefore this step confirmed its added value for practice. The effectiveness of the protocol can best be described by presenting the results, hence the validation process will be discussed together with the findings and recommendations.

To summarize, 6 out of 10 standards were assessed with a '*medium/high security risk*'. Although this is not an ideal score for the exam program, it does show that the protocol can flag security gaps in the examination process and due to the open nature of the criteria it was also possible to provide several concrete recommendations in order to limit the chances of security risks in the future. In addition, the remaining 4 out of 10 standards were assessed with a '*low security risk*'. This indicated that the standards were developed in such a way that proper security measures also get rewarded by the protocol. Although exam fraud can never be fully banned, these findings advocate the current content of the protocol, since it seemingly provides standards covering the entire process of examination.

4   Conclusion

This design research started on the premise of developing a set of standards, enabling practitioners to prevent and detect possible fraud during the process of examination. In the end, the research provided a set of standards aimed at achieving a well-secured exam process as well as increasing awareness in doing so. This paper reported on the theoretical base of developing the EDF protocol and the development considerations along the way.

By means of the five design steps carried out in this study, the main research question is unambiguously answered by stating that the EDF protocol provides sufficient direction and guidance in securing the entire process of examination. To summarize these standards: (1) Security plan, (2) Tasks and responsibilities, (3) Exam development and maintenance, (4) Security of examination, (5) Security of results, (6) Data forensics I, (7) Incident response, (8) Internet screening, (9) Data forensics II, (10) Security audit. Continuous application of the protocol in the future must determine whether the current set of standards and underlying criteria is sufficient. To illustrate, within this study the protocol was used for an exam program that did not have a security plan. Although this was well illustrated by applying the protocol, which emphasizes the usability of the protocol, we do not yet know how the protocol responds to a well secured exam program in terms of evaluating and measuring the possible security risks.

To answer the second research question, during development, several conditions have been considered to provided practitioners with the ability to act on indications of exam fraud based on these standards. By adding an 'evidence-table' for each standard, organizations are given the opportunity to provide concrete insights per standard on how each criterion is currently dealt with, meaning they can now include their own practice in the protocol. Secondly, it provides the foundation for an internal discussion. By doing so, security awareness is being encouraged on a personal level, and at a policy level, again, the foundation is laid for a well secure exam program. Also, the implementation of the protocol results in a 'protocol report', including findings for each standard as well tailor-made recommendation (e.g., short term or long term). A deliberate choice was made not to include a set of fixed recommendations into the protocol, on the contrary, these recommendations are now the result of implementation. In doing so the protocol can be used more widely in various exam programs, without compromising or limiting the quality of implementing the EDF protocol for individual exam programs.

5   Contribution to Practice

5.1   Establishing a Tailor-Made Protocol

The starting point for the EDF protocol was to develop a set of universal standards and underlying criteria for securing the process of examination. This would allow the protocol to be deployed more widely within different organizations or on a diverse set of exam programs. A remark on this idea however, is that although the standards describe the entire process properly, the underlying criteria often lacked a certain amount of concrete examples or conditions.

That is why it is recommended to first go through the entire protocol and provide evidence and arguments for the entire set of standards. Doing this, you will create a baseline, or a frame of reference for each exam program or organization in which the protocol is used. From this point, it can then be determined whether improvement is needed in current practice. As a result the added workload for the exam organizers would differ based on the improvements needed. Based on the current study we cannot estimate how much additional workload is created by applying the standards. Therefore, one has to consider the organizational climate and exam conditions for the actual implementation.

The added value of this method is that each exam program can determine when conditions are truly sufficient, also considering the impact for their exam. In this way, the universal character of the EDF protocol is retained, but at the same time the various examination programs are given the tools to use the protocol in a both sustainable and concrete way, hence securing the process of examination through empirical implementation.

5.2   The Practical Value of the Protocol

Besides providing practitioners with a set of standards and criteria for securing the examination process, the added value this protocol offers in comparison with other available guidelines lies in the possibility of assessing potential security risks based on the users' current practice. Despite this promising potential, an assessment model generally also has a downside. Namely, when using this protocol in an audit, some standards or criteria may not appear to be 'fit' or even suitable because of their broad description. For this reason, it is important to recall the proper value of these standards. The EDF Protocol provides standards, underlying criteria, and the possibility to provide evidence if these criteria are sufficiently met. However, those who will apply this protocol must continue to thoughtfully examine to what extent the provided criteria are applicable, because the applicability can be bound to the context of the exam or exam process.

5.3   Proper Use of Data Forensics

An important consideration for policy making is how to proceed if there are statistical indications of misconduct based on the data forensic on the examinee, proctor or location level. When using the data forensic results, caution is strongly advised. Unless the data can be supported by more direct evidence, such as reported irregularities by a proctor, punitive actions are not directly advised. Ideally, communicating in advance that data forensics are conducted would be sufficiently deterrent, however in a high stakes exam setting the risk taking might be high as well. In this respect the use of multiple indices is especially important. Also, it is important that the use of data forensics operate as deterrents and detectors rather than judge and jury.

In addition to the mentioned consideration for policymaking on indications of misconduct, also decisions on the most effective way of communicating these indications must be considered. Before examination, the communications should emphasize a positive message mentioning the use of sophisticated data forensics to ensure that everyone is treated equally and fair during examination. While brought in a positive manner, the underlying message is that test tampering or misconduct will be detected and acted upon. Finally, care must be taken that the rights and privacy of the involved individuals is being protected.

5.4   Final Words

The EDF protocol is a quality assurance system, aimed at the prevention (i.e., the prevention of exam fraud as much as possible in advance) and detection (i.e. by means of data forensics after examination) of misconduct in the exam process. Although exam fraud can never be fully banned, the protocol provides standards covering the entire process of examination in order to limit the chances of security risks. That is why the interaction with the EDF monitor as described earlier, is vital, because together they can flag possible misconduct and potential security gaps. The full research paper is available through e-mail. Please contact the first author. Also, the final version of the EDF protocol can be requested via Xquiry's website (www.xquiry.com).

References

1. McCabe, D.L., Butterfield, K.D., Trevino, L.K.: Academic dishonesty in graduate business programs: prevalence, causes, and proposed action. Acad. Manag. Learn. Educ. **5**(3), 294–305 (2006)
2. McCabe, D.L.: CAI Research. Center for Academic Integrity (2005). http://www. academicintegrity.org/cai_research.asp
3. Murdock, T.B., Hale, N.M., Weber, M.J.: Predictors of cheating among early adolescents: academic and social motivations. Contemp. Educ. Psychol. **26**, 96–115 (2001)
4. Novotney, A.: Beat the cheat. Am. Psychol. Assoc. **42**(6), 54 (2011)
5. Witherspoon, M., Maldonado, N., Lacey, C.H.: Undergraduates and academic dishonesty. Int. J. Bus. Soc. Sci. **3**(1) (2012)
6. Yee, K., MacKown, P.: Detecting and preventing cheating during exams. Center for Academic Integrity, Rutland Institute for Ethics, Clemson University (2010). http://www. academicintegrity.org
7. Marianti, S., Fox, J.P., Avetisyan, M., Veldkamp, B.P., Tijmstra, J.: Testing for aberrant behavior in response time modeling. J. Educ. Behav. Stat. **39**(6), 426–451 (2014). https:// doi.org/10.3102/1076998614559412
8. Impara, J.C., Kingbury, G., Maynes, D., Fitzgerald, C.: Detecting cheating in computer adaptive test using data forensics. In: National Council on Measurement in Education and the National Association of Test Directors, Montreal, Canada (2005)
9. Plackner, C., Primoli, V.: Data forensics: a compare and contrast analysis of multiple methods. Presented at the 2012 Conference on Statistical Detection of Potential Exam Fraud in Lawrence, KS (2012)
10. Van Noord, S.: Detecting cheating in computer based multiple-choice testing. Master thesis, University of Twente, The Netherlands (2018)
11. Fremer, J.: Data Forensics, [Blogpost] (2011). https://www.fsbpt.org/FreeResources/ NPTEArticles/articleType/ArticleView/articleId/40/Data-Forensics.aspx
12. Howell, S.L., Sorensen, D., Tippets, H.R.: The New (and Old) News about Cheating for Distance Educators (2016). https://www.researchgate.net/publication/268359500
13. Xquiry: XQUIRY Whitepaper 1.0. Xquiry, Amersfoort (2017)
14. Moher, D., Liberati, A., Tetzlaff, J., Altman, D.G.: Preferred reporting items for systematic reviews and meta-analyses: the PRISMA statement. PLoS Med. **6**(6), e1000097 (2009). https://doi.org/10.1371/journal.pmed1000097
15. Cassell, C., Denyer, D., Tranfield, D.: Using qualitative research synthesis to build an actionable knowledge base. Manag. Descision **44**(2), 213–227 (2006)
16. McKenney, S., Reeves, T.C.: Conducting Educational Design Research. Routledge Education, New York (2012)
17. Piercy, K.W.: Analysis of semi-structured interview data (2004). https://www.scribd.com/ document/249952429/Piercy-Analysis-of-Semi-structured-Interview-Data
18. Wools, S., Sanders, P.F., Eggen, T.J.H.M., Baartman, L.K.J., Roelofs, E.C.: Evaluatie van een beoordelingssysteem voor de kwaliteit van competentie-assessments [Testing an evaluation system for performance tests]. Pedagog. Stud. **88**, 23–40 (2011)
19. Wohlin, C.: Guidelines for snowballing in systematic literature studies and a replication in software engineering (2014). http://dx.doi.org/10.1145/2601248.2601268
20. Wollack, J.A., Fremer, J.J.: Handbook of Test Security. Routledge, New York (2013)
21. Cizek, G.J., Wollack, J.A.: Handbook of Quantitative Methods for Detecting Cheating on Tests. Routledge, London (2017)

22. Kingston, N.M., Clark, A.K.: Test Fraud: Statistical Detection and Methodology. Routledge, New York (2014)
23. American Educational Research Association, American Psychological Association, and National Council for Measurement in Education: Standards for educational and psychological testing. American Educational Research Association, Washington DC (2014)
24. Oleck, J.: Most high school students admit to cheating. Sch. Libr. J. (2008). http://www.schoollibraryjournal.com/article/CA6539855.html

Assessment of Collaboration and Feedback on Gesture Performance

Dimitra Anastasiou[1]([✉]) [ID], Eric Ras[1], and Mehmetcan Fal[2]

[1] Luxembourg Institute of Science and Technology,
5 Avenue des Hauts-Fourneaux, 4362 Esch-sur-Alzette, Luxembourg
{dimitra.anastasiou, eric.ras}@list.lu
[2] Turkish Aerospace, Ankara, Turkey
mehmetcan.fal@tai.com.tr

Abstract. This paper proposes gesture performance as one main channel for assessing collaboration skills, while multiple users solve a problem collaboratively on a tangible user interface. Collaborative problem solving incorporates two dimensions, complex problem solving and collaboration. Thus, the technology-based assessment of collaborative problem solving includes assessing both problem solving and collaboration skills. Particularly, for assessing collaboration skills, we consider gesture performance as an important indicator. We differentiate between physical 3D mid-air gestures and manipulative gestures; for the latter, we developed a gesture recognition application using Kinect. The method we follow for object and gesture recognition is to merge the logging files from our tangible interface software framework (object recognition) with the Kinect log files (gesture recognition) in one file. The application can analyze the number of object manipulations with respect to timing axis, subject/participant, and handedness.

Keywords: Assessment framework · Collaboration · Feedback ·
Feed-forward · Gestures · Performance · Tangible user interfaces

1 Introduction

Humans use gestures as a very intuitive means of communication and usually receive feedback from their partners, either orally or also with gestures. However, when it comes to human computer interaction, gesture interaction is still at its infancy, since gesture detection, analysis, and recognition has still many challenges to overcome.

In our research we focus on tangible interfaces and collaborative problem solving, and this paper studies particularly the assessment of collaborative problem solving skills. Collaborative problem solving (CoIPS) incorporates two dimensions: (i) *complex problem solving* as the cognitive dimension and (ii) *collaboration* as the interpersonal dimension. CoIPS is not just the sum of those two dimensions, but represents the interaction of their skills (OECD [1]). Assessment of *complex problem solving* is related with task performance and is well researched in the literature, but assessment of *collaboration* unfortunately is not. Collaboration has various definitions, is a subjective dimension, domain-specific, and accordingly its assessment is a difficult challenge.

© Springer Nature Switzerland AG 2019
S. Draaijer et al. (Eds.): TEA 2018, CCIS 1014, pp. 219–232, 2019.
https://doi.org/10.1007/978-3-030-25264-9_14

In the project GETUI (Gestures in Tangible User Interfaces) we have been investigating the use of gestures on tangible user interfaces (TUIs) in the context of technology-based assessment of collaborative and complex problem solving skills. Within GETUI, we define *collaboration* as "the overall social group interaction in a coordinated effort to solve a collaborative problem on the tangible user interfaces". We run exploratory case studies at secondary schools in Luxembourg and Belgium, where groups of three users solved a problem collaboratively on the TUI [2]. Early enough during these experiments, we experienced that participants during the user studies were unsure about their past as well as their future actions, so they were requesting feedback from the experimenters. Thus we decided to follow up our research focusing on feedback and feed-forward, particularly by connecting gesture analysis with our assessment framework for collaboration.

In this paper we present our assessment framework, including our interactive feedback strategy and our gesture recognition application. The paper is laid out as follows: We begin with literature review (Sect. 2) on three related sub-fields of our research: collaboration, tangible interaction, and gestures. Section 3 highlights our own research related to the assessment framework and interactive feedback strategy. In Sect. 4 we describe our gesture taxonomy on tangible user interfaces and in Sect. 5 follows the technical part about recognizing manipulative gestures. We conclude the paper with a few future prospects in Sect. 6.

2 Related Work

Our research is about assessment of collaboration and provision of feedback based on gesture performance on tangible user interfaces. As this research is interdisciplinary, we present related work on collaboration on tangible interfaces (Sect. 2.1), gesture taxonomies and recognition (Sect. 2.2), as well as design artifacts including feedback on gesture performance (Sect. 2.3).

2.1 Collaboration on Tangible Interfaces

As far as collaboration in tabletop interaction is concerned, Hornecker and Buur [3] designed a framework related to the social user experience of tangible interaction, including the aspects of tangible manipulation, spatial interaction, embodied facilitation, expressive representation. We focus particularly on embodied facilitation which highlights how the configuration of objects and space affects emerging group behaviour.

When multiple users are working collaboratively on a tangible interface, there are many challenges that appear, such as spatial position of the users, clear roles/objectives, simultaneous actions (speech/gesture), etc. Gutwin and Greenberg [4] call *mechanics of collaboration* "the small-scale actions and interactions that group members must carry out in order to get a shared task done" (p. 98), such as communicating information, coordinating manipulations, or monitoring one another. Schmidt and Bannon [5], talking about Computer-supported Cooperative work, argued for supporting *articulation work* as an integral part of cooperative work, by *articulate* they mean divide, allocate, coordinate, schedule, mesh, interrelate, etc. their distributed individual activities (p. 15). They added that in order to articulate these distributed activities, access to appropriate means of communication is needed.

As for the technology in group settings, Scott et al. [6] suggested eight collaborative design guidelines systems for co-located tabletop collaboration; according to these guidelines, "technology must: (1) support interpersonal interaction, (2) support fluid transitions between activities, (3) support transitions between personal and group work, (4) support transitions between tabletop collaboration and external work, (5) support the use of physical objects, (6) provide shared access to physical and digital objects, (7) consider the appropriate arrangements of users, and (8) support simultaneous user actions" (p. 163).

Regarding complex problem solving specifically, O'Neil et al. [7] added the collaboration dimension and defined collaborative complex problem solving as "searching for the path from the initial state to the goal state while interacting with others working on a shared goal". The full definition provided by the OECD [8] follows: "Collaborative problem-solving competency is the capacity of an individual to effectively engage in a process whereby two or more agents attempt to solve a problem by sharing the understanding and effort required to come to a solution and pooling their knowledge, skills and efforts to reach that solution". Humans intuitively often assume that effective collaboration brings mostly positive effects to task performance and learning. Thus we share the implicit assumption in Evans and Wobbrock [9] that effective collaboration leads to positive learning outcomes, while ineffective collaboration hinders learning, although that may not always be true in practice (Dillenbourg and Evans [10]).

2.2   Gesture Taxonomies and Gesture Recognition

We differentiate between gestures studied in psychology and gestures studied in computer science. In psycholinguistics, the most prominent gesture taxonomy is that of McNeil [11], based on Kendon's continuum [12]. McNeil [11] categorized the gestures into *gesticulation, emblems, pantomimes*, and *sign language. Gesticulation* is further classified into *iconic, metaphoric, rhythmic, cohesive*, and *deictic* gestures.

From a human computer interaction (HCI) perspective, Karam and Schraefel [13] provided a taxonomy of gesture interaction research since the early 90s. There already exist many gesture taxonomies in HCI [14–16]. Hinrichs and Carpendale [17] have examined gestures "in the wild" on multi-touch interfaces. Higgins et al. [18] provided a review about multi-touch interfaces in educational settings to support collaborative learning. There is a lot of related work on gesture data sets on surface and interactive tabletop computing [19–21], but there is not a systematic analysis or dataset of gestures with regards to TUIs.

Regarding recognition of gestures, Rautaray and Agrawal [22] wrote a meta-analysis on vision-based hand gesture recognition. Gesture recognition is researched in the area of touch interfaces [23], but gesture recognition on TUIs is still a young field [24–26]. Schneider and Blikstein [26] examined students' interaction around a TUI and made a link between their active or passive positions and learning gains. Their hypothesis was that more engaged students move their body more than less engaged ones. We disagree with the one-sided rationale of this hypothesis, since we believe that the purpose of the interaction has to be linked with the hand movements' performance and should accordingly be taken into account in the analysis.

To sum up, there is a literature gap on gesture datasets analysis and gesture recognition pertaining to TUIs specifically, let alone when this is used for CoIPS. Moreover, in our opinion, gesture analysis can have certain benefits only if the two fields of psychology and HCI are combined, since the fine-grained categories of gestures in psychology can be detected and recognized as soon as ICT technology and particularly gesture recognition is being advanced.

2.3   Feedback on Gesture Performance

In this section we present a few devices/artefacts based on three output feedback modalities: visual, auditory, and tactile. The feedback in these artefacts is mainly an output for gesture performance.

Ahmaniemi et al. [27] examined through two experiments the perception of audio-tactile feedback to gesture input with a handheld device. In the first experiment they assessed the discrimination performance regarding modality conditions, texture designs, and gesturing behaviour. In the second experiment they investigated the role of noise used for masking the leakage sound of the tactile actuator in the first experiment. The modality conditions were tactile, audio, or audio-tactile. They found that the audio alone led to best detection performance and gesturing behaviour was affected by the modality condition. Tactile feedback induced subjects to do more energetic movements, while audio feedback led to slower gesturing. Lucchese et al. [28] developed *GestureCommander*, a touch-based gesture control system for mobile devices capable of recognizing gestures in real-time. Continuous recognition allows the system to provide visual feedback to the user and to anticipate user actions before completion. *GestureCommander* allows users to perform gestures while displaying textual feedback of what the system predicts to be the three most likely gestures; as a second form of visual feedback, the application also traces out the anticipated continuation of the most likely gesture using Viterbi calculations. Oh et al. [29] proposed and evaluated two techniques to teach touchscreen gestures to visually-impaired users: (i) corrective verbal feedback using text-to-speech; (ii) gesture sonification based on finger touches, creating an audio representation of a gesture. They concluded that a combination of the two may ultimately be useful for a gesture training system. Most recently, Grosse-Puppendahl et al. [30] combined a semi-transparent capacitive proximity surface sensing with an LED array. After gesture recognition, this array provides visual feedback on the actual interaction status.

In this section we have seen many design artifacts which provide verbal, visual, audio, or tactile feedback to user gesture performance. Similarly, we plan to provide multimodal (audio-visual or visual-tactile) feedback in real-time depending on the collaborative skills of the users while solving a collaborative problem on the TUI.

3   Assessment Framework and Interactive Feedback Strategy

Feedback is tightly coupled with assessment in the overall learning process. Evans [31] defined assessment feedback as "all *feedback exchanges* generated within assessment design, occurring within and beyond the immediate learning context, being overt or covert (actively and/or passively sought and/or received), and importantly, drawing from a range of sources" (p. 71). Formative assessment refers to assessment that is specifically intended to generate feedback on performance to improve and accelerate learning (Sadler [32]).

Apart from feedback, at least equally important is feed-forward. Higgins et al. [33] suggested to move to feed-forward, since discussion, clarification, and negotiation between student and tutor can equip students with a better appreciation of what is expected of them. In the context of HCI and Interaction Design, the term feed-forward was firstly given by Djajadiningrat et al. [34]: "Feedforward informs the user about what the result of his action will be".

Figure 1 depicts our proposed **Assessment Framework** and **Interactive Feedback Strategy** for collaborative problem solving environments on tangible interfaces.

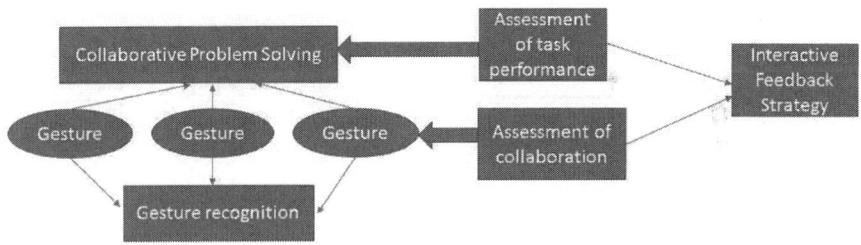

Fig. 1. Assessment framework and Interactive Feedback Strategy

Firstly, a group of users solve a collaborative problem on a TUI and performs intuitively hand gestures during that session. The gestures are both free-hand/in the air and manipulative gestures (with the tangibles); both these gesture kinds are detected and analysed through our gesture recognition application (see Sect. 4). During the session, the group as a whole, but also individual users are evaluated about their task performance and their collaboration.

On one hand, the assessment of task performance is partially based on the microDYN framework [35]. The *micro-DYN* methodology allows for independent microworld scenarios that rely on structural linear equations as underlying model in order to assess complex problem solving. On the other hand, the assessment of collaboration around tangible user interfaces is currently our research topic; the input parameter (at this stage) is the gesture performance.

Currently, the assessment of task performance is performed real-time, while the assessment of collaboration requires high gesture recognition accuracy and is under development. After the overall assessment (task performance and collaboration), multimodal feedback and feed-forward is provided to the users also at real time.

For example, when a group is positively collaborating, then a green ambient light is lit, etc. This green light informs, but also encourages users to continue. On the contrary, when a group is negatively collaborating, a red light or an audio effect will make clear to the users to make another action (feed-forward). Different kinds of feedback can be integrated into the application that use different multimedia channels. More information about the feedback representation on TUI during collaborative problem solving can be found in Schwarz et al. [36]. We call it *interactive* feedback strategy as the feedback is planned to be performed real-time taking into account the group *interaction* dynamics, i.e. interaction among users, and between the users and the tangibles or the TUI. We also follow the *Interactive Tutoring Feedback* (ITF) model, developed by Narciss [37] which reflects theoretical and empirical insights of feedback frameworks and research as well as research on formative assessment. ITF refers to feedback types providing strategically useful information that guides the learner towards successful task completion. Our feedback is also multimodal, as various feedback modalities are represented (audio, visual, tactile), various feedback output sources (tangible tabletop, external lamp, smart watch) can be implemented, and last but not least, feed-forward is included in addition to feedback.

4 Gesture Taxonomy

In this section we present our gesture taxonomy, the main result of the GETUI project. We followed [11, 12, 38–41] to create this gesture taxonomy for ColPS on TUIs. All the gestures included in this taxonomy have been used in the user studies we conducted, where groups of three users solved a problem collaboratively on a TUI. We focus on hand gestures and sub-categorize gestures into two main categories:

(1) 3D mid-air free hand gestures;
(2) Touch-based and manipulative gestures.

The former category is about gestures which are done in the mid-air (see Fig. 2), while the latter are in combination with the tangible objects or the tabletop (see Fig. 3). As the former include fine-grained gestures, often including multiple fingers, are difficult to recognize automatically, thus we did manual gesture coding (see Sect. 4.1).

The first four gestures (placing, removing, tracing, rotating) have to do with tangible objects, while the last five can be applied also to interactive GUIs (without tangibles).

4.1 Manual Gesture Coding

For manual gesture coding/annotation, we use the software ELAN [42], which is a professional tool for the creation of complex annotations on video and audio resources. The coding has the following procedure: we upload in ELAN the video of our user study as well as a template file where the taxonomy of free-hand gestures is saved. While the video is running, we stop and annotate the kind of gesture a user performed

Pointing	object(s)
	TUI
	other participant(s)
	self-pointing participant
Iconic	encircling with whole hand
	encircling with index finger
	moving an open hand forward/backward
	moving an open hand downwards vertically
Adaptor	head scratching
	mouth scratching
	nail biting
	hair twirling
Emblems	thumps up
	victory sign
	fist(s) pump

Fig. 2. Taxonomy of free-hand gestures while solving a collaborative problem on a tangible interface

Touch-based/manipulative	placing
	removing
	tracing
	rotating
	resizing
	tapping
	sweeping
	flicking
	holding

Fig. 3. Taxonomy of touch-based gestures

in the exact time frame (see Fig. 5). We perform this analysis for all three users of a group. ELAN can provide descriptive statistics. The coding can, of course, be done, both for free-hand and touch-based gestures. However, as manual gesture coding is very time-consuming thus costly, we have developed an automatic gesture recognition application using Kinect^{TM} for the touch-based gestures; the application is described in Sect. 5. The results of the manual video coding in our user studies are outside the scope of this paper (Fig. 4).

Fig. 4. Pointing hand gestures during collaborative problem solving

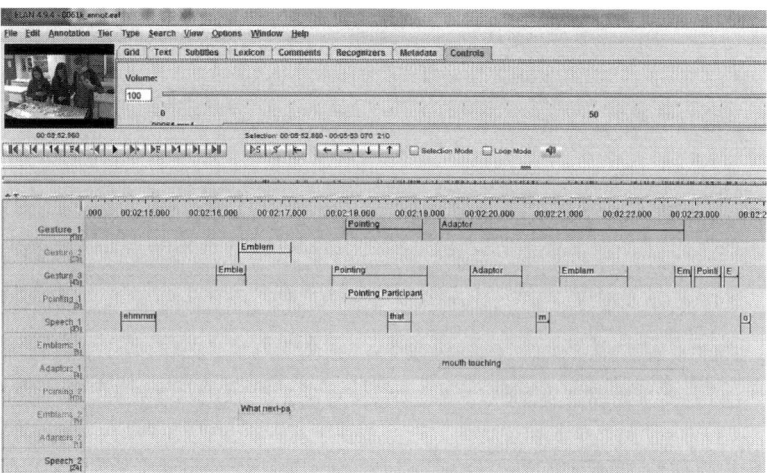

Fig. 5. Manual gesture coding with the software ELAN

5 Gesture Application on Tangible User Interfaces

Here we present our gesture recognition application for the touch-based/manipulative gestures. It is an object (tangible) and gesture recognition application which can automatically recognize object manipulation in real time with regards to (i) *which object* has been manipulated, (ii) *when*, (iii) by *whom*, and (iv) using *which hand*. The application is fully replicable for Kinect™ SDK users and TUI holders with a tracking software framework. The method we follow for object and gesture recognition is to merge the logging files from our TUI software framework, COPSE (Maquil et al. [43]) (object recognition) with the Kinect log files (gesture recognition) in one file. The application converts the TUI objects' screen coordinates to the Kinect coordinates system. All active objects are continuously controlled by the application in order to check whether the participants' hand coordinates collide with the objects' coordinates. The application consists of two main parts: (i) the first part is at the TUI side; it creates a UDP socket and sends the object ID and the TUI's coordinates of the objects, and (ii) the second part takes these coordinates and converts them into Kinect coordinates by using a transformation matrix. This matrix is created by a calibration procedure, where the TUI location and its plane are transformed into the Kinect coordinate system. Figure 6 presents the overall data flow of human-object interaction and the functionalities of the client data reader (TUI) and body reader (Kinect). Moreover, these data can be visualised through the connectivity protocol *mqtt* at an external monitor, something that is more attractive for participants instead of raw data.

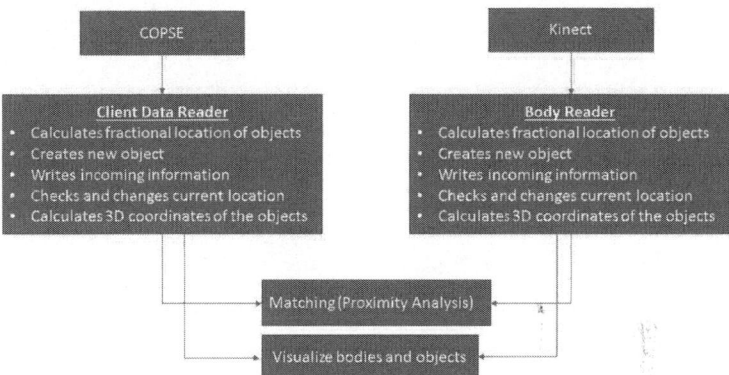

Fig. 6. Data flow of human-object interaction

5.1 Calibration Procedure

The calibration provides 3D coordinates of the TUI surface plane. Therefore, an experimenter needs to complete this procedure for each new position of Kinect or the TUI. In order to locate the TUI's plane, the experimenter should be close to the short edge of the TUI table and (s)he needs to locate their right hand and left hand at the corner of the TUI's screen. The left hand must be on the side of the pixel (0, 0) and the right hand on (0, 1080). At this phase, the application takes the average of the left and right hand coordinates of the experimenter and assumes that these two hand positions correspond to the TUI table's screen (0, 0) and (0, 1080) coordinates. The second step is the location of "other" corners' coordinates of the TUI table, i.e. the opposite of the first located corners. As a similar procedure, the experimenter has to locate right and left hands at the other corners of the TUI table, which correspond to (1920, 0) and (1920, 1080) screen coordinates. In Fig. 2, the position of Kinect and TUI table are presented; the arrows represent the corners of the TUI. The presented relative positions of Kinect and TUI table are crucial for a successful object and gesture recognition (Fig. 7).

In the end, the system extracts the information about the physical location of the first and the last pixel of the TUI screen. By this method, we can easily locate each

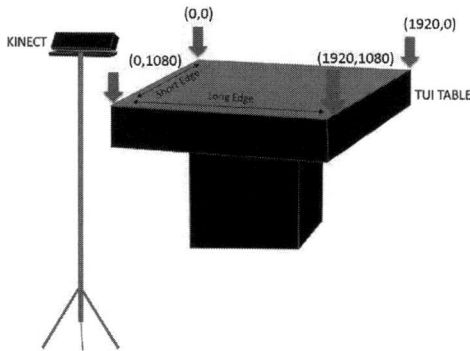

Fig. 7. Calibration procedure

object location in the physical coordinate system of Kinect. The rest of the analysis has been done by using proximity analysis. This algorithm checks the x, y, z coordinates of the hands of the participants and each active object(s) x, y, z coordinates, and then decides whether these coordinates are close to each other or not.

5.2   Interpretation of Log Files

In this section we describe the output log files of the application. Each group is associated with its own data files: *mainlog, outputleft, outputright, outputleft1, outputright1, outputleft2, outputright2,* and *pointingout*. The *mainlog* file presents information about the objects pertaining to the TUI:

5*417*319*ROTATING*63599356325442

5: Object ID
417: horizontal coordinate of the objects
　　 with respect to TUI coordinates
319: vertical coordinate
ROTATING: manipulative state of the object
63599356325442: application system time (Kinect-based)
*: delimiter

Fig. 8. Logging file description

The information provided in Fig. 8 refers only to the TUI table; there is no tracking information of participants. However, logging the objects information on Kinect PC provides a way to synchronize the TUI table events and Kinect events. Therefore, this log file is called *fusion log*. The *outputleft* log file and similarly the other files (*outputright, outputleft1, outputright1, outputleft2, outputright2*) present information on human-object interaction:

```
Object No: 5*Participants No: 1*
left hand*63600200530167
Object No: 5*Participants No: 1*
```

```
left hand*63600200536523
Object No: 5*Participants No: 1*
left hand*63600200541587
```

In this example, the object ID number, participant's ID, hand indicator, and the system time are presented. The drawback in this tracking, and accordingly logging, is the number of records that participant 1 interacts with the object 5. One single continuous interaction can create a lot of tracking "noise". At this point, the identification of each discrete interaction of a participant and an object has to be defined. The system time can solve the problem that each record line has its own system time and the experimenter can decide about the interval between two records. This decision can be made through statistical reasoning or naïve reasoning. Since consecutive records have a homogeneous system time difference, and statistical methods can provide a meaningful mean that belongs to mostly same interaction, outliers of this mean can be used as a discriminative metric. If the difference between two consecutive system times is higher than the mean or higher than the mean + (2 * Standard Deviation), then the record can be considered as another interaction.

As far as free-hand gestures are concerned, the *pointingout* file provides the following information: participant's ID; status of gesture detection; kind of gesture; system time:

```
Participants No:3*GestureDetected*
pointingTUI*635993456313995
```

Currently in our application we have included one commonly used gesture, i.e. a user points with stretched index finger at the TUI. We use the Visual Gesture Builder (VGB)[1] to generate data that our application uses to perform gesture detection at run time. Other target gestures can be created within VGB and must be then embedded to the application.

6   Conclusion and Future Prospects

Assessment of collaboration entails measurement of collaborative skills and being a new research field, it has many dimensions that have to be considered, such as clear definitions of positive/negative collaboration, relation of collaboration to learning outcomes, consideration of various input collaboration channels, etc. In our research, we take as an input channel the gesture performance of the users. Nevertheless, apart from gesture, there are other aspects that have to be taken into account in a multi-users interactions analysis, e.g., emotion recognition, distance from the table, sound level, speech, eye gaze, etc. Furthermore, the relationship between collaboration and task performance has to be thoroughly investigated.

In this paper we proposed our assessment framework, including assessment of task performance and collaboration as well as our interactive feedback strategy. We presented

---

[1] https://msdn.microsoft.com/en-us/library/dn785529.aspx, 10.08.2018.

our developed application that can merge the logging files from our TUI software framework (object recognition) with the Kinect log files (gesture recognition) in one file. It analyzes the number of object manipulations with respect to the timing axis, the subject, and the handedness. Our application is very promising with regards to real time object and gesture recognition on TUIs, as it combines TUI with Kinect tracking.

The main limitation of the application is the recognition of continuous gestures. Defining the starting and end points of a kinematic event is a difficult challenge. In our application, we have to define the kinematic and temporal boundaries of a gesture. Therefore, in the log files especially related to pointing gestures, gestures' logs are taken continuously. In other words, it is difficult to distinguish whether these logs represent one discrete pointing gesture or two/more different interactions from one continuous gesture, particularly when these interactions have a short time interval between them. In the long-run, ELAN or other manual video coding tools can be enriched with a plug-in, so that manipulative gestures are annotated in real time during experiments when connected with Kinect, for instance.

Moreover, awareness has to be raised to the HCI community that 3D mid-air gestures have many sub-categories that should also be taken into account when gesture recognition algorithms are being developed. Last but not least, we plan to use machine learning, to define time-shorted gesture sequence in order to recognize patterns. For instance, when participants perform a specific type and amount of gestures in 5 min, it is most probable that this pattern of gesture repeats later on.

Acknowledgments. This project has received funding from the European Union's Horizon 2020 research and innovation programme under the Marie Sklodowska-Curie grant agreement No. 654477.

References

1. OECD: PISA 2015 Collaborative Problem Solving Framework (2017). http://www.oecd.org/pisa/pisaproducts/Draft%20PISA%202015%20Collaborative%20Problem%20Solving%20Framework%20.pdf. Accessed 18 Nov
2. Anastasiou, D., Ras, E.: Case study analysis on collaborative problem solving using a tangible interface. In: Joosten-ten Brinke, D., Laanpere, M. (eds.) TEA 2016. CCIS, vol. 653, pp. 11–22. Springer, Cham (2017). https://doi.org/10.1007/978-3-319-57744-9_2
3. Hornecker, E., Buur, J.: Getting a grip on tangible interaction: a framework on physical space and social interaction. In: Proceedings of the SIGCHI Conference on Human Factors in Computing Systems, pp. 437–446 (2006)
4. Gutwin, C., Greenberg, S.: The mechanics of collaboration: developing low cost usability evaluation methods for shared workspaces. In: Proceedings of the IEEE 9th International Workshop on Enabling Technologies: Infrastructure for Collaborative Enterprises, pp. 98–103 (2000)
5. Schmidt, K., Bannon, L.: Taking CSCW seriously. Comput. Support. Coop. Work (CSCW) 1(1–2), 7–40 (1992)

6. Scott, S.D., Grant, K.D., Mandryk, R.L.: System guidelines for co-located, collaborative work on a tabletop display. In: Kuutti, K., Karsten, E.H., Fitzpatrick, G., Dourish, P., Schmidt, K. (eds.) ECSCW 2003, pp. 159–178. Springer, Dordrecht (2003). https://doi.org/10.1007/978-94-010-0068-0_9
7. O'Neil, H.F., Chuang, S.H., Chung, G.K.W.K.: Issues in the computer-based assessment of collaborative problem solving. Assess. Educ. **10**, 361–373 (2003)
8. OECD: PISA 2012 assessment and analytical framework mathematics, reading, science, problem solving and financial literacy. OECD Publishing (2013)
9. Evans, A., Wobbrock, J.: Filling in the gaps: capturing social regulation in an interactive tabletop learning environment. In: Proceedings of the 11th International Conference of the Learning Sciences (2014)
10. Dillenbourg, P., Evans, M.: Interactive tabletops in education. Int. J. Comput.-Support. Collab. Learn. **6**(4), 491–514 (2011)
11. McNeill, D.: Hand and Mind: What Gestures Reveal About Thought. University of Chicago Press, Chicago (1992)
12. Kendon, A.: The study of gesture: some observations on its history. Rech. Semiot. Semiot. Inq. **2**(1), 25–62 (1982)
13. Karam, M., Schraefel, M.C.: A taxonomy of gestures in human computer interactions. Technical report (2005)
14. Lao, S., et al.: A gestural interaction design model for multi-touch displays. In: Proceedings of the British HCI-Group, pp. 440–446 (2009)
15. Murphy, K.M.: Building meaning in interaction: rethinking gesture classifications. Crossroads Lang. Interact. Cult. **5**, 29–47 (2003)
16. Quek, F.: Toward a vision-based hand gesture interface. In: Proceedings of the Virtual Reality, Software and Technology Conference, pp. 17–31 (1994)
17. Hinrichs, U., Carpendale, S.: Gestures in the wild: studying multi-touch gesture sequences on interactive tabletop exhibits. In: Proceedings of CHI 2011, pp. 3023–3032 (2011)
18. Higgins, S.E., et al.: Multi-touch tables and the relationship with collaborative classroom pedagogies: a synthetic review. Int. J. Comput.-Support. Collab. Learn. **6**, 515–538 (2011)
19. Djajadiningrat, T., Buur, J.: Look mama, with hands! On tangible interaction, gestures and learning. In: Proceedings of DIS 2002, Designing Interactive Systems, p. 417. ACM, London (2002)
20. Marquardt, N., Jota, R., Greenberg, S., Jorge, J.A.: The continuous interaction space: interaction techniques unifying touch and gesture on and above a digital surface. In: Campos, P., Graham, N., Jorge, J., Nunes, N., Palanque, P., Winckler, M. (eds.) INTERACT 2011. LNCS, vol. 6948, pp. 461–476. Springer, Heidelberg (2011). https://doi.org/10.1007/978-3-642-23765-2_32
21. Wobbrock, J.O., Morris, M.R., Wilson, A.D.: User-defined gestures for surface computing. In: Proceedings of the SIGCHI Conference on Human Factors in Computing Systems, pp. 1083–1092 (2009)
22. Rautaray, S., Agrawal, A.: Vision based hand gesture recognition for human computer interaction: a survey. Artif. Intell. Rev. **43**(1), 1–54 (2015)
23. Martinez-Maldonado, R., Yasef, K., Kay, J.: TSCL: a conceptual model to inform understanding of collaborative learning processes at interactive tabletops. Int. J. Hum.-Comput. Stud. **83**, 62–82 (2015)
24. Wu, M., Balakrishnan, R.: Multi-finger and whole hand gestural interaction techniques for multi-user tabletop displays. In: Proceedings of the 16th Annual ACM Symposium on User Interface Software and Technology, pp. 193–202 (2003)
25. Julià, C.F., Earnshaw, N., Jordà, S.: GestureAgents: an agent-based framework for concurrent multi-task multi-user interaction. In: Proceedings of TEI, pp. 207–214 (2013)

26. Schneider, B., Blikstein, P.: Unraveling students' interaction around a tangible interface using gesture recognition. In: Educational Data Mining, pp. 320–323 (2014)
27. Ahmaniemi, T., Lantz, V., Marila, J.: Perception of dynamic audiotactile feedback to gesture input. In: Proceedings of the 10th International Conference on Multimodal Interfaces, pp. 85–92 (2008)
28. Lucchese, G., et al.: GestureCommander: continuous touch-based gesture prediction. In: Proceedings of CHI Extended Abstracts on Human Factors in Computing Systems (2012)
29. Oh, U., Kane, S.K., Findlater, L.: Follow that sound: using sonification and corrective verbal feedback to teach touchscreen gestures. In: Proceedings of the 15th International ACM SIGACCESS Conference on Computers and Accessibility (ASSETS 2013) (2013)
30. Grosse-Puppendahl, T., Beck, S., Wilbers, D.: Rainbowfish: visual feedback on gesture-recognizing surfaces. In: Proceedings of CHI Extended Abstracts on Human Factors in Computing Systems, pp. 427–430 (2014)
31. Evans, C.: Making sense of assessment feedback in higher education. Rev. Educ. Res. **83**(1), 70–120 (2013)
32. Sadler, D.R.: Formative assessment: revisiting the territory. Assess. Educ. **5**(1), 77–84 (1998)
33. Higgins, R., Hartley, P., Skelton, A.: Getting the message across: the problem of communicating assessment feedback. Teach. High. Educ. **6**(2), 269–274 (2001)
34. Djajadiningrat, T., Overbeeke, K., Wensveen, S.: But how, Donald, tell us how?: on the creation of meaning in interaction design through feedforward and inherent feedback. In: Proceedings of the 4th Conference on Designing Interactive Systems: Processes, Practices, Methods, and Techniques, pp. 285–291 (2002)
35. Greiff, S., et al.: Complex problem solving in educational settings – something beyond g: concept, assessment, measurement invariance, and construct validity. J. Educ. Psychol. **105**, 364–379 (2013)
36. Schwartz, L., Ras, E., Anastasiou, D., Latour, T., Maquil, V.: Designing a collaborative problem solving task in the context of urban planning. In: Ras, E., Guerrero Roldán, A.E. (eds.) TEA 2017. CCIS, vol. 829, pp. 223–234. Springer, Cham (2018). https://doi.org/10.1007/978-3-319-97807-9_17
37. Narciss, S.: Informatives tutorielles feedback. Entwicklungs-und Evaluationsprinzipien auf der Basis instruktionspsychologischer Erkenntnisse. Waxmann, Münster (2006)
38. Bavelas, J., et al.: Gestures specialized for dialogue. Pers. Soc. Psychol. Bull. **21**(4), 394–405 (1995)
39. Kipp, M., et al.: An annotation scheme for conversational gestures: how to economically capture timing and form. Lang. Resour. Eval. **41**(3–4), 325–339 (2007)
40. Lausberg, H., Sloetjes, H.: The revised NEUROGES-ELAN system: an objective and reliable interdisciplinary analysis tool for nonverbal behavior and gesture. Behav. Res. Methods **48**, 973–993 (2015)
41. Morris, M.R., et al.: Cooperative gestures: multi-user gestural interactions for co-located groupware. In: Proceedings of CHI 2006, pp. 1201–1210 (2006)
42. Wittenburg, P., et al.: ELAN: a professional framework for multimodality research. In: Proceedings of the 5th Conference on Language Resources and Evaluation, pp. 1556–1559 (2006)
43. Maquil, V., Tobias, E., Anastasiou, D., Mayer, H., Latour, T.: COPSE: rapidly instantiating problem solving activities based on tangible tabletop interfaces. Proc. ACM Hum.-Comput. Interact. **1**(1), 6 (2017)

Author Index

Druck:
Customized Business Services GmbH
im Auftrag der KNV-Gruppe
Ferdinand-Jühlke-Str. 7
99095 Erfurt